André Maurois

America in
the Market Place

America in the Market Place

Trade, Tariffs and the Balance of Payments

BY PAUL H. DOUGLAS
United States Senator from Illinois

Holt,
Rinehart and Winston
New York   Chicago
San Francisco

Designer: Ernst Reichl
81912-0116
Printed in the United States of America

To My Wife
Emily Taft Douglas

Contents

vii

Preface

During the past decade, I have necessarily become involved in matters dealing with both the economics and politics of our foreign trade. This book, in a sense, is a by-product in some depth of my efforts to deal with these issues.

I hope it may be of some help to others as we decide in these coming years about our tariff policies, aid to the underdeveloped countries of the world, our balance of payments, and the development of an international monetary system.

I am greatly indebted to Dr. James Knowles and Dr. Gerald Pollack for aid in assembling and analyzing material, offering criticism, and in reading proof, and to Howard Shuman for assistance with Chapter 6. Mary Frances de la Pava and other members of my staff have worked hard and long in typing the various redrafts and in deciphering my somewhat illegible handwriting.

Paul H. Douglas

Washington, D.C.
March, 1966

*America in
the Market Place*

Part One

Trade and Tariffs

1
The
Basic Advantages of
Broadened Trade

Mankind would produce little beyond bare subsistence if each family were compelled to raise its own food, build its house, tend and sheer its sheep and then spin and weave the wool into cloth and make this up into clothes. Such a family would also have to tan the hides of animals and make the leather into shoes and act as its own blacksmith, toolmaker, and teacher. Under these conditions, the food would be scanty and restricted, the housing poor, and the clothes ragged and ill-fitting. Few, if any, of the arts and graces of life could be cultivated. Life under these conditions would indeed be scanty, nasty, and brutish.

Men soon learned that it was better to specialize and then exchange the products of their labor than to try to be jacks-of-all-trades. Some gave most of their time to farming, others to tending sheep, and still others to spinning, weaving, and tailoring. Some became carpenters, others masons and shoemakers, while some were blacksmiths who made the rough tools with which the others worked.

In slave societies, this division of labor was carried on

by compulsion within the estate or plantation. In other
societies, it was achieved by the patriarchal head of the
family assigning specialized functions to his male and fe-
male descendants and to his in-laws.

Even under those conditions, plantations and patriarchs
could not be entirely self-sufficient. They could not themselves provide everything they wanted and, as a result,
they had to exchange with outsiders something of what
they produced in return for other items which they desired. Even in the most primitive societies, therefore,
there was some trade and exchange. Originally this took
the form of barter, or the direct exchange of commodity
for commodity, according to terms which were fixed by
the relative amounts supplied as against the relative intensities with which the bargainers desired the others'
products, together with the comparative trading skills of
the bargainers. Even the mutual exchange of gifts, if it
were to continue over a long period, involved a rough
approach to barter. For a purely one-sided series of dona-
tions can seldom, if ever, permanently endure.

Under primitive conditions, the coming of specialization and the subsequent trade and exchange raised the
general standard of living and helped men and women to
satisfy their wants. This movement toward an increasing
division of labor was speeded up, moreover, as the huge
patriarchal families, with their rigid subordination of the
younger sons and of their women, began to break up and
as islands of freedom, in the form of towns, began to
emerge in the midst of the slave and serf societies.

In the towns most men followed some manual trade.
Family names in every language still bear witness today
to this fact, as for instance Carpenter, Mason, Smith,
Taylor, Glover, Cook, Butcher, Baker, Shoemaker, Cooper,
and Brewer. By specializing, these men gained greater

skill in their particular trade than if they had scattered their attention over many jobs. They also saved time which would otherwise have been lost in moving from one occupation to another and they devoted themselves to those trades which were best suited to their own abilities and desires. More and better goods were therefore produced.

In turn, the farmers gave up their efforts at self-sufficiency and concentrated on raising crops, cattle, hogs, sheep, and timber. Once more family names such as Farmer, Shepherd, Hogg, Barnes, Countryman, Forester, Field, and Wood reveal past occupations.

As a result of this specialization, production increased and the standard of living rose. Men ate better, dressed better, and lived in better houses. Some even had time to cultivate the needs and desires of the mind and the spirit.

All of this specialization was based on exchange and trade, in the form of direct barter such as the exchange of wheat, meat, eggs, and milk for clothing and shoes. But the great difficulty with barter is to find people who want each other's products, or have what the economists call "coincident desire." A must not only want what B has to offer, but B must have a like desire for A's product. This was simple when only two persons and two products were involved, but it became complex and time consuming when a man had to satisfy his need for a wide variety of articles by bartering with many people for the one or two products which he turned out. This difficulty gave rise to market days when men came together with their varied products from town and country. On a larger scale, fairs with their goods from faraway places served the same purpose. Specialized traders and merchants naturally came to these fairs to show their wares. A trading class developed, now reflected in such family names as Merchant and Sellers.

The clumsiness of barter led inevitably to the invention
of money as a common medium of exchange, which did
away with the necessity that each man must desire the
other's product. No longer did a seller have to find a pur-
chaser who could satisfy his personal needs. Even if the
trader loathed eggs himself, he would pay money for
them because he could resell them to someone else. The
merchants would buy with money and sell for money,
and gradually the metals, at first silver and then gold,
universally acceptable in themselves, were used as means
of exchange, and were in a sense suspended purchasing
power.

Trade enabled men to dispose of goods of which they
had a surplus for those which they valued more. It was
therefore not sterile, as the Greek and medieval writers
held, but productive, in that it increased the sum total
of the satisfactions of men. For while the trader did
not physically produce commodities, he added to the
pleasures of mankind by enabling people to obtain and
enjoy articles which would not have been produced if his
function had not existed.

But this was not all. Increased trade also encouraged
and indirectly created a demand for greater quantities.
This forced the craftsmen from whom the traders bought
to specialize more minutely. When the traders purchased
only a small quantity of shoes from a rural shoemaker,
the latter could still continue to be primarily a farmer.
But as the sales of the merchants increased, they naturally
increased their purchases. This helped the farmer to cut
himself loose from farming and to concentrate more fully
on shoemaking. In this way, the widening market has-
tened the division of society into separate crafts.

But as the market was further widened by the improvement of roads and by the greater use of rivers and water-

ways, the division of labor was then carried into the crafts themselves. Instead of one man making the entire shoe, this now became the work of several; one would make the sole, another the uppers, and a third would sew them together. Then further subdivisions were carried out until many occupations went into the making of the shoe. The same process was going on in the production of cloth. Originally the women of a family carded, combed, and spun the yarn and the men then wove the yarn into cloth. But, as the market expanded and the volume of sales increased, separate but allied crafts of carders, pullers, dyers, and so forth developed.

What was happening to shoes and cloth was also happening to swords, firearms, hats, clothes, pins, needles, and a myriad of other products. As Adam Smith wrote, in 1776 before the factory system was really underway, "the division of labor is limited by the extent of the market." As the market grew, the division of labor within a craft became ever more minute.

By subdividing their work, men were then able to concentrate more fully upon one simple set of operations. They not only learned how to do their jobs more quickly, but how to perform them more effectively. This saved time which they would otherwise have lost in moving from one operation to another, and it also enabled them to develop and utilize to the full any special talents which they might have.

Even more important than these personal advantages was the fact that, as the work became more and more subdivided, it was possible to develop and use highly specialized tools for these operations which increased the efficiency of the workers. Finally, machines performed the operations, for a machine is merely a tool which generally obtains its motive power not from men but from a generating mechanism. The falling of water over a wheel was one of the more primitive sources of power used in the United States for the grinding of wheat and the manufacture of cotton and woolen cloth. This was soon followed by steam-powered engines and this power was transmitted to the tools by shafts, pulleys, and so forth. Factories were built to house and utilize these machines and their transmitting mechanisms. Thus, to the advantages of the division of labor, there were added the productive advantages of the factory system and of machinery. Supervision became more minute and exacting.

But these gains were only realized because the market was expanding. This expansion was the major dynamic force which both revolutionized production and expanded output. The market grew along with improvements in roads, with barges traversing the rivers and ships the high seas. This complex of causes led to a rapid growth in the total volume of production and in the average standard of living. Just as the division of labor between producers enabled each man to do what he could do best, so the specialization between geographical areas enabled the workers, the enterprisers, and the capitalists of each area to concentrate upon those products which they could turn out most effectively.

Adam Smith pointed out that, even in the cold and cloudy climate of Scotland, good grapes could be grown in greenhouses and good wine made from them. But this could only be achieved at an expense of thirty times as much labor and capital as in the sunnier climes of foreign countries. In other undertakings, such as fishing or raising sheep, on the other hand, the Scotch had an advantage over the peoples of the southern countries. There would be more wine and more woolens for all if each region specialized in that which it could do best. Each could then exchange its products for that of the other.

This is the first and most important lesson for us all to learn that, instead of trying to be self-sufficient, all groups prosper most when they concentrate on producing and selling what they can do best, and buying those things in which others excel.

This basic advantage of a broad market has been one of the strongest forces in merging clans into states and then these small states into the larger and more modern nations. The division of labor could progress further after Scotland, Wales, and Ireland were added to England to form Great Britain. The development overseas of the English-speaking colonies of Canada, Australia, and New Zealand provided still broader markets and increased demand. All this in turn led to greater specialization, a more minute division of labor, and higher prosperity.

In the same way, the continued growth of the United States was not caused solely by population pressures and by political considerations, but also by the desire for broader markets. This helps to explain the Louisiana Purchase by Jefferson, the purchase of Florida, and the Mexican War. These broader markets, in turn, forced a greater division of labor, and caused the productivity of the workers and the prosperity of the United States to rise. This was stressed at the time by such Western expansionists as Thomas Hart Benton and Stephen A. Douglas.

These same influences were also powerful in Germany and Italy. After the Napoleonic Wars there were no less than thirty-nine separate North German States. Since each had its own high tariff, they were forced to be largely self-sufficient. This meant that the German markets were chiefly local, the manufacturing enterprises small, while very little division of labor was possible within the crafts. All these factors kept production and the German standard of living at a relatively low level. The contrast between the economically divided Germany, on the one hand, and a unified Great Britain and our own new nation on the other, stimulated German statesmen and writers, such as Friedrich List, to propose a customs union (Zollverein) between the German states. This union was to abolish all duties which the separate states levied against each other and, thus, internally to achieve completely free trade. Unfortunately, another ultimate feature of the customs union was to be a high external tariff on imported products from outside the union, which in turn limited the possibilities of a still broader trading area.

The creation of this greatly broadened market led to the familiar growth in specialization and production which both Adam Smith and List had forecast. At the same time, the Germans built a railway web which further bound the different states into an economic unity.

The German Zollverein led within forty years to political unity. After the Franco-Prussian War, in 1871, the German Empire was created out of the former customs confederation. Bismarck had indeed cemented the country by blood, but he had also done so by iron—iron from the blast furnaces to build the railways and machines.*

The Italian story followed the same pattern although there political unity came first. Between 1860 and 1870 the efforts of the great patriots of the Risorgimento—Garibaldi, Mazzini, and Cavour—were finally crowned with success. The elimination of the numerous separate states and the creation of a unified railway system broadened

---

* For a graphic description of this process see Werner Sombart, *Die Deutsche Volkswirtschaft im Neunzehnten Jahrhundert und im Anfang des 20. Jahrhunderts.*

the markets for manufactures that had been predicted by the advocates of a united Italy. During the next forty years, the prosperity of all parts of Italy, except the south, rose markedly.

These wider markets not only helped to create nations out of separate states but they also were a source of encouragement to the industrial nations to embark upon colonialism. The British pushed for domination outside the English-speaking colonies and took control over a large part of Africa and of sections of Asia. The French went into Algeria, Tunis, and Morocco in north Africa, into large sections of central Africa, and also into what became known as French Indochina in southeast Asia. While Germany came late into the race for empire, she nevertheless found some footholds in southeast and southwest Africa and in the scattered islands of the Pacific.

Many other motives contributed to this imperialistic drive, among them the desire for greater absolute and relative power, as well as the urge "to paint the map red" and thus increase national prestige. Expanded markets, trade, and productivity were certainly not the only motives, but they were real forces. This is well illustrated in a speech by the celebrated African explorer, Henry M. Stanley, who, after describing the economic benefits to the British textile mills of getting the Africans to wear more clothes, proclaimed: "Birmingham foundries are glowing with the metal which will be made into trinkets to adorn those dusky bosoms and the ministers of Christ are waiting to gather them into the fold."

All these advantages have not only helped to create nations but have also provided some of the cement which has held them together. Thus, the United States was subjected by the Civil War to internal strains which were probably greater and more terrible than those suffered by any other modern state. Certainly, devotion to the Union and a will to wipe out the great moral crime of slavery were key factors in marshaling the forces of the North to victory. But discerning Northerners also saw that a politically divided country would not only lead to continuing wars but would prevent the realization of the economic advantages of a broad continental market.

We have in fact within the United States the greatest free trade area in the world today and much of our prosperity is based upon this fact. This permits North and South Dakota, Kansas, Nebraska, and Oklahoma to specialize in wheat; Illinois, Iowa, and Indiana in corn and hogs; Wisconsin and Minnesota in dairy products; Mississippi and Alabama in cotton; Florida in citrus fruits; the mountain states in cattle and sheep; and the Pacific Northwest in timber. If each of these states were compelled to be self-sufficient, instead of specializing where it has an advantage, the sum total of all products would be much less and the standard of living in each and every state would be far lower.

Raw materials, labor supply, and good transportation help to locate industries. The manufacture of steel, for example, is chiefly confined to a strip of the country extending from Chicago to Pittsburgh, where coal and iron ore meet. The skilled workers of New England gave to their area a head start in the production of textiles and of boots and shoes, while the nimble fingers of the eastern and southern Europeans helped to concentrate the clothing industry in New York and Chicago. The advantages of an early start came to much of New England industry, the glove factories of Johnstown and Gloversville, and the shirt and collar industry of Troy.

But whatever the reasons for the localization of industry, and these reasons shift with time, there is a consequent general benefit to the entire nation. The nationwide market of 195 million people makes possible specialization as well as the greater productivity of each worker. So great is our internal division of labor and the wide range of our natural resources that our vast wants are mainly satisfied from within our borders. Our total export of goods only amounts to about four percent of our gross annual product while our imports are slightly less.

Appeals are frequently made that we should trade only with state or local concerns. "Patronize home industry," it is urged, "and give employment to local labor right here in our home state." But these slogans overlook the larger advantages of the people to whom they are addressed. By buying only from their home industries, families would lose the advantages of buying at the lower prices from other states where costs are lower. The advocates of home industry also ignore the fact that, were their policy to become general, the markets for the products which are produced locally in Hometown or Homestate would be shut off. Labor and capital in the home area would then be forced to turn to occupations in which they would be less productive. The same forces would be at work elsewhere so that national productivity and prosperity would decline.

An allied fallacy is the belief that one state or locality can discriminate against others without suffering the same reprisals. In real life, this sort of discrimination spreads like wildfire and in the end boomerangs against the producers in the state or locality which started the policy. The final result is that all are losers.

A brilliant and satirical economist, John Ise of the University of Kansas, has reduced the home market argument to its essential absurdity by showing what would happen if it were applied first to a state, then to a county, then to a town, and finally to a block or family. With each move, the "buy locally" slogan becomes more restrictive and the final damage increases until its essential absurdity becomes clear.

Most people now admit the advantages of broad internal markets and freedom of trade within a nation, but the majority still balk at recognizing that the same economic advantages of specialization and trade exist among nations. "That," they object, "is another matter. Mississippi and North Dakota may supplement each other but not Great Britain, Germany, and the United States, nor Argentina, Brazil, and the United States."

While not insisting that a man should buy only the products of his own state, they still insist that we should "buy American." "Only in this way," they argue, "can we employ American labor and prevent our products from being displaced by those made with low-wage foreign labor."

This argument ignores the fact that from a purely economic standpoint, the advantages of broad international markets are the same as those of an internal market. They are simply spread over a wider area among regions which have different flags and currencies. It would be absurd, for example, for us to try to raise bananas and grow coffee, cocoa, and tea. It is far better for us to let Central America grow the bananas, Brazil and Latin America the coffee, Africa the cocoa, and India and Ceylon the tea. We should also buy sugar from the islands of the Caribbean where the richest sugar soils in the world are located and where sugar can be produced at half the cost of the American yield.

In the same way, the French are experts in turning out

laces, gloves, and wine, the Italians leather goods, the Germans chemicals and small automobiles, and the Scots whiskey and woolens. Solely from the standpoint of ultimate prosperity and, for the moment, disregarding other difficulties, we would have to agree that world-wide free trade is desirable, since it would encourage production in the most advantageous areas and lead to freer competition in the market. Individual families would be able to buy more cheaply and, hence, each dollar would buy more. The employed would work where they could produce most, and national, as well as world, real income would rise.

Marcus Aurelius, one of the few saints who was also an emperor, had a clear idea of the basic interdependence of mankind when he wrote in his Meditations: "For we are made for co-operation, like the hands, the feet, the eyelids, like the rows of the upper and lower teeth."

Mankind has been slow to recognize this basic truth.

We have stressed the positive advantages of the division of labor which follow from ever broader markets, but it has been much harder for people to recognize that the same principle holds good in those cases where the person or unit has not an absolute but rather a "comparative advantage." This principle was well stated by the Irish economist, Bastable, when he wrote, "A doctor may be a better gardener than the gardener whom he employs, but he may be a still better doctor and he would lose if he did not restrict himself to the highest type of work he could do. His advantage over the gardener is the greatest not when he is acting as a gardener, but when he exercises his functions as a doctor." *

Translated into money terms this means that a doctor

* Bastable, Charles Francis, *The Commerce of Nations*, 1892, p. 10.

will increase his real income if he hires someone else to tend his garden so that he can take care of more patients. He will receive more from the increased fees paid by patients then he will pay out in wages to his gardener.

Bastable then continued: "A country may be able to produce everything better than another country, but it will pay it best to concentrate on those articles in which its comparative advantage is greatest, while the inferior country must restrict itself to those products in which its comparative disadvantage is least."

The Swiss economist, Michael Heilperin, has worked out the logic of this same principle in more detail.* "Let us assume," he writes, "that the economic universe consists of two countries, one of which has an industry which is in terms of technical efficiency greatly superior—in all fields—to that of the other. According to the principle of comparative advantage, there will nevertheless be commercial transactions between the people of Superia and those of Inferia. . . . If in Superia the most efficient industries are so expanded as to supply buyers in Inferia with some of their products, and if the least efficient industries are at the same time reduced in scope or liquidated and their place is taken by imports from Inferia, several consequences will follow:

1. In Superia a larger proportion of the labor force will be employed in the most efficient industries;

2. In Inferia the part of the labor force employed in its most efficient industries will expand;

3. Productivity will grow in both countries; so will standards of living."

By the same logic, a day's labor in the United States will produce more hemp than in India, but it will produce

* Heilperin, Michael A., *The Trade of Nations*, New York: Alfred A. Knopf, 1952, pp. 8–9.

even more wheat. It is therefore wise for us to specialize in the latter and import the hemp we need from India.

The broader the area of trade, the greater is the division of labor and the higher the total output. The division of labor permits both men and regions to specialize in that which they can do best. It reduces the time needed to learn a job and lessens the time spent in passing from one occupation to another. Moreover, as processes are subdivided, it becomes easier for machines to carry out the simplified work. In this way mechanical power multiplies the effectiveness of human power.

But the widening of trade takes place only through traders. They, in turn, have been able to enlarge the scope of their operations with improvements in the means of transportation and communication. The advantages of extending the size of markets, as measured in money terms, are limited by the costs of transportation to obtain goods from afar. Transportation and all forms of trade have to yield a money surplus if they are to be used.

But the extension of the market also helps to dissolve former local monopolies in trade and manufacture. It is true that the extension of the market is often followed by national monopolies, but usually the final degree of control is less than when the markets were purely local. In the same way, the development of international trade lessens the power of purely national monopolies. H.O. Havemeyer, of Sugar Trust fame, may not have been completely accurate when he said, "the tariff is the Mother of Trusts," but it is certainly a nurse. When foreign competition is reduced, industrial combinations behind the national tariff walls are encouraged. In the long run, therefore, broader trade benefits the overwhelming majority of the people in all areas. Its positive, comparative, and competitive advantages will increase total production and the general standard of living.

The degree to which the various sections and countries will share in this general advance is determined by highly complicated factors such as the relative degree to which the different regions possess natural resources, an efficient and sufficient labor force, adequate capital, and the state of the industrial arts and techniques. It also depends on two other factors: the relative degree to which outputs in the different areas and countries respond to changes in the values or prices of the articles in question; and the relative intensities of demand on the part of the people of each country for the products of others.

Thus, when two countries begin to trade, Country A's terms of trade will be most favorable if its demand for the products of other countries is relatively inelastic while that of the other countries for its products is elastic. For this will appreciably lower the prices of the imports into Country A while producing only slight decreases in the prices of its exports. Many subtle analyses of these forces have been carried out by economists starting with John Stuart Mill. This book is too brief to go into them in any great detail, but the important fact to understand is that nearly all groups will benefit from expanded trade even though they may do so in varying degrees.

2
The Arguments
for Protective Tariffs
Considered

There are many ways in which trade between nations can be discouraged. The cost of transportation is a natural barrier to the movement of commodities, for an article must be able to meet not only its production costs but also its handling and transportation costs before it can profitably be sold in another area or country. The higher these are, the less commodities can be moved. For example, sand, gravel, and stone move only within relatively limited areas.

Tariffs create the most common additional barrier on goods entering a country. They are an added financial cost which must be paid to a government on foreign goods before they can find a market. The higher the tariff, therefore, the greater the handicap and the fewer the goods which will come in. The tariff wall can in fact be raised so high as to stop all imports.

Tariffs can be of two main kinds: a flat levy, called a "specific duty," of so much in dollars and cents for each pound, ton, yard, or quart brought into the country; or a levy of a given percent upon the sales values of each article imported into the country. These are *ad valorem* duties, and are commonly computed on the basis of wholesale prices in the country of origin.*

But tariffs are not the only barriers to international trade. Another barrier is a flat limit or quota imposed upon the amount of a given commodity which can be imported. It is a common practice to distribute these quotas among the various countries which are possible suppliers. After the second World War the European countries imposed rather rigid quotas upon the quantities of American goods which we could sell to them. Some of these quotas still remain. Germany, for example, still permits only six million tons of foreign coal to enter her country duty free, five million of which can be American. All coal imported in excess of this figure has to pay a duty of five dollars a ton. In the field of services, the limitation on American actors who can appear on the English stage is another instance of quantitative restrictions. On the other hand, for some years we imposed quotas on lead and zinc which restricted the amounts which Canada and Peru could sell to us, and we also impose a quota on residual fuel oil from Venezuela, on the amounts of sugar which we can import from various countries, and on cotton textiles from Japan, Hong Kong, and other countries.

For political reasons also, complete or partial prohibitions are sometimes imposed upon the imports from or exports to a given country. These embargoes are practiced in varying degrees between the countries of the Free World and those of the Communist world, and vice-versa. Russia and its satellites impose severe restrictions on the goods which they will import from or export to the Western World; so does Communist China. The democracies have followed suit. They properly do not want to swell the

* Though sometimes they are computed on the basis of prices in the country of destination.

military strength of those countries, which, by propaganda, subversion, and at times naked force, are seeking to overthrow the Free World.

There are more subtle ways than tariffs and quotas to restrict international trade. The French, for example, carry out a hidden form of discrimination against American automobiles by levying a tax of two hundred dollars on all cars with engines of more than sixteen horsepower, while cars with lesser horsepower are taxed at no more than thirty dollars. Since nearly all American autos have greater horsepower than this and many French and other European cars have less, this rule amounts to a high protective tariff against American-produced automobiles. The British use a similar method.

Another way of discouraging imports is to require specific licenses or permits before goods can be brought into a country. This requirement can then be used to delay or prevent the importation of goods. When complaints are made, they can be shrugged off as exceptional cases and not as indicating a general policy—which, in fact, they are. France followed this practice for many years and, upon occasion, still does, while the British, as has been pointed out, use it in certain fields of employment. It is a common practice in Mexico.

Excessive sanitary requirements can also be interpreted so strictly as to bar the entrance of otherwise qualified goods. Argentina has complained for years that we have prevented good fresh beef from being brought into the United States under legislation which precludes any such imports from a country in which the hoof and mouth disease exists. If we raised spices, we might impose rigid standards against the condiments which we now import from the islands of southeast Asia. But we do not do so, even though the imports often arrive in an impure condition, because there is nowhere else for us to get these products.

There are still other ways of preventing the full and fair competition of goods. One is to apply *ad valorem* duties to unrealistic prices when computing tariff changes. Recent studies by the Congressional Joint Economic Committee have shown that, for a wide range of articles, ocean freight rates are much higher on articles which we export than on identical articles imported on the same ship and involving the same ports. Curiously enough, this practice so harmful to American trade was enforced for years by our Maritime Board and later by the Maritime Administration which punished any shipping line which broke away from the international shipping cartel by withholding government subsidies from it.

Finally, international cartels at times map out markets between big producers and agree not to poach on each other's preserves thus diminishing the international competition which would lower prices.

We can now consider some of the arguments for protective tariffs and other restrictive practices. We have already mentioned the most common of these, namely that by restricting or stopping the entrance of foreign goods, we give employment to native labor which would not otherwise be employed.

It is true that a higher tariff on cotton or woolen cloth would increase employment in our textile mills. The existing mills would produce more and hire more labor and sooner or later additional mills would probably also be built in the United States. Those who would benefit either directly or indirectly from this policy would then call attention to the new plants with their smoking chimneys and to the increased throngs of workmen going in and out of the factory gates. These would be the seen consequences of the higher tariff. They would have a powerful and, in many cases, an overriding influence on the minds of the public.

Other consequences of the higher tariff, however, would tend to be unseen, but they would be real. The prices of cotton and woolen cloth would be higher and consumers would have to pay more for them. They would buy a smaller quantity than before and they would therefore be less well dressed. They would have less money to spend on other articles and their demand for these other goods would decrease. Less of these other commodities would be produced, and fewer workers would be employed to produce them. There would be less prosperity elsewhere. This would be further accelerated by the fact that, since foreign countries would sell less to us, they would be unable to buy as much from us. Our export industries would be hurt and sales, production, and employment in these lines would also decrease.

These bad effects would be harder to see because they would be widely diffused. But, on the whole, there would be no net increase in employment. What would happen, instead, would be merely a transfer of labor from more to less productive lines, with a consequent decrease in the real national income.

The French publicist and economist, Frédéric Bastiat, satirized this argument of the protectionists when he drew up an imagined petition from the manufacturers of candles and lamps asking the Chamber of Deputies to protect them against the light of the sun by ordering everyone to shut all windows and skylights.* The supposed petitioners then pointed out that such action would create more work for them by increasing the demand for artificial light. Writing before the days of gas and electricity, Bastiat went on to point out that this would promote the produc-

*Bastiat, F., *Fallacies of Protection* (*Sophismes Economiques*), 1909, Stirling translation, pp. 60–65.

tion of cattle to furnish tallow for the candles and the development of a whaling fleet to provide whale oil, and so forth. And to those who objected that this was an absurd example, Bastiat correctly pointed out that it differed not in kind but only in degree from the arguments for the protective tariffs which favored the less economic lines of production and handicapped those which were more productive.

Underneath all the exaggerations of Bastiat's analogy, there is a solid residue of truth which citizens, consumers, workers, businessmen, and politicians should take to heart but which, unfortunatly, they all too often neglect.

The average man of affairs will probably dismiss this analysis as too theoretical. He may object that we have treated the differences in output between men, areas, and countries almost entirely in terms of physical units whereas in real life commodities compete against each other in terms of price. "The workers in one country," he will object, "may be less efficient than those in another, but their wages will be lower so that their products can still undersell." The argument continues that even if their output be only half as much per hour, but their wages only one quarter as high, their labor costs per unit of output will still only be one half as great as in the first country, and they will be able to undersell the products of the more efficient country and drive them from the market both at home and abroad.

The modern defender of high protective tariffs then compares the average American wage in manufacturing of approximately two and a half dollars an hour with the much lower wage rates of Europe and Japan and concludes that, with free trade, foreign imports would swamp our country, drive our goods from the market, and create vast unemployment.

There are several answers to this argument. It ignores the fact that fringe benefits are both more widespread and proportionately more costly abroad than they are in the United States. Hourly money wages, therefore, do not fully measure hourly labor costs, and actual differences in wage costs per hour are less than is indicated by wage rates alone.

It also ignores the all important consideration that labor costs per unit of output rather than labor costs per hour are the real measure of labor costs. The high hourly wages in the United States are generally caused by high productivity. It is the high output per man-hour and the comparative skill of our management which make it possible for us to pay high hourly wage rates. The result is that actual labor costs per unit of output are lower in many cases here than in Europe and Asia. This allows many of our products to compete successfully with those countries even after meeting transportation costs. As an example, we export approximately 26 billion dollars of commodities each year and import only about 21 billion. We export not only farm products such as wheat, soybeans, cotton, tobacco, and powdered milk, but also farm and earth-moving machinery, electrical equipment, and many other items. Conversely, the low wages of other countries are largely due to their low productivity and their unit labor costs are often, therefore, actually higher in most types of goods. (While this is still the general rule, there are notable exceptions which I shall shortly discuss.)

We have also a commonly overlooked advantage, namely, our raw material and power costs are appreciably lower than those of most European and other countries. For instance, we have a big advantage in the price of coal because of our thick seams of the mineral and our mechanized mining. An American miner turns out about thirteen tons of coal a day as compared with about one ton in Great Britain and about three tons in Germany. The cost of electrical power is also less in the United States than it is abroad. Our basic cereals also cost less than on the continent of Europe. Wheat sells here at about $1.70 a bushel, compared with $2.50 in France, and over $3.00 in Germany.

In general, the lower wage countries specialize in commodities where the amount of machinery and capital used is comparatively slight and where the labor content of the article is comparatively high. Thus, India has been able to dominate the market for jute and hemp, as has Japan for silk.

But one serious qualification must be made to all this. Since World War II, the industrial techniques of the advanced nations have been rapidly introduced into the less developed countries. Labor has been taught to use this machinery and, while there are continuing difficulties, a unique combination is developing whereby the most modern machinery is being handled by low-paid labor operating under skilled management. The wages in these countries are, in turn, kept low by the stern facts of there being little alternative employment. In these less developed countries, population presses sharply against natural resources and the total quantity of capital available. This causes the marginal productivity of labor and, hence, of wages, in agriculture, handicraft, and the more retarded manufacturing industries to be low. While the new and highly modern industries in these countries have to pay for the costs of training, they are nevertheless able, in many instances, to reach Western standards of production at labor costs which are much below the prevailing American scale. In such cases, foreign wage costs per unit of output are lower than ours.

Japan is today a conspicuous example of this trend and the same situation may be true tomorrow in some of the African states as well. We must watch these trends although they are not yet widespread. In many cases the low wages are still offset by higher material and power costs. On the other hand, the European economies are developing technical improvements in many lines at a faster rate than we. The oxygen process for blast furnaces and the continuous casting process are being widely used in the European steel mills where they increase output, eliminate many intermediate steps, and lower production costs. These developments are stimulating our steel companies to adopt like methods although they have been slow to do so because of certain technical problems and the huge new investments of capital which they would require.

But, even if overall manufacturing costs—that is, wages and material costs combined—were lower in other countries than here, there would still remain the transportation costs which constitute a natural belt of protection around a country. These are especially great for such a country as our own which is separated from most foreign competitors by broad oceans. But the effectiveness of this protective belt has been lessened by the practices of the international shipping cartels which, as we have said, charge much lower rates on articles coming into the United States from foreign ports than on those going out. This practice, which until recently had actually been encouraged by the U.S. Maritime Administration, is an artificial barrier to our exports and an artificial stimulus to our imports.

The most conclusive answer, however, to the argument that a country may be swamped with goods produced by cheap labor lies in the mechanism through which deficits in international payments are ultimately eliminated. If, in fact, a country's markets were being flooded by goods being produced at lower cost abroad, that country would tend to have a deficit in its balance of payments because its purchases from abroad would exceed its sales and it would have to pay for this excess with some form of monetary purchasing power. Market forces would then be set into motion which would tend to eliminate the deficit and restore equilibrium between the country's international purchases and sales.

In the pre-World War I days of the gold standard, international movements of gold triggered this mechanism of adjustment. In those days men could receive gold from the monetary authorities of a country in return for the national currency. Then there was a ready answer to those who argued that under free trade lower costs abroad would cause wholesale unemployment here. The answer was that there would ultimately be a compensatory movement of prices which would correct the original excess of imports.

Thus if the volume of our imports was so much greater than our exports that we owed foreign countries more than they owed us, and if this excess of debt was not offset by non-commodity transactions such as investments, interest payments, remittances, foreign travel, and the like, then the balance of payments would have to be met by our shipment or transfer of the international currency, namely, gold, to our foreign creditors.

Under the monetary conditions which formerly prevailed, such an outflow of gold would contract the quantity of money here and consequently cause the general level of prices in this country to fall.* This fall in prices

---

* The general price level is determined by the ratio between the quantity of money (including checks) times the velocity at which money and checks circulate on the one hand and the volume of goods and services for which money and credit are paid.

and contraction in available money within the country which had an unfavorable balance of payments would naturally discourage imports into it and cause its exports to increase. Similarly, gold would then move into the lower price country and the net exporting nation would consequently expand its money supply and cause its own price levels to rise. This would make it more difficult for it to export and at the same time would encourage imports into it. This process of readjustment would continue until equilibrium in the balance of payments was restored.

Under the gold standard there was, therefore, a self-correcting and self-regulating mechanism which in the end produced a balance in international payments between countries and which prevented any continuing excess of international payments by any one country or any long continuing drain of gold from it. There was no need, therefore, for a technically advanced country to fall into panic over a short-term excess of imports or to forfeit the advantages given to it by the international division of labor and by the law of comparative costs.

There were other consequences of these compensatory price movements. As prices rose in the trade surplus country and fell in the deficit country, the surplus country would be priced out of world markets altogether with respect to some commodities, and it would suffer an impairment of its competitive position with respect to others; the trade deficit country, on the other hand, would begin to export products for which it had not earlier found international markets, and its competitive position in general would be enhanced. Thus the compensatory price movements were associated with shifts in productive resources —into export industries in the deficit country and out of such industries in the surplus country.

This process of adjustment resulted in a tendency towards an equality in prices among countries—or what the Swedish economist, Gustav Cassel, termed "purchasing power parity" of the international currency—and exercised an influence toward equality of wages per unit of output. The same tendency toward equalization is more clearly and directly seen within a country where the expanding regions with lower wage costs tend to bid up the price of labor in order to attract labor and where, conversely, competition and the immigration of workers tend to decrease wages in the high-cost areas. Recent wage movements in the Southern textile industry and in New England illustrate these tendencies. The same forces, in a weakened form, also operate between countries. Such a compensatory movement of labor and of wages is, however, largely offset both by the natural reluctance of laborers to leave their home country and by the restrictions on immigration imposed by many of the high-wage countries, our own included.

We have spoken of "tendencies" toward an equality of prices and of wages between countries as a result of this adjustment process. But such a movement is very slow to develop in the case of wages, and in the meantime lower costs can prevail in those exporting countries which have advanced techniques but low wages. Consequently, they can undersell the more advanced countries for a considerable period of time and, in the process, both industry and labor in the advanced countries will suffer. Even here, however, the consumers in the countries with higher costs will benefit from the reduction in prices effected by the added imports. This will increase their real income and enable them to buy more of both the articles imported and of others produced at home.

In other words, the compensatory and equalizing tendencies in international trade and immigration operate "in the long run" while, in the short run, real damage may be done to many people. It is, of course, hard for those affected adversely to think in terms of the long-run benefits to the general public. The human race has never been noted for its ability to subordinate its immediate and special interests to the long-run general benefit. This is particularly true where the general benefit extends into the future, but where the individual losses are immediate and direct. Governments are inclined to follow the same pattern.

This is why many people support high tariffs and other protective devices. It takes but a short time for most college graduates to forget their textbook lessons and to espouse the short-run interests of their own industries and class. The pure theory of international trade has been taught in the colleges and universities of New England for nearly a century, but most of the graduates who have gone out into business rather speedily became ardent protectionists.

In 1791 Alexander Hamilton, in his Report on Manufactures, urged that the United States adopt a protective tariff to encourage industries which would otherwise be killed off at birth by competition from the more industrially advanced nations, such as Great Britain. He also urged that by creating manufacturing industries and a city population divorced from the soil we would then provide a home market for the surplus products of agriculture. During the early years of the Republic, these protectionist views did not make great headway. After 1815 however, English manufactured goods coming from their newly established factories began to pour in upon us and the "infant industry" argument was then renewed in strengthened form. The textile magnates of New England and the iron manufacturers of Pennsylvania were the driving forces behind this protective movement while the Whig Party and, in particular, its rising leaders, Daniel Webster and Henry Clay, were its political exponents. In the same way, profiting from American experience and the arguments of Hamilton, the German manufacturers under the intellectual leadership of Friedrich List used this argument from 1830 on and were finally successful.

There is a certain measure of truth in this infant industry argument. Enterprises which would ultimately become productive and stand on their own feet can be discouraged from starting or prevented from surviving by competition from foreign firms which have the initial advantages of an early start. Almost the same disadvantages exist within a country, although this is less noticed. Infanticide is properly a crime under our codes of ethics and laws and we restrain adults from abusing children. In this way, among other ethical advantages, we get an adult population which can compete on more equal terms. Why then, it is argued, should we not do the same with our infant industries? Later, it is said, these tariffs can be removed after the industries have grown up and can stand on their own feet.

This argument is theoretically correct. But, in practice, there are several crucial difficulties connected with it. In the first place, it is almost impossible to predict which industries will become self-supporting and which will fall by the wayside. Since the claims of promising infancy will be advanced for a wide range of industries, uncritical acceptance of the argument could and would lead to encouraging a multitude of new industries which ultimately would not be able to hold their own. In the meantime, we would have wasted some of the resources of the nation on industries which could never grow up and reduced our national and individual prosperity in the process.

Yet, the very costs of these parasites would have been spread so widely that they would probably escape public notice. If threatened, they could so marshal their lawyers and lobbyists and those dependent upon them as to resist successfully any attempt to wean them from their economic nursing bottle. It would be better, therefore, if we wished to encourage well-chaperoned industries, if we did so by public subsidies rather than by protective tariffs. This would bring the true costs out into the open and would enable the public to decide more wisely as to whether or not they should be continued.

This leads us to the second great weakness in the infant industry argument. Those who benefit from the tariff will refuse to admit that they ever grow up, and even in hoary age will continue to demand protection. The textile and metal industries first raised their infant cries after the War of 1812. These pleas have continued for a century and a half. They were successfully made during and after the Civil War, and again at the turn of the century, and they reappeared with full vigor in the 1920's. Today, the very same groups are still beating the drums for further protection. The textile and steel manufacturers argue as though they were indeed in a perpetual state of infancy. Instead of welcoming the chance to grow up and fend for themselves, they refuse to be weaned and insist rather on drawing sustenance from the breast of an indulgent mother, although they wear the whiskers of old age.

If these industries cannot grow up in one hundred fifty years, it may be asked, "when, if ever, will they?" Sometime the silver cord of dependency should be broken and the industry should learn to stand on its own feet and be self-reliant. The manufacturers in these tariff-protected industries are fond of urging these sturdy virtues upon the poor, but they are extremely reluctant to see this same principle applied to themselves.

The early free traders were charged with being too cosmopolitan and of putting the interests of all mankind above those of their own nation. They were lampooned as loving every country but their own and of diluting national patriotism in a vague sea of internationalism.

In reality, the advocates of free trade have always been vitally concerned with the economic welfare of their own nation by emphasizing the unseen advantages to consumers and to exporters of lower tariffs and of freer trade. But they have also urged more universal advantages. They have correctly believed that trade was mutually beneficial and have felt that it was unnecessary to injure others in order to benefit themselves. While they wanted their own country to benefit from freer trade, they were happy that in the process the people of other countries also prospered. Their patriotism was therefore expansive and not dominated by hostility towards others. They also recognized that, if the nations became more interdependent economically and were tied together by the peaceful exchange of goods, there would be far less danger of war. Thus, the great English orator, John Bright, who, more than any other man, created the sentiment for free trade in Great Britain, was a deeply convinced Quaker whose concern for international peace was the dominant purpose in his life. Even the somewhat pedestrian Richard Cobden declared, "When I advocated Free Trade, do you suppose that I did not see its relation to the present question [of peace] or that I advocated free trade merely because it would give us a little more occupation in this and that pursuit? No, I believed Free Trade would have the tendency to unite mankind in the bonds of peace and it was that more than any pecuniary interest which sustained and actuated me, as my friends know, in that struggle." *

To all this, the nationalists have replied, "But as a matter of fact we do live in a real world of bitterly competitive national states. While mutual trade may mitigate some of these conflicts of interests, there are deeper roots of war such as rivalries for power, religious and racial prejudices, and struggles between conflicting political and economic systems. In the light of these conflicts, it would be foolish to become dependent on foreign countries for goods which would be essential for national survival in case of war but which would not then be available."

The national interest, it is argued, requires a large degree of self-sufficiency. Part of this need, it is said, can be met by stockpiling an adequate minimum of raw materials such as minerals, food, and possibly fibers. But part can only be provided by building up vital national industries behind import quotas and tariff walls.

It is hard to deny this contention with the world divided as it is between power blocs. At the same time, the case for import restrictions on national security grounds does not seem to have won wide application. At the present time, only petroleum and certain of its derivatives receive protection for reasons of national security, even though the statutory authority for relief in such cases is broad and permissive.†

If a nation faces a determined and malevolent enemy, it is certainly unwise to furnish that foe with the goods which it could later use against the country. In the days before the rise of aggressive Nazism and Communism, these dan-

---

* *Speeches of Richard Cobden,* edited by John Bright and Thorold Rogers, Vol. 2, p. 421.

† Section 232 of the Trade Expansion Act of 1962.

gers were far less acute than they are today. We cannot disregard such perils now, however, while Communist nations continue to preach and seek the destruction of the democratic nations.

Trade with the Communist world should, therefore, in my opinion, be carefully restricted until clear evidence is given that the Communists have abandoned their plans for world revolution. On the other hand, the Free World should encourage wider trade and economic co-operation within its own areas. For this will not only yield economic advantages, but it will also help to create the mutual support and the fellowship which we need to resist the spread of the police state and the loss of freedom.

And freedom is more than a word. I cannot subscribe to the slogan, "Better red than dead," or as Arnold Toynbee is reported to have intellectualized the same position, "Existence is more important than freedom." For in the face of an aggressive and well-armed force determined to take over the world, the adoption of any such philosophy would mean the victory of the police state with all its denials of individual freedom. This would be neither a wise nor a proper choice.

If the Soviet Union and its satellites were to give clear, convincing, and prolonged proof that they are abandoning their plans for world conquest and are content to live at peace with the democracies of the world, then the circle of trade can and should be further enlarged. But until then, the democracies should, in my judgment only make cautious and tentative probings.

A nation may want to lower its tariffs provided its neighbors and associates will reduce theirs, yet be afraid that the other nations will not follow. One solution of this difficulty is through a treaty or trade agreement between two or more countries under which they reciprocally agree to reduce the tariffs on each other's products. Such arrangements have often been useful and, as we shall see, have had great success since 1934, but at times they are as hard to negotiate as mutual disarmament agreements.

When a country finds that its neighbors do not want to co-operate and will not agree to a satisfactory treaty, it has two possible lines of action. It can either launch reductions on its own initiative in the hope that by example and logic it will in the end induce its neighbors to follow suit or, on the other hand, it can apply economic pressure by threatening to increase its own tariffs if they do not lower theirs. The people of Great Britain chose the first way in the 1840's and prospered both as consumers and exporters because of it.

But nations are not always moved by example. Sometimes, in fact, they try to benefit from the low tariffs of other countries without giving anything in return. Nevertheless, these same countries might reduce their tariffs reciprocally if they knew that their refusal would provoke reprisals. Force and toughness in bargaining may create a willingness to co-operate which magnanimity cannot evoke. This is a hard lesson to accept for those who believe in the innate goodness of man, but the bitter school of experience confirms that it is frequently true, particularly when one deals with states rather than with individuals.

Threatened retaliation has, of course, its own dangers. It may stiffen rather than reduce the opposition of the other nations and lead to tariff wars which will injure everyone. Retaliation should never be threatened unless a country is prepared to carry it out. Adam Smith wisely said about such a policy, "There may be good policy in retaliations of this kind, when there is a probability that they will procure the repeal of the high duties or protections complained of . . . To judge whether such retaliations are likely to produce such an effect, does not, perhaps, belong so much to the science of a legislator, whose deliberations ought to be governed by general principles which are always the same, as to the skill of that insidious and crafty animal, vulgarly called a statesman or politician, whose councils are directed by the momentary fluctuations of affairs." * Despite the invidious words by which Smith downgraded politicians, he had apparently greater faith in their tactical judgments than in those of philosophical legislators. But, unfortunately, they are seldom swayed by magnanimity.

A final defensive argument of the American protectionists is the plea that our foreign trade is relatively unimportant and that consequently any damage which might be done by high protective tariffs would be comparatively insignificant. It is true that our foreign trade comprises the smallest proportion of the national product of any of the major nations in the Free World. In 1963 we exported 22.1 billion dollars' worth of commodities and imported 17.0 billion dollars.† Since our Gross National Product in that year amounted to 589 billion dollars, these transactions came to four and three percent, respectively, or to a combined total of about six and two-thirds percent, or approximately one-fifteenth of the national product. Since the Gross National Product, however, included 152 billion dollars of services paid for by individuals and probably at least another 81 billion dollars by all levels of government, this meant that exports formed about six and a half percent

* Smith, Adam, *The Wealth of Nations,* Cannan edition, Modern Library, p. 435.

†See *Federal Reserve Bulletin,* October 1964, pp. 1366–67. This does not include the export of grant-aid military equipment and supplies under the Mutual Security Program.

of our output of goods with the imports amounting to another five percent.* While the totals were higher in 1965 than in 1963, the proportions were substantially the same.

This is in sharp contrast with such countries as the Netherlands and Great Britain whose exports alone amount, respectively, to approximately one-half and one-quarter of their gross national products. Along with Russia and China, we are, in fact, one of the three relatively self-sufficient nations of the world. This self-sufficiency is not primarily created by artificial barriers in the form of tariff walls, quota restrictions, or import licenses, but instead by the abundance of our resources and the skill of our industry. Spanning a continent we are able to produce a wide variety of products in great abundance.

Nevertheless, our foreign trade is not insignificant and what we and other nations do about it is of real importance to our nation and our people. First, it is certainly important to many industries and localities. Thus, in 1962, thirty-four percent of our cotton was exported, thirty-nine percent of our tobacco, fifty-seven percent of our wheat, and thirty-five percent of our soybeans. All of these had a total money value of some 3.2 billion dollars. If we were to lose the foreign markets for these products, our farmers and farm communities would suffer a heavy direct loss while, in addition, because the former exports would be thrown back upon the home market, domestic prices would break badly and, hence, would inflict further damage.

In the same year, 1962, we also exported 8.2 billion dollars' worth of all kinds of machinery. The exports of electrical machinery alone came to 1.25 billion dollars; construction, mining, and oil equipment to 800 million

* See *Economic Indicators*, December 1965, p. 2. Total governmental expenditures for goods and services came to 123 billion dollars. I estimate that roughly about two-thirds of these outlays were for services.

dollars; automobiles and trucks to 1.2 billion dollars; aircraft and parts to over 1.4 billion dollars; agricultural machinery and tractors to 500 million dollars; and other machinery to around 1.8 billion dollars. About forty percent of the sales of the Caterpillar Tractor Company, which dominates the industrial economy of Central Illinois, are, for example, made abroad and were these markets to be lost, the results would be catastrophic for that area and indeed for others as well.

Second, there are many American products which, with proper promotion and with co-operation from both our shipping interests and foreign governments, have a potentiality for much larger exports. Among these are air conditioning and refrigerator equipment, beef, books, canned foods, sporting goods, high pressure boilers, toys, and whiskey.

Third, on the import side, we are completely dependent upon Latin America, Asia, and Africa for our coffee, cocoa, and tea, to the amount of 1.2 billion dollars a year. We import thirty-five percent of our sugar and all of our bananas. Under complete freedom of trade, we could indeed import virtually all of our sugar from the Caribbean and do so at a saving of several hundred million dollars a year. Nor is our dependence on foreign supplies confined to the breakfast table. We also import most of our raw and semi-manufactured wool from Australia, to the tune of about 300 million dollars a year, and we are dependent upon Canada for wood pulp, lumber, and paper in amounts equal to 1.75 billion dollars annually. We import another 1.75 billion dollars' worth of petroleum products, mostly from Venezuela, but increasingly from the Persian Gulf. We are becoming more dependent upon copper from Chile, bauxite from the countries of the Caribbean, and aluminum from Canada. The iron mines of Labrador are taking the place of those on the Iron Range of Northern Minnesota. Other crucial minerals which we import are cobalt, chrome, and manganese. Fifteen years ago the Paley Committee predicted that we would become more and more dependent upon foreign countries for minerals and oil, and this prediction is coming true. Had our tariffs been lower and our quotas less restrictive, we would have drawn a larger quantity of zinc, lead, and petroleum from abroad than we did.

Fourth, there are political reasons why we should interest ourselves in international trade. Whether or not we welcome the fact, we are the strongest nation in the democratic Free World. That world is challenged by the police state of communism. Our alliances with the democracies cannot be solely based on either force or sentiment. They need to be reinforced by solid economic ties which can best be created by trade across national lines between individuals and democracies.

Both economic and political considerations should therefore make us realize the importance of our foreign trade and we should not allow the protectionists to downgrade it in any cavalier fashion. In addition, our position as the center of the world's capital and financial markets lends a further importance to our foreign trade. We cannot be the world's banker if we are not a world trader.

Part Two
The Historical Development of Tariffs and Trade

3

Mercantilism

As small European states began to be formed in the later Middle Ages and the Renaissance, they almost universally adopted the economic system which has come to be known as mercantilism. This has been well defined by the Swedish economic historian, Eli F. Heckscher, as the philosophy and practice of state power.* It flourished for some centuries along with the growth of nations and nationalism. In its internal policies it sought to weaken the hold of the feudal lords as well as that of the guilds and towns and to increase the powers of the central or national state. Barriers to internal trade, such as excessive tolls, were discouraged and uniform commercial law and practices were imposed. Mercantilism, therefore, sought to broaden internal trade within the newly developing states. Externally, it tried to cut the state loose from its cosmopolitan ties with the universal Roman Catholic Church and the Holy Roman Empire. It was indeed the instrument by which the rulers of the emerging states sought to increase their power and was a means of state making. To use a modern expression, the mercantilists believed that man was made for the state and not the state for man. It is probably true that even today most

* Heckscher, Eli F., *Mercantilism*, 2 vols. New York: Barnes and Noble, Inc., 1955.

men tend to be mercantilists in their thinking, and it is still a force in the policies of nations.

In their economic dealings with foreign countries, the mercantilist states followed a series of assumptions, most of which were wrong and some of which were mutually contradictory. These may be summarized as follows:

That (as Heckscher has observed) production, incomes, and the standard of living were all static and neither did nor could increase. The idea of general world growth was totally alien to the mercantilists. A state, it was thought, could only go forward at the expense of its neighbors. It gained as they lost and lost as they gained. Any dealings between states were, therefore, a case of dog eat dog. The same principle was equally true between individuals.

These tenets were openly stated by the writers of the time, as, for example, by the celebrated French essayist, Montaigne, in 1580, "The profit of one man is the damage of another. . . . No man profiteth but by the loss of others." Forty-five years later, the jurist and philosopher, Francis Bacon, observed, "Whatsoever is somewhere gotten, is somewhere lost." The French minister, Jean Baptiste Colbert, writing on the rivalry between the maritime English and Dutch concluded: "England cannot increase the scope of employment for the ships of her subjects or increase their number other than by the diminution of those of the Dutch. . . . It must be added that trade causes perpetual strife both in time of war and in time of peace between all the nations of Europe to decide which of them shall have the greatest share."

This belief encouraged the mercantilists to use every means, whether political or economic, to take something away from their rivals. Since power was relative and not merely absolute, a state could consequently improve its position by weakening other states even if in so doing it did not add at all to its own total wealth or if it merely lost less than its rivals. Statecraft was ruthless and aimed at national power, but it was unrelated to the happiness and prosperity of its people.

The mercantilists believed that the state must, at all costs, be made strong. In order to build a navy, shipping and shipbuilding were to be encouraged as were the growing and cutting of tall timbers for masts and the breeding and training of sturdy sailors. Commodities which were required in order to wage war were either to be produced internally or, if necessary, imported but their export was to be discouraged. A high birth rate, particularly amongst country folk was to be encouraged in order to provide soldiers and, as we shall see, to keep wages low.

The mercantilists believed that production was far more important than consumption. Production meant strength while consumption meant pleasure. Since individuals grew rich by producing more than they consumed, it was thought that this rule also applied for states. The Frenchman, Antoine de Monchretien, wrote in 1615, "He who wishes for good order in the arts and to maintain their standing must never decrease profits through abundance. The brightness of the lamp is dimmer if it be too plentifully filled with oil."

It followed that the mercantilists thought that sale was more important than purchase. This was also held to be as true for the state as the individual. Thus, Charles D'Avenant, the English mercantilist of the late seventeenth century, wrote: "It is to the interest of all trading nations that their consumption should be little . . . and their own manufactures should be sold at the highest markets and sent abroad, since by what is consumed at home, one loseth only what another gets and the nation in general is not at all the richer, but all foreign consumption is a clear and net profit." Thomas Mun, likewise, declared that "We must ever observe this rule, to sell more to strangers yearly than we consume of theirs in value." Similarly, Becher, the German mercantilist, wrote, "It is always better to sell goods to others than to buy goods from others, for the former brings a certain advantage and the latter inevitable damage."

The mercantilists apparently never realized that each sale normally requires a purchase and that it is impossible to universalize the practice of selling more than is bought. For they always refrained from considering matters from a general point of view and instead chose to think only in terms of individual or national advantage.

The mercantilists taught that so far as possible a state should be economically self-sufficient. This was largely due to their paramount purpose of strengthening the state in time of war. Because of their belief in the superiority of production over consumption, they also thought that this would give a greater volume of employment. They held that more people would be employed if all the goods which a nation consumed were produced at home. If some were produced abroad, the mercantilists believed that the associated employment would be lost. That such a lack could or would be made up by producing and then exporting more of the home products in which a country had a positive or comparative advantage was never recognized.

Nevertheless, the practical advantages of mutual trade and the division of labor were so great that the mercantilistic goal of complete self-sufficiency was impossible. The very fact of trade required exchange. The mercantilists, therefore, tried to turn the terms of trade to the advantage of their state and also to that of the economic class of which they were a part. As Richard Jones pointed out, this began with what he termed "the balance of bargains," namely, that each trader should sell more abroad than he bought. When this was found to be impossible, the emphasis was shifted to the "balance of trade" where the state as a whole was expected to export more than it imported and to receive the balance in gold and silver. This desire for a surplus of exports over imports followed in part from the belief that production was superior to consumption and sales to purchases. Some of this same belief lingers on in the concepts of "favorable and unfavorable" balances of trade and of payments.

The mercantilists also stressed the importance of hoarding as much money as possible. Money was suspended purchasing power and in those days it consisted almost entirely of the so-called precious metals, namely, gold and silver. Money was especially valuable in financing wars and in meeting the expenses of sovereigns and states. Since individuals strove to accumulate money, so it was reasoned should the state. By accumulating stores of the precious metals, a state could better finance its neverceasing struggle to gain greater power both internally and externally. This emphasis upon the possession of money made many of the mercantilists confuse money with wealth, although to the more sophisticated, money was a means but not entirely an end.

In earlier days, the export of gold and silver was discouraged or prohibited, while the importation of these metals was directly encouraged. Later, this same end was sought through obtaining a "favorable" balance of trade under which exports exceeded imports. It should have been clear, of course, that all nations could not export more than they imported and that what was a "favorable" balance for some was an "unfavorable" balance for others. In fact, the mercantilistic theory was not capable of being successfully universalized.

But this did not disturb the mercantilists. That was the way the world ran—what one nation gained, another lost. The important thing was that one's own country, one's own class, and oneself should always be the gainer and never the loser.

The mercantilists, therefore, tried to stimulate exports and to discourage imports. The purchase of foreign luxury goods was especially frowned upon, and high tariffs and outright prohibitions were imposed in order to reduce or to stop such trade. But where a nation had a short supply of raw materials, such as wool which was needed for later processing and fabricating, importation from the outside was encouraged. Then, the export of the fabricated article, such as cloth, would be encouraged, sometimes by means of bounties. It was believed that in this way employment would be created in the processing trades such as spinning, weaving, and dyeing. Even today, groups which want a high tariff in order to keep out foreign manufacturers will support the free entrance of the raw materials which are needed for fabrication.

This principle was explicitly stated by Colbert, the seventeenth-century minister of Louis XIV of France, when he wrote, "The whole business of commerce consists in facilitating the import of those goods which serve the countries' manufacture, and placing embargoes on those which enter in a manufactured state."

This argument was particularly strong in those countries which had a large pool of unemployed labor which, it was thought, could only find work through such means. In the same way, the export of improved tools and machinery was almost universally prohibited, because of the fear of helping competing industries in foreign countries. England did not abandon this prohibition until well into the nineteenth century. This was evidenced by the fact that the plans for the first cotton mill in the United States at Pawtucket, Rhode Island, had to be smuggled into this country by Samuel Slater.

The mercantilistic attitude toward colonies was similar. A state wanted and fought for colonies if they could produce gold or silver. That was why Spain, in the sixteenth century, conquered Mexico, Central America, Peru, and Northern South America, while English freebooters, such as Drake, Hawkins, and Henry Morgan, with help from their mother country, "hijacked" many of the homeward-bound Spanish treasure galleons and bore their booty back to England. Despite the piratical nature of their profession, these men were rewarded, if successful, by Elizabeth and the Stuarts and were allowed to retain much of their booty. The line between piracy and patriotism was indeed not only thin but at times nonexistent. A man was a patriot if he stole from other countries; a pirate if he stole on the high seas from his own countrymen.

With respect to other commodities, the aim of the mercantilists was to restrict the colonies to the production of those raw materials which would go to the mother country for processing or resale. The colonies, in turn, were to furnish a market for the manufactured goods of the mother country. In the seventeenth and eighteenth centuries this was the chief principle of the British colonial system under which the American colonies were to produce timber, fish, and tobacco for England, but were not to engage in manufacturing for themselves.* Interestingly

* See Beer, George L., *Origins of the British Colonial System; The Old Colonial System;* and *British Colonial Policy.*

enough, the Russians are trying to follow this same policy today in respect to their Communist satellites.

As a justification for his policy of ruling Ireland with an iron hand, Lord Strafford said, "I am of the opinion that all wisdom advises to keep this Kingdom as much subordinate and dependent on England as is possible and holding them from the manufacture of wool . . . and then in forcing them to fetch their clothing from thence and to take their salt from the King (being that which preserves and gives value to all their native staple commodity) how can they depart from us without nakedness and beggary."

Such policies were not likely to win the friendship and support of the colonies. Nor did they. They were, in fact, one of the causes of the American Revolution and they helped to arouse justified bitterness on the part of the Irish toward their English overlords. A vestigial remain of this thinking is our own insistence that about a million tons of raw sugar shall not be processed in Puerto Rico, but sent instead to American refineries.

Finally, as Edgar Furniss has correctly pointed out,* the laborers were to be treated as agents of national enrichment and not as human beings to be valued for their own sake. The population was to be expanded as rapidly as possible, since, as one mercantilist wrote, "in the multitude of the people is the strength of the King." William Temple in 1770 proposed that the poor man was to be seized and locked in a workhouse "where he shall labor fourteen hours a day." Similar proposals were made by many others, and the British system of workhouses was devised to give partial effect to this program. Nor were

---

* Furniss, Edgar, *The Position of the Laborer in a System of Nationalism.* New York: Augustus M. Kelley.

the children of the poor to be spared. On the contrary, every step was to be taken "to insure them to the lowest and most early labor."

Wages, in turn, were to be forced down to the barest minimum in order to lower costs. For to do this would expand exports and enrich their employers. Such a lowering of hourly and daily wages would also force the laborers to work harder to maintain the same standards of life. This was thought to be a good policy. The utmost output was to be squeezed out of the manual workers who were to be kept as poor and as miserable as possible.

Thus, Arthur Young wrote as late as 1771, "Everyone but an idiot knows that the lower classes must be kept poor or they will never be industrious. . . . they must like all mankind be in poverty or they will not work." Weyland, nearly four decades later, came to the same conclusion; "The lowest orders should endure a state bordering on want in order that a necessity may exist for their labor."

Mandeville and Mun accurately summarized the opinions of the mercantilists and ruling classes. Mandeville declared in the *Fable of the Bees* that "it is requisite that great numbers be poor" in order that society might be happy, while Mun wrote that "plenty and power do make a nation vicious and improvident, so penury and want do make a nation wise and industrious." Adversity was considered beneficial for the poor. Arthur Young became highly indignant because the wives of the English workers wanted to drink an occasional cup of tea and eat a piece of bread. This he thought was unpardonable.

It is thus apparent that mercantilism was a cold-blooded and utterly immoral body of doctrine. While the rulers, the administrators, and the merchants wrote and spoke in terms of national advantage, they had, in fact, an alert eye to their own personal enrichment and power. Lower wages to the workers meant higher profits to their employers and to those traders who handled and exported the goods which were thus manufactured.

Moreover, the monarchs created monopolies for the benefit of their favorites and sometimes of themselves. James I and his son, Charles I, were especially addicted to this form of favoritism, and these practices helped to feed the fires of the Puritan Revolution. The colonial monopolies given to certain favored groups such as the British East India Company, which was the trading monopoly for India, and the Hudson's Bay Company, which was awarded the fur trade of Canada, helped to enrich the insiders who were granted these favors.

These gains for the favored few helped to arouse the resentment of the exploited many and paved the way for the ultimate decline of mercantilism. Those excluded from the right to trade were anxious to have the entrance gates thrown open so that they might come in. Moreover, with the rise of the democratic spirit and of popular government, people properly came to be considered as ends in themselves and not merely as means for the enrichment of others. It was no longer possible for men to write in such chilling and heartless terms of the poor.

But we should not exult prematurely over the death of mercantilism. Many traces of it remain. Perhaps every man is naturally a mercantilist and believes that his gain must come at the expense of others and that nations can only advance by forcing others backward. Hitler aimed to create a self-sufficient German empire in which Slavs and Latins were to be serfs. Politicians still speak as though an excess of exports is the supreme good of economic policy. Money is still confused with wealth, and there are still many, even in this country, who secretly think of the wage workers as subjects of the state and not as citizens and equal members of society. But, despite all this, the influence of mercantilism has declined for reasons which we shall now consider.

4

The Decline of
Mercantilism
and the Growth of
Economic
Liberalism

The Scottish philosopher, David Hume, was the first important writer who openly challenged the basic monetary doctrines of the mercantilists, namely, that a country can achieve continuing increases in both its prosperity and its stock of precious metals through surpluses in its balance of payments. Hume's aim was instead to show that the supply of money in a country would take care of itself and that action by the state was neither needed nor of any real help. To illustrate this, Hume traced the consequences under two differing sets of assumptions.

His first assumption was that the supply of money within a country such as Great Britain had decreased to one-fifth of its former volume. This, Hume said, would cause "the price of all labor and commodities to sink in proportion." "What nation," he continued, "could then dispute with us in any foreign market or pretend to . . .

sell manufactures at the same price which to us would afford sufficient profit?" *

This excess of British exports would be paid for by the foreign countries in the form of money. But this inflow of money would, in turn, raise British prices and this process would continue until the "levels" of British prices and of money were once more compatible with those abroad.

Conversely, if the quantity of money in Great Britain was suddenly multiplied fivefold, British prices would "rise to an exorbitant height." The result would be that "no neighboring nation could afford to buy from us, while their commodities, on the other hand, became comparatively so cheap that in spite of all the laws which could be formed they would be run in upon us." A large amount of money would, therefore, flow out of Great Britain and this process would continue until price and money levels in England were again appropriate to those abroad.

Nor was it necessary to have such catastrophic changes in the quantities of money and the level of prices as Hume originally assumed to create these results. The same forces would operate even if there were only slight variations. Hume also realized that fluctuations in the exchange rate could have the same effect as movements of currency. "When we import more goods than we export," he wrote in a footnote, "the exchange turns against us and this becomes a new encouragement to export as much as the charge of carriage and insurance of the money which becomes due would amount to." †

Hume concluded that there was a self-regulating mech-

---

* Hume, David, *Essays, Moral, Political, and Literary* (1898 edition) Vol. I, Part II, Essay V, "On the Balance of Trade," p. 337.

† *Ibid.*, p. 337.

anism in international trade which resulted in a comparative equality in the price levels of the various countries and in such a distribution of money between them as to maintain this relationship. Governmental measures to increase the importation of the precious metals and to diminish their exports were, at best, unnecessary and, at worst, actually harmful. If let alone, prices and money, according to Hume, would find their natural levels through the medium of international trade. "All water," he wrote, "wherever it communicates, remains always at a level." Hume, therefore, probably deserves to be regarded as the first important quantity theorist of modern times and as the most influential formulator of the modern theory of international trade.

Hume's attack on the mercantilistic doctrine that a country should strive at all costs to increase its supply of money greatly influenced his friend and fellow Scotsman, Adam Smith. Smith, therefore, somewhat imperfectly took over Hume's concept of the self-regulating mechanism of trade, prices, and the distribution of the money supply.

Smith not only added his clear exposition of the positive advantages of the division of labor but also emphasized that trade between, as well as within, countries was productive. He, therefore, concluded that the efforts of that time to restrict trade between Britain and France were economically wrong.

As he wrote, "All commerce that is carried on betwixt any two countries must necessarily be advantageous to both. The very intention of commerce is to exchange your own commodities for others which you think will be more convenient for you. When two men trade between themselves, it is undoubtedly for the advantage of both. . . . The case is exactly the same betwixt any two nations. The goods which the English merchants want to import from France are certainly more valuable to them than what they give for them."

Smith went on to say, "A nation that would enrich itself by foreign trade is certainly most likely to do so when its neighbors are all rich, industrious, and commercial nations." It followed, therefore, that efforts to impoverish one's neighbors were suicidal and worked to the ultimate disadvantage of the countries which practiced them. If France and Great Britain would only trade freely with each other, Smith argued, it would be to their mutual advantage.

In a sardonic fashion, Smith pointed out why this policy had not been followed. "Being neighbors," he wrote, "they are necessarily enemies and the wealth and power of each becomes on that account more formidable to the other and what would increase the advantage of national friendship serves only to increase the violence of national animosity. They are both rich and industrious nations and the merchants and manufacturers of each dread the competition of the skill and activity of those of the other. Mercantile jealousy is excited and both inflames and is itself inflamed by the violence of national animosity. And the traders of both countries have announced with all the passionate confidence of interested falsehood the certain ruin of each in consequence of that unfavorable balance of trade which they pretend would be the infallible effect of an unrestrained commerce with the others." But, as Smith pointed out, no country was ever impoverished by a so-called "unfavorable balance of trade" and those countries, such as Holland, which had the freest trade had profited the most.

The Wealth of Nations was first published in 1776, the same year as our Declaration of Independence. It was the

beacon light for the liberation of commercial intercourse
and economic liberalism as was Jefferson's preamble for
political liberalism. The doctrines of Smith, in fact, converted most of the few economists of the times and made
a distinct impression on such statesmen as Pitt in England, and on Jefferson, Madison, and Gallatin who were
the leaders of the nascent Democratic Party in this country.

But these principles were slow to permeate the popular
mind and the Napoleonic Wars with their sharp national
rivalries and hatreds gave economic liberalism a sharp
setback. Both France and Great Britain used commerce
as a weapon in their military struggle. Napoleon sought
to shut off all trade with Britain, while the British tried
to isolate that section of the continent which was controlled by France. But, underneath the passions created
by the wars, the doctrines of Smith were making intellectual headway and, after Waterloo, exponents of freer
trade began to appear in many countries.

David Ricardo, in his *Principles of Political Economy*,
which was published in 1817, made perhaps the greatest
contribution to the theoretical development of free trade
by stressing the doctrine of "comparative cost." But this
concept did not have as much political effect as his theory
of distribution. The rapid increase in population which
Malthus had postulated in his celebrated essay and which
was being witnessed in Great Britain was forcing both
the cultivation of the poorer soils and the more intensive
cultivation of the better soils. This meant a decrease in
the yield of farm produce which a combined unit of labor
and capital could produce at the margin of cultivation.

Ricardo held that labor and capital would receive together, as their combined share, this ever decreasing

marginal yield. The owners of land, on the other hand, would receive the increasing differentials between the yields on the better soils and those at the margin. The share of rent in the distribution of the national product would, therefore, increase, and the combined share of labor and capital taken together would fall. Ricardo further assumed that, under the Malthusian theory, the wages of labor could never permanently rise above a relatively bare minimum of existence nor fall below it. Consequently, he concluded that wages would remain relatively constant. This, in turn, meant that the full force of the increase in rents would fall upon the profits of capital. These would continue to diminish as population grew and as the margin of cultivation was pushed downward.

In other words, rents would rise at the expense of profits, and the landowning class would appropriate an ever larger share of what had been the profits of the rising capitalistic class of manufacturers and merchants. Without explicitly saying so, Ricardo, therefore, postulated a basic antagonism between the landlords, who were the inheritors of the old feudal system and, hence, largely constituted the nobility and the "establishment" of England, and the rising lords of the loom, the barons of steel and iron, the rulers of the factories which were mushrooming over the landscape of northern England and of the midlands.

There was not only an economic but also, originally, a social antagonism between the established gentry and the rising industrialists, merchants, and bankers. The former looked down upon the latter as the newly rich and had a contempt for their pushing ways and rough manners. This clash of interests expressed itself politically in a conflict between these two classes which were respectively represented by the Tory and Whig parties. The manufacturing and mercantile classes had been originally almost completely excluded from Parliament and "rotten boroughs" under the control of the aristocracy abounded. But the rising middle class won representation in the Reform Act of 1832. They then used their newly found political power to agitate for the removal of the high tariff duties on foodstuffs from abroad. Foreign wheat, for example, was much cheaper than British wheat and, as a result, British bread was more costly than it was abroad. The fact that foreign countries were prevented by the British high tariffs from exporting wheat and other foodstuffs to Britain meant, in turn, that they did not have the purchasing power with which to buy any large volume of cotton and woolen cloth or other manufactured articles from England. If England were to import wheat and pay for it in gold, the consequent increase in prices abroad would then also increase the demand for and the export of English manufactured goods.

The British mills had already largely supplied the basic needs of the home market and their owners were looking abroad for an added outlet. In order, therefore, to promote their export trade, they wanted to bring in more foodstuffs from abroad and this could only be done by a drastic reduction or elimination of tariffs. There was also another consideration in the background which those who stress the economic basis of politics have properly emphasized. This was the doctrine of the classical economists, such as Nassau Senior, that the wages of the factory workers and of the urban population could be reduced by lowering the price of food. The rising capitalistic class would therefore profit from a cut in costs as well as from an increase in the demand for its products. While this motive was real, it could not be openly stressed because the new capitalistic leaders were seeking support from the urban workers against the landlords and the nobility, and perhaps it was not consciously realized by some of the more idealistic proponents of free trade.

The political leaders of this movement for free trade were Richard Cobden and the Quaker, John Bright. Bright was the most eloquent orator in British politics and a man of great sincerity and nobility of character who later had the courage to stand alone against the Crimean War. Cobden was a skilled debater and pamphleteer. The two made a powerful team and by their campaigns both inside and outside of Parliament, they began to change the mind of Great Britain. In these two men, idealism merged with economic class interest and, as always, made a powerful amalgam.

Finally, spurred on by the horrors of the Irish famine, the Tory leader, Sir Robert Peel, yielded and, joined by the new forces represented by Bright and Cobden, repealed the protective duties on food in 1846. Great Britain thus became the first free trade country in the world. Under free trade, British exports flourished and Britain became the world's foremost industrial nation. While the price of food was greatly reduced, the wages of the British working classes did not fall as the classical economists had expected but instead rose markedly because of the increased prosperity of the country. All classes, except the landlords, benefited from the new policy.

The two parties then began to shed their former names of Whigs and Tories and came to refer to themselves instead as Liberals and Conservatives. At the same time, they began to compete with each other in an effort to gain the political support of the working classes. The Tories were largely successful in passing protective legislation for women and children, and, in 1867, under the

artful Disraeli, they extended the ballot to the urban
workers. The Liberals responded in the 1880's by en-
franchising the agricultural workers. Each side was trying
to win favor with the enemies of its enemies. On the
whole, the British industrial workers preferred the Liberals to the Conservatives until shortly after the turn of
the century when they began to create a party of their
own. While they were doing so, Liberal and Tory families
began to intermarry and their children to attend the same
private schools. The industrialists, in order to gain the
social prestige attached to the ownership of land, started
to buy country estates and to fancy themselves as members of the feudal nobility. The owners of industrial and
of agricultural property, therefore, began to draw together
socially, economically, and politically and the children of
the wealthy industrialists began to enter the ruling estab-
ment.

The successful transition of Britain from a protectionist
to a free-trade nation and its resulting prosperity strengthened the free-trade forces everywhere. In the United
States, the Walker Tariff Act, which was also passed in
1846, put us closer to a free-trade basis and our prosperity
rose rapidly during the next few years. In France, Bastiat
and Michel Chevalier were the chief exponents of the
liberation of trade and, in 1857, Cobden and Louis Napoleon negotiated a treaty of reciprocity between Great
Britain and France which opened up a much wider area
of trade between them.

At the same time, the German Zollverein was ending
internal tariffs and establishing complete freedom of trade
within the North German states and the industrial expansion of the United States was creating a continent-wide
area of complete free trade. Japan was also being opened

up for trade with the West and the China trade was grow-
ing and profitable. Trade was expanding everywhere.
Prosperity was increasing. The threat of war was receding.
Political absolutism was on the wane. Well might Robert
Browning sing with Pippa:

> The year's at the spring;
> The day's at the morn;
> Morning's at seven;
> The hill-side's dew pearled;
> The lark's on the wing;
> The snail's on the thorn;
> God's in His heaven;
> All's right with the world.

And under the influence of the Prince Consort, England
opened the first World's Trade Fair in the new Crystal
Palace to spur the movement on.

The greatest immediate source of profits in this expanded
trade lay in the substantial differences between the relative
prices in the developed and undeveloped economies. For
example, ice was of low value in New England but of high
value in China, while Chinese silks were low in value
there but high in value here. Therefore, there were big
profits for Yankee traders and shipowners to buy ice
cheap here and sell it high there, and then, with the
profits, to buy silk cheap there and sell it high back home.
Such disparities in values accounted for the great profits
made by British East India Companies and by the Dutch
in trading with Java, Sumatra, and the Spice Islands.

Similarly, low cost whiskey, flannel, rifles, and car-
tridges could also be exchanged with the Indians on this
continent for rare furs, so that by such trading the Hudson's Bay Company in Canada and American traders like
John Jacob Astor were able to make high profits.

These disparities tended to be reduced with the continued exchange of commodities, but for a long time great profits were made by the traders from the more advanced countries.

Before we condemn the Anglo-Saxon traders too severely, however, and pity the guilessness of the poor Chinese and Indians, we should remember that the latter also thought that they were getting the better of the bargain. The wealthy Chinese were receiving ice to cool their thirst in return for silk which they had in such excess that any given piece had little value to them. The Indians probably also smiled at trading off furs, of which they had excess, for rifles and ammunition, striking red flannel, and, as Caliban, for the nectar of "firewater." In these exchanges, the traders served to increase immediate satisfactions and to help equalize values between countries. In the process, they did well for themselves.

During this period it seemed that the doctrines of Adam Smith and Cobden would conquer the world and win universal acceptance. As the nations became more closely joined together in trade and became more dependent on each other, the future seemed to promise not only material prosperity for all, but the coming of universal peace. In the spirit of the age, Tennyson, the favorite poet of the Victorians, wrote of the time:

> When the war drums beat no longer
> And the battle flags are furled
> In the Parliament of man
> The confederation of the world!

But, across this rosy vista fell first a shadow and then a clap of thunder which swept away the idyllic pastoral.

5
The
Revival of Nationalism
and the Rise of
Modern Protectionism

The thunderstorm of war began to beat in upon the world
as it does in Beethoven's Pastoral Symphony. The West
had enjoyed nearly a half century of peace since Napoleon had been defeated at Waterloo. But in 1861 the
bloody Civil War broke out in America and Walker's free-
trade system of 1846 was replaced by high protective
duties in this country.

During the next decade, Bismarck cemented Prussia's
domination over Germany by a successive series of wars
with Denmark, Austria, and France, respectively. In the
course of these, Schleswig-Holstein was detached from
Denmark and both Alsace and Lorraine from France.
Bavaria was tied to Prussia rather than to Austria. But
this policy of blood and iron forged a French passion for
revenge which discouraged economic co-operation between these two great European powers. Neither France
nor Germany wanted to be dependent upon the other.
This was particularly true in the case of foodstuffs. As a
safeguard against another possible conflict between them,

both France and Germany, therefore, gradually became high-tariff countries,* and each increasingly protected its own farmers.

Nor did the mischief stop there. The unification of Italy in 1871 and the end of internal tariffs were quickly followed by the levying of higher external tariffs. In the late 1880's these policies erupted into a tariff war between Italy and France from which the mutual trade between the two countries was slow to recover.

During this period, all of the European countries were, as I have intimated, sucked into colonial and imperialistic ventures which intensified the competitive strains between them. Britain had begun in the eighteenth century with India and had gone on to settle the dominions of Canada, Australia, and New Zealand. She now vied with France for the control of Africa. The projected English line of control ran from north to south, starting with Egypt, the Sudan, and Nigeria, and running down through the heart of the continent to South Africa, which she took over at the end of the century in the bloody Boer War.

The French tried to build up their African empire from east to west and to cut the Cape to Cairo axis so dear to the heart of the British imperialist, Cecil Rhodes. This almost led to war, but a compromise was finally reached which allowed France to have wider territories in central and west Africa. Germany also took slices of southeastern and southwestern Africa. King Leopold of Belgium organized a private company to exploit the Congo and, in order to gain the maximum amount of rubber and of profits, permitted and perhaps encouraged cruel atrocities upon the helpless natives. Little Portugal, under the protection of its historical ally, Britain, strengthened its hold

* This development is well traced in Percy Ashley's *Modern Tariff History.*

on strategic sections in both southeast and southwest Africa.

The same struggle went on in Asia. As far back as the seventeenth century, Holland had taken possession of Java, Sumatra, and the Spice Islands of the Dutch East Indies. Spain had made itself master of the Philippines, and Britain extended her control over Burma and Ceylon with a dominating influence over Malaysia just north of its great naval base at Singapore. France took Indochina with its three subdivisions of Vietnam, Cambodia, and Laos. The great powers were then on the point of dividing up China, but United States protests helped to prevent this. Only Japan among the nations of the Orient kept its independence. It did so by combining German militarism with British industrialism, cemented by a mystical worship of the Emperor.

At the turn of the century, the United States abandoned its continental isolation and joined the race for empire. As a result of our war with Spain, we took control over Puerto Rico, the Philippines, and Guam and assumed a virtual protectorate over Cuba. At the same time we annexed Hawaii in the Pacific and took over Eastern Samoa. By 1900 most of the world was parceled out among the big powers—a process glorified in the poems and stories of the apostle of imperialism, Rudyard Kipling, and his lesser follower, Sir Henry Newbolt.

The European powers in their colonial policies now relapsed into the practices of the mercantilists of previous centuries. They encouraged the colonies to furnish foodstuffs and raw materials for the imperial country and, in return, they used the colonies as markets for the manufactured goods of the dominant nations and as outlets for their capital investments. The colonies were indeed treated again as happy dumping grounds for the capital and manufactured goods of the controlling powers. Rivalry between the European countries for these economic opportunities was one of the causes for the increasing international tensions, although the desire for greater relative power and dominance and to "paint the map red" may have been an even stronger motive among such imperialists as the German Kaiser Wilhelm II, the British Lord Salisbury and the French statesman, Delcassé.

By 1905, the centers of conflict had shifted to the Balkans and the Middle East. In the former, the primary rivalry was between Austria and Russia, while in the latter, Germany and Great Britain were the contestants. France allied herself with Russia, and Germany with Austria and Italy. The fears of war deepened. Great Britain tried at first to keep itself neutral and to hold the balance of power between the rival continental alliances. But Germany then began to build a big navy with the intention of taking the control over the seas away from Great Britain, or, at the very least, sharing that control with her. Britain could not endure such a possibility and the race in battleships began.

As the rivalry grew keener, Britain formed a tacit defensive alliance with France under which it was understood by the two foreign offices that Britain would come to the aid of France if the latter were attacked. This agreement was kept secret both from Germany and from the British people. In 1914 when Germany invaded Belgium in order to attack France, the British government felt that both its interests and its honor required it to help France. The First World War had started and soon spanned the globe. In 1917 when the scales were somewhat tipping in favor of Germany, the United States entered the war on the side of Great Britain and France.

This alliance finally triumphed in the next year and Germany was defeated.

When the war ended, Great Britain was almost the only country which still clung to free trade. The rest of the world had gone over to protection both for industrial and agricultural products. As countries such as Poland and Czechoslovakia gained their independence, they imposed tariffs on manufactured goods in order to build up their home industries and to become more self-sufficient. The same trend developed in the English-speaking colonies as they progressed from mere colonial dominions to self-governing commonwealths. Russia turned Communist and shut itself off from the rest of the world by a system of rigid state control over both imports and exports.

Finally, Great Britain could maintain free trade no longer. Because of the marked decrease in her exports of cotton and woolen goods and of coal and steel, she suffered from high unemployment throughout the 1920's. The development of internal monopolies and cartels and an unwise monetary policy also helped to choke off demand, production, and employment within the British Isles. With the advent of the worldwide depression in 1929, British production fell still further and unemployment soared. England's balance of payments became steadily more adverse. Her exports suffered from the high protective tariff passed by the United States in the summer of 1930. A year later she was carried off the gold standard and soon afterwards gave up free trade and adopted a protective tariff on manufactured goods under a general system of Empire preference. Under these agreements finally negotiated at Ottawa in 1932, Britain sought and obtained a preference for her manufactured goods in the countries of the Commonwealth, notably Canada, Australia, and New Zealand, and in return gave favored treatment on wheat, meat, and dairy products from these commonwealths and colonies. The earlier enthusiasm for free trade had largely evaporated and English industrialists no longer had the buoyant self-confidence of the previous century. They sought shelter within their widespread empire instead of seeking to conquer the trade of the world in the competition of the market.

Hitler took power in Germany in the winter of 1933 and immediately launched his program of autarchy, or economic self-sufficiency similar to a policy Mussolini had been following for a decade. Just as economic internationalism had won out in the 1850's, so now economic nationalism and a revival of mercantilism was for a while in the ascendant. During the next six years, as Hitler and Mussolini went from one apparent triumph to another, while unemployment was still intense in the Anglo-Saxon democracies, one trade restriction after another was placed upon the international exchange of commodities. Books were written proclaiming the end of free trade and the coming of managed commerce. Under the shadow of war, the world seemed to be reverting to the most restrictive and violent forms of mercantilism. The only liberalizing tendency in world trade during the period after 1934 came from an unexpected quarter, namely, the United States, hitherto a high-tariff country.

6

The Tariff in America
from Alexander Hamilton
to Cordell Hull

The tariff has been one of the basic issues in American
politics. From the very beginning, the vast majority of
manufacturers have wanted a high tariff on imported textiles, on iron, steel, and other fabricated articles to protect
them from foreign imports and to allow them to obtain
higher prices for the goods they manufactured. The American lords of the loom and the magnates of iron and steel,
therefore, became the driving forces behind the movement for a protective tariff. They first used the Whig and,
later, the Republican party as the vehicles for their political action. The banking and professional groups affiliated
with the manufacturing interests naturally followed their
lead. All these factors helped to make, first, Whiggism
and, then, Republicanism dominant in southern New
England, in most of the middle states and, after the Civil
War, in northern New England as well. Hamilton laid the
intellectual foundation for American protectionism in
his Report on Manufactures, while Clay, Webster, and
Mathew Carey were, later, its chief exponents.

On the other hand, the Southern planters who grew

cotton and tobacco did not want high tariffs, for these meant higher prices for the cloth and tools which they had to buy. Moreover, by directly restricting the amount of goods which the European countries—notably England —could sell to us, tariffs also tended to limit the amount of cotton and tobacco which we could sell to them. Such a curtailment of the European markets reduced the prices of these commodities inside the United States, and the dominant economic and social groups in the South therefore came to oppose protection as strongly as the corresponding dominant group in the North were favoring it.

This conflict between South and North over trade policy was not as important as that over the expansion of slavery, nor did it involve such a grave moral issue. But it was a source of friction which contributed to the final cleavage between the sections, and, on this point, the Southern lords of the lash were more nearly correct than the Northern lords of the loom.

In the Virginia and Kentucky Resolutions of 1799, Madison, reversing his earlier nationalism, had developed the doctrine that states might refuse to comply with the edicts of the federal government. Later, this doctrine was repeated by the New England Federalists who opposed the War of 1812, but it was first put into open effect by South Carolina in 1832, in protest against the protective features of the so-called "tariff of abominations" which had raised the average import duties to nearly forty-four percent. Only the threat of force by President Andrew Jackson caused the South Carolinians to back down. The doctrine of "Nullification" which Calhoun had learned from the conservative Federalists as a student at Yale and then at the Litchfield Law School were first applied by him in the cause of free trade and later in his defense of slavery and inequality.

This conflict over the tariff was one of the main differences between the Democratic Party, led successively by Jackson, Van Buren, and Polk, and the Whigs, led by Webster and Clay. Some of the worst abuses of the "tariff of abominations" were later reduced in the Jackson administration, but in 1842 another Whig tariff was passed under the Tyler administration. The Democrats came back to power in the election of 1844 when Polk was chosen President. Under the sponsorship of Robert J. Walker, the free trader from Alabama who was Secretary of the Treasury in Polk's cabinet, protective tariffs as such were largely abolished by the Act of 1846, and almost completely so by the Tariff Act of 1857, passed during the Presidency of Buchanan. The fifteen years from 1846 on were indeed the golden age of free trade. Great Britain, as we have pointed out, had turned from protection to free trade at the same time and had opened its doors to American foodstuffs and raw materials.

During this period, the prosperity of both the United States and Great Britain soared. During the twenty years from 1840 to 1860 our population almost doubled—from 17 million to 31.4 million people and the proportion of our people living in cities of over eight thousand people rose from 12.5 to 16.1 percent.

At the same time, the production of wheat also doubled from 85 million to 173 million bushels. Of course, this was not only because America could now sell in European markets as a result of the free trade between the United States and Great Britain, but was also due to improvements in farm machinery, such as McCormick's reaper and the iron plow. The production of corn more than doubled, from 377 million to 839 million bushels. The annual cotton crop increased from 1.3 million to 4.5 million bales, a total not to be reached again until 1877.

The value of manufactured products rose from 1.0 billion in 1850 to 1.88 billion dollars in 1860—or an increase of eighty-eight percent in ten years. Much of this was due to new inventions and to better transportation, but the stimulus of broader international trade was also important.

The coal output increased from 1.8 million to 13 million tons—or a sevenfold increase in twenty years. The annual output of pig iron rose by three fold during this period —or from 287 thousand to 821 thousand tons. The production of steel rails increased ninefold between 1842 and 1860—namely, from 24 thousand to 205 thousand tons. The number of cotton spindles in operation went up from an estimated 2.3 million to 5.2 million in 1860. This is an increase of 126 percent.

The volume of foreign trade greatly expanded. In the ten years from 1847 to 1857—the years of the Walker Tariff—our exports doubled, rising from approximately 163 million to 306 million dollars, while our imports multiplied three times from 127 million to 363 million dollars.

During this period our customs revenue rose from 27.5 million dollars, under the protective tariff of 1843, to 64 million dollars under the Walker Tariff. In practice, therefore, the low tariff meant greater revenues, cheaper products for consumers, and greater prosperity.

Having adopted an ambiguous attitude on far too many issues, the Whig Party died in the 1850's and was succeeded by the Republican Party. Because the Republicans took a direct and forthright stand against the territorial extension of slavery, they attracted the idealistic men and women of the North and West. Furthermore, by pledging to give 160 acres of public land to anyone who would homestead beyond the Mississippi, they became "free soilers" in a double sense. But, along with the desire to contain slavery and to build the Mississippi Valley upon the basis of small independent farmers, the Republicans were also the spokesmen for the manufacturing interests of the East. These groups wanted to restore and, if possible, to increase the protective duties which had been cut under the preceding Democratic administrations. Protection was, therefore, one of the basic planks of the Republican platform of 1860.

When the Republicans came to power in 1861, they promptly moved to carry this policy into effect. By the successive Morrill Acts of 1861, 1862, and 1864, the tariffs were raised to an average level of forty-seven percent.*

The manufacturers whose products bore a wartime internal excise tax were given a more than compensatory subsidy in the form of increased tariffs. This meant that the consumers bore a double burden. They paid for the excise taxes levied on domestic manufactured goods and also for higher import prices resulting from increased tariffs. The decrease in imports from abroad also caused higher cost American goods to be produced. In addition, everyone

---

* The party lineup on the Morrill Acts is extremely interesting. In the final vote on the Morrill Act of 1861, 89 of the 105 yea votes in the House were from Republicans and Whigs. Seven were from Democrats and nine from minor parties. Of the 64 nays, 59 were from Democrats. In the Senate, 22 of the 25 yea votes were from Republicans, two were from the allied party of Free Soilers while only one was a Democrat. On the other hand, 13 of the 14 negative votes were from Democrats. In the vote on the Morrill Act of 1864, 73 of the 82 affirmative votes were from the Republicans and their satellites. The Democrats furnished 23 of the 26 opposition votes. In the Senate all but one of the affirmative votes for protection came from the Republicans and their allies and all five negative votes were from Democrats. These votes indicate where the party responsibility lies for the origins of modern protectionism.

paid higher prices under the rampant inflation caused by financing so large a proportion of the costs of the War by the issuance of greenbacks rather than by levying direct taxes.

Despite the belated efforts of Lincoln to compensate in part for these burdens by enacting a Federal income tax, the lower- and middle-income groups bore the major share of the financial as well as the human sacrifices of the war. In contrast, the business groups did very well and many of the great American fortunes were created during these very years.

The passions aroused by the Civil War were so strong that, despite close elections in 1876 and 1880, the Republican Party stayed in power throughout the next twenty years. In 1872, the internal excise taxes on manufactured goods were ended, but most of the external protective tariffs which had been partially defended as a compensatory device for them were retained. This still further helped the business interests. The high tariffs during this period produced an annual surplus of around 100 million dollars, which was a large sum for those days.

In protest against this, a movement by farmers and consumers to reduce the protective duties gained headway in both South and West, but this drive was blocked by the manipulation of the Southern Congressional vote, which was still under military control. Instead, cuts in the tariff were limited to an average of about one-tenth, or a decrease from forty-seven to forty-three percent overall. Furthermore, these decreases were largely confined to articles which we did not manufacture and the reductions, therefore, did not weaken the protective aspect of the tariff structure. Finally, these same cuts were restored in 1875 while the fall in the general price level from 1873 to 1897 greatly increased the relative protection given by the specific duties. As for the troublesome government surplus, this was taken care of by the payment of liberal and widespread pensions to the veterans of the Civil War. The emotional alliance between the G.O.P. (Grand Old Party) and the G.A.R. (Grand Army of the Republic) was thus cemented by strong economic ties.

Nor was this high level of protection reduced by the Tariff Act of 1883. After a minute examination, the tariff historian, F. W. Taussig, concluded that, "looking at the tariff system as a whole, it retained, substantially unchanged, the high level of duties reached during and after the Civil War." In 1884, however, the Democrats broke the virtual Republican monopoly of political power by electing Grover Cleveland as President. The forces of change were gathering strength.

As Grover Cleveland was finishing his first term, he decided to make the tariff the paramount issue for the coming campaign and devoted his entire annual message of 1887 to the subject of tariff reform. In this message he called the tariff "a vicious, inequitable, and illogical source of unnecessary taxation." The Republicans won the subsequent election (although Cleveland received a slight popular majority) and they took this as a mandate not merely to maintain the existing rates but actually to raise them. This was done in the McKinley tariff of 1890 which increased the general average to approximately fifty percent.

The Democrats won the next election in 1892 and Cleveland came back for his second term. In 1894, the somewhat unsatisfactory Wilson Act was passed which reduced duties by an average of about one-fifth. This was the rough equivalent of a forty-percent tariff. But the tariff lobbies were sufficiently strong inside both parties so that many protective features were retained.

The fundamental economic and political forces behind both the protective- and low-tariff forces remained largely the same. The Republican protectionists were supported by the manufacturers of the North and East, while the low-tariff Democrats drew their chief strength from the cotton and tobacco exporters of the South, plus the importing houses of the Northern coastal cities. The Northern manufacturers, in turn, were successful in convincing many of the urban workers that a low tariff would throw them out of work.

Conflicting loyalties were at work in the wheat-exporting centers of the Middlewest. The economic interests of the farmers were definitely injured by protection, for this raised the prices of the goods which they bought and, by reciprocally contracting the amounts of foodstuffs they could sell abroad, reduced the prices of what they produced. Nevertheless, the memory that it was the Republican Party which had fought the Civil War, pensioned the veterans, and given homesteads to the farmers served to keep them basically loyal to the party which also espoused protection.

The growing number of the independent and middle-class professional workers was a more complicating factor. Many college professors and teachers, editors, lawyers, and doctors became convinced that protection was uneconomic. They had also been repelled by the corruption of the Grant Administration and by the way Tilden had been maneuvered out of the Presidency in 1876. Led by such journalists as Godkin of the *Nation* and Samuel Bowles of the *Springfield Republican*, and by such leaders as Carl Schurz and George William Curtis, they became politically independent and were derisively styled "Mugwumps." They supported Cleveland in his first campaign of 1884 and stayed with him in 1888 and 1892 as he made low tariffs and civil service reform his dominant issues.

But the development of Populism in the Western states and the nomination of Bryan in 1896 by the Democrats turned this group back to the Republicans. For while Bryan was a low-tariff man, his basic program was to expand the currency and raise the price level by the unlimited coinage of silver at a ratio with gold of sixteen to one. While he united the South and the states west of the Mississippi, he lost those east of the Mississippi and north of the Ohio and was defeated.

When the Republicans came back to power in 1897 under McKinley, they promptly raised the tariff once again. By the Dingley Tariff of 1897 the rates were increased on such commodities as iron and steel, sugar, tobacco, steel rails, petroleum, lead, copper, salt, matches, whiskey, tin cans, locomotives, glassware, rubber, and leather goods. At the same time, the movement towards monopoly was gathering headway with an increasing number of pools and mergers and the restriction of foreign competition made it easier for American concerns to control output and to raise prices.

By the turn of the century and with the formation of the U.S. Steel Corporation, the merger movement gathered further speed. Bryan tried to rally the country behind an antitrust and anti-imperialistic program in 1900, but was unsuccessful and was once again defeated in 1908. After twelve years under the Dingley rates, despite rumblings of opposition, the Republicans refused to lower the tariff schedules and passed the Payne-Aldrich tariff of 1909. The duty on hides was abolished to help the shoe industry, but those on iron and steel were maintained and the rates on silk and cotton goods and many minor items were actually increased.

Taussig well summarized the realities of the Payne-Aldrich Tariff when he wrote, "This act, as finally passed, brought no real breach in the tariff wall and no downward revision of any serious consequence. . . . In the Senate things went on in star chamber fashion and the familiar logrolling and manipulation was once again to be seen."

Instead of vetoing the bill as many had hoped, President Taft not only signed it, but on a Western tour endorsed it in ringing terms. All this deepened the split in the Republican Party and helped to lead to the formation of the Progressive Party in 1912 and the nomination by this party of Theodore Roosevelt. It also increased the popular drift toward the Democrat Party.

As a result of the cleavage in the Republican Party and general discontent over Republican policies which were believed to favor big business, the Democrats won a sweeping victory in 1912 and elected Woodrow Wilson President. Wilson swiftly moved to reduce tariffs. After a severe struggle in Congress, during which Wilson denounced the pressures of the tariff lobbies, the Underwood Tariff was passed. This was the first real breach in the protective tariff since the Civil War. The trend of a half century was reversed by a sharp reduction in rates down to an average of about thirty percent—a cut of approximately two-fifths.

During the first two years of Wilson's Administration, the Federal Reserve System was established, the Federal Trade Commission created, and the Clayton Act passed, along with a system of rural credits. Tariff reform was, therefore, not an isolated achievement but was accompanied by a wave of other reforms as well.

World War I broke out in 1914 and for the next six years Wilson's attention was turned from domestic to international problems. With our entrance into the struggle in 1917, the conduct of the war and later the problems of the peace absorbed virtually all public energies.

The post-war reaction swept the Democrats out of power in 1920 and the Republicans took control for the next twelve years. During this period the tariff was twice increased. By the Fordney-McCumber Tariff of 1922, the reductions which had been made in 1913 were canceled and the rates were raised back to the Payne-Aldrich level of 1909. One feature of this Act was the power given to the President to raise or lower duties by fifty percent to equalize production costs. Of the thirty-seven times in which this authority was used, in no less than thirty-two cases duties were further increased.

However, one change made by executive action in 1923 was curiously a step towards broader trade. This was the unconditional interpretation given to the so-called "most favored nation" clause. Formerly, the clause had been interpreted to limit the application of any tariff concession, in the first instance, to the country with which it was originally negotiated. Other countries could then receive the same concession upon granting the United States a *quid pro quo* equivalent to that originally received by the United States. The most-favored-nation clause was now inserted into treaties of friendship, navigation, and commerce in an unconditional form, whereby a tariff concession granted to *any* country would automatically be generalized to all countries with which we had such treaties. But since our tariffs consisted almost entirely of single rate schedules without differentiation between countries, the difference between the old and the new interpretations was more important in theory than in practice.

But even the Fordney-McCumber rates were thought inadequate by the dominant industrial and political interests of the country and, after the sweeping Republican victory of 1928, the Smoot-Hawley-Grundy Act of 1930 raised the tariff once more, this time to a schedule which was greatly above the Payne-Aldrich level, in fact, the highest level in our history. It was the remedy which the protectionists believed would check the deepening depression and give employment to more labor. By keeping out foreign goods, it was argued, more jobs would be created for American workers and more business and higher profits for American business.

Over a thousand economists signed a petition of protest. They pointed out that the new tariff would not only curtail our exports through the normal processes of international trade, but would also cause other nations to raise their tariffs in retaliation and consequently wreak double damage. The real national revenue would be reduced and the consumers injured, declared the petitioners, and unemployment, which was already heavy, would also be increased.* Despite these protests, President Hoover, like Taft twenty years before him, signed the bill.

The results bore out the predictions of the economists. Other countries rapidly raised their tariffs. Even Great Britain went protectionist and the Commonwealth countries adopted empire preference. International trade slumped and so did production and employment until by the end of 1932 there were some sixteen million unemployed in our country alone. Every bank in the country had to be closed temporarily to control the increase in the already large number of bank failures. The increase in our tariff was, of course, not the exclusive and probably not

* I hope I may be pardoned if I mention that I had a leading share in drafting this statement.

even the major cause for these unfortunate developments, but it was a powerful contributing force.

Just as there had been a popular revulsion in 1912 from the protectionist and other policies of the preceding years, so the Great Depression brought another economic and political revolt. The Democrats came back into power and Franklin Roosevelt embarked on his New Deal. The veteran freetrader, Cordell Hull of Tennessee, became Secretary of State, and the Administration immediately launched a program to reduce tariffs and to expand international trade.

7

The Hull Program of
Reciprocal Trade Agreements
1934 - 1960
and Our Relations with
GATT

Under Cordell Hull's leadership and with the support of President Roosevelt, our country now reversed its previous policy of high protection. This occurred while the rest of the world was moving rapidly in the direction of higher tariffs, rigid import quotas, and exaggerated economic nationalism. Hull chose the method of reciprocal trade agreements as the instrument with which to combat this world-wide movement toward restricted trade.

His first great change was in method. Instead of seeking to reduce the whole range of tariff schedules through legislation, as Cleveland and Wilson had done, Hull proposed to accomplish the same result by giving to the President the power to negotiate reciprocal reductions with other countries. These reductions were to be carried out through the medium of executive agreements, which, unlike either tariffs or commercial treaties, did not have to be ratified by the Senate. Past experience had abundantly demonstrated that when Congress acted upon the whole gamut of tariff schedules it had been so overwhelmed by the special interests that it could not properly defend the general interest. Special private and industrial interests stood to gain large sums by protection, and therefore they spent huge amounts in lobbying, hiring attorneys and public relations men, and in stirring up popular sentiment in their favor.

In contrast, the interests of the consumers were so diffused and fragmented that any one family did not stand to lose appreciably by increases in the duties on any one group of commodities. The consumers were therefore relatively uninformed and apathetic about the fate of specific tariff schedules. Moreover, the importers and exporters who were actually hurt by protective restrictions were far weaker than the groups demanding protection.

And yet the interests of the people and of the nation as a whole are directly hurt by the general policy of protection. The whole process is an example of the ability of special interests to triumph over diffused general interests. The pennies taken from every family did not furnish an adequate defense against the fortunes amassed from them by the few. This is still one of the gravest weaknesses in our democratic system, demonstrating that the theory of countervailing checks exercised by differing occupational groups, which Madison had expounded in the tenth essay of the *Federalist,* cannot be relied upon to work adequately in practice.

The Hull Trade Agreements Act of 1934 was an attempt to overcome this difficulty by giving to the President the power for three years to negotiate mutual tariff-cutting agreements with foreign countries. Reciprocal rather than unilateral reductions were therefore to be the apparent vehicle through which the tariffs were to be lowered.

They were to be mutually bargained down rather than initially lowered by us alone.

But these reductions were to be further extended to other countries by the broadest possible policy of nondiscrimination and an extended interpretation of the "most favored nation" principle. The 1934 Act was very specific on this point, although it is not certain that this feature was fully understood at the time either by the general public or by some of the writers upon the subject. It declared that tariff concessions resulting from such agreements should also be granted to "all foreign countries," provided only that they did not discriminate against our goods and commerce or otherwise act contrary to the purposes of the Act. In other words, if we made an agreement with one country under which we mutually lowered tariff rates on each other's products, our concessions would then be granted to all other countries even though they did not grant us any specific concessions in return. It was enough merely that they did not specifically discriminate against us. While tariff reductions were to be triggered by such reciprocal agreements between the United States and individual foreign countries, they were thereupon subsequently automatically extended to virtually all countries.

This was a vigorous move in the direction of expanded world trade. It went far beyond the Harding-Hughes policy of 1923. For this had committed us only to extending the concessions granted to any one country to those other countries with which we had concluded treaties of friendship, navigation, and commerce containing the most-favored nation clause. Secretary Hull hoped that by his policy of actively negotiating trade agreements he could offset the restrictive practices of other nations. His program differed essentially from earlier attempts to reduce the U.S. tariff.

He did not propose a unilateral reduction in the tariff as had been effected legislatively by the Wilson-Underwood tariff of 1913. Instead, American tariffs were to be lowered only in return for comparable, or reciprocal, reductions in the tariffs of other countries. Then concessions granted to one country were to be extended to all. But, if a nation *did* openly discriminate against us, the President could deny it the benefits spelled out in the new agreements and maintain the Smoot-Hawley schedules on its products. This penalty was, however, only to be imposed for outright discrimination against our trade and commerce and not because of the continuance or even the further increase of generalized high tariffs, as such. In this sense, the policy of nondiscrimination established by the Act was far broader than that which had been generally practiced by the European powers. Their usual practice was, at most, to extend specific trade favors to other countries with whom they had specific tariff agreements. Within a few years the United States therefore moved from an extremely restrictive interpretation of the most favored nation principle to a unique position at the other extreme.

The Hull Act was successively renewed for additional periods of three years in 1937 and 1940, then for two years in 1943, and for three years in 1945. During these twelve years from 1934 through 1946, agreements were concluded with no less than twenty-nine countries of which those with Canada, Cuba, Belgium, the Netherlands, France, Great Britain, and various Latin American countries were the most important. The totalitarian countries operating within the economic orbits of Germany, Russia, Italy, and Japan would not sign such agreements so that, in practice, the system was confined to the so-called Free World. In 1951, the Soviet bloc was specifically excluded from the principle of nondiscrimination.

The Canadian agreements were perhaps the most important since they succeeded in breaking through the restrictions which we had imposed on our side in 1930 by the Hawley-Smoot-Grundy tariff and they by the Empire Preference, or Ottawa Agreement of 1932. The concessions made to Canada were thereafter automatically extended to all other nations and the same principle was followed as successive agreements with Great Britain and other countries were concluded.

But the outbreak of the Second World War in the summer of 1939 suspended the ordinary processes of peaceful competitive trading and led everywhere to strict governmental control of both the kinds and quantities of goods which could be exported and imported. In such a world of closely regulated state trading, which was necessarily concerned almost entirely with national survival and power, reciprocal trade between nations had an archaic and obsolete meaning.

After the Democrats had won their fourth consecutive Presidential victory in 1944 with a substantial majority in both the House and Senate, Congress not only extended the trade agreements for another three years in 1945, but also gave to the President the power to reduce tariffs by a further cut of fifty percent. Thus, if a given tariff had already been lowered by fifty percent, the President was authorized to conclude agreements which could further lower it to a figure only one-quarter as high as the original schedules. This Act of 1945 was indeed a major milestone in the movement for reciprocal trade.

During the latter part of World War II, we began to lay plans with our allies for the trade policies and practices which all should follow after the war. Along with this went plans for the maintenance of stable currencies and adequate international investment. The war had so disrupted the ordinary processes and channels of trade that, by and large, export and import trade was carried out under government controls and, except in Canada, goods were only being exported and imported under license. The Roosevelt Administration was therefore properly afraid that these severe restrictions would be continued or tightened when peace came again and that Hull's policies would be submerged in the quicksands of mercantilistic nationalism.

We moreover wanted a general or multilateral agreement among the nations of the Free World so that trade would be conducted under a broad set of rules governing international commercial relations and under which we would get as well as give. Therefore the United States sought to place the whole process of tariff bargaining in a multilateral frame of negotiation instead of continuing with the previous pattern of a wide series of separate individual agreements under which we automatically extended concessions to nonparticipating countries but had no reciprocal assurance that equal concessions would be given us in return. These proposed simultaneous and multilateral negotiations would be at once simpler to conduct and take less time to carry through than a long series of individually bargained agreements.

By requiring simultaneous concessions from all of the participating countries, such a procedure reduced the weaknesses created by our somewhat overgenerous application of the most favored nation principle. For, as we must again emphasize, this had extended reductions to countries which, while they had not explicitly discriminated against us, had nevertheless not provided adequate reciprocal reductions. Under a general agreement, however, everyone who came to the common bargaining table was to be required to grant what the other countries regarded as equivalent concessions in return for the general benefits which were to be granted to them. A many sided process of mutual bargaining and of concessions conducted in one place and at one time would therefore become possible.

Largely under American leadership, such a General Agreement on Tariffs and Trade (GATT) was finally completed in October, 1947, with twenty-three other countries which had either been wartime allies or friendly neutrals. This Agreement went into effect in January, 1948, and not only provided for mutual concessions by many countries on thousands of specific commodities, but also laid down the general principles of international trade which the countries agreed to follow in the future. The nations pledged themselves to reduce trade barriers by lowering tariffs and to do away, as a general principle, with quotas, licenses, and other impediments to trade between nations. Certain carefully defined exceptions to this general rule were permitted, such as in the case of farm products, necessary sanitary regulations, and, most importantly, where countries were suffering from balance of payment difficulties. The countries also agreed under Article XIV that they would not discriminate against each other except in special circumstances and, under Article I, adopted the unconditional form of the most favored nation clause for its members.

GATT provided relief to the European countries which had been devastated by the war. Since they had little foreign exchange in the form of gold or American dollars, they were permitted to impose quotas on the importation of foreign goods and these were primarily consumers' goods from the United States. These exceptions were probably justified at the time, but, as we shall see, they were continued by the European countries long after they had recovered from the effects of the war and after their balances of international payments had become favorable. The United States was then forced into the position of having extended tariff reductions to our allies while they made their reciprocal reductions to us largely inoperative by applying strict quotas against the importation of our goods.

This was bad enough when practiced by our former allies but, as our former opponents gradually entered GATT and obtained the right to impose quotas because of "exchange difficulties," this unfairness was compounded. Despite the reductions in the explicit tariff schedules, there was not therefore real mutuality in the total arrangements.

It is to the credit of our government and people that, despite the disadvantages which we have suffered, we have nevertheless persisted throughout the postwar period in giving vast amounts of economic and military aid to the other nations of the Free World, aid now amounting to more than 115 billion dollars. At the same time, we have patiently borne discriminatory acts against our trade while we have worked for the reduction of trade barriers and for broader and more extensive commerce between the countries. In a world of political and economic realities, no nation could have acted more unselfishly, or with greater concern for the long-run welfare of the world. It is not improper, therefore, for us to ask for some reciprocal consideration and co-operation from the other nations of the Western World.

It is true that the intensity with which we have pursued these high-minded ends has ebbed and flowed. The ever present and powerful protectionist interests have always been opposed to this policy and have exercised a strong restraining influence. This has been strengthened by the justified feeling that, under the reciprocal trade program, we have made concessions to others which have not been fully returned. We could certainly have made more progress towards freer trade had other nations co-operated more fully.

While the concrete details of GATT, as it came to be called, were being developed, the United States was also pushing for the creation of another and still more ambitious body with even broader powers, namely, the International Trade Organization (ITO). The charter for this organization was completed at Havana in late 1947. This charter included rules which paralleled the GATT provisions on international trade, but it also added further provisions restricting cartels and monopolies, regulating commodity agreements, fostering economic development and investment, and providing for the creation and government of the ITO itself.* The new organization was designed to discourage international cartels and monopolies among the industrialized nations which would restrict output and raise prices and, at the same time, to permit commodity agreements or cartels for raw materials from the tropical and underdeveloped countries on such raw materials as coffee, sugar, cocoa, and jute. As Clair Wilcox remarked, these two latter provisions were, in a sense, mutually contradictory.

But the ITO was stillborn. The United States did not ratify the treaty nor did any other nation formally join it. The trade provisions, however, were salvaged and GATT was set up with its headquarters in Geneva. In view of the cold reception which the ITO had received at

* The best description of this proposal is in Clair Wilcox's *A Charter for World Trade*.

the hands of the Senate, the Administration decided that it would not submit the GATT agreement for formal Senate ratification but would instead put it into effect by executive agreement.* Although this action could be justified under the 1934 Reciprocal Trade Act, such a bypassing of the Senate helped to strengthen the movement for the so-called "Bricker Amendment" to the Constitution.

This amendment was designed to outlaw such agreements by the executive and to require in their place either Senate ratification or, in many cases, state action. While this resentment was not only understandable and indeed to some degree justified, the Bricker amendment was far too cumbersome and restrictive. By requiring the states to act on treaties of commerce where the privileges granted to foreigners were, under our Constitution, matters for state regulation, the Bricker amendment would have made it almost impossible to negotiate such treaties with the other countries of the world where it was the central governments which universally had the power to grant such internal rights to foreigners. The submission of a modified version of this amendment to the states was defeated in the Senate by a margin of only one vote.

Before we continue with an account of negotiations under GATT, let us return to the political developments inside the United States as they have affected tariffs and trade. After fourteen years of political dominance, the Democrats suffered a crushing defeat in the Congressional

---

* The refusal of the Senate, after World War I, to ratify our entrance into the League of Nations and the two-thirds majority which is required by the Constitution for such ratification also undoubtedly caused the Executive branch to turn to executive agreements rather than to use formal treaties.

elections of 1946. While the Republican 80th Congress deserves credit for not repealing the Reciprocal Trade Act, it was extended in 1948 for only one, instead of for the customary three years. The Hull program was, therefore, placed under a limited period of probation. More important still, the so-called "peril point" provision was written into the Act. This provided that, before the President could carry through any further reductions in tariffs, he was required to notify the Tariff Commission in advance on what articles he proposed to negotiate. The Commission was then to investigate, take testimony from interested groups, and fix the points below which the domestic industries would be put in peril by reductions in the tariff rates. While this process could be carried on concurrently with other preparatory work, the general effect was to slow down negotiations and to fix practical limits to the cuts which the President could authorize in the tariff schedules. For, while the President had the ultimate power to disregard the peril point findings, their declaration put great pressure on the President not to go below the limits fixed. The peril point provision was added to an "escape clause" first introduced in the 1942 trade agreement with Mexico and extended by executive order in 1947. This permitted the President to increase specific rates if a severe injury could be proved in any industry, and was, of course, intended to make it more difficult for the President and the low-tariff forces to reduce duties.

Nearly everyone expected that the swing toward the Republicans and protection would continue with full force into the 1948 elections. But, surprisingly enough, this did not happen. President Truman was instead elected and the Democrats won a majority in both Houses of Congress.

In 1949, therefore, the Democrats and the low-tariff

forces had sufficient strength not only to renew the Act for a further period of three years, but also to repeal the peril point provision. But this hold on Congress was severely weakened in the Congressional elections of 1950 and, at the same time, large sections of the South began to defect from their former low-tariff beliefs. This was primarily caused by the fact that the textile industry was rapidly moving into the South from New England and the middle states and was carrying its protectionist beliefs and influence with it. The highly protectionist chemical industry was also developing in the Southern states.

All this helped to erode the historic Southern opposition to protection which had largely been based upon the export of cotton and tobacco. In consequence, the Democratic leaders, in order to get even a two-year extension of reciprocal trade in 1952, agreed to restore the peril point provisions and to tighten further the "escape clause."

Then, in the fall of the same year, the twenty years of almost continuous Democratic victories were finally ended by the election of General Eisenhower to the Presidency and by the Republicans' gaining control of Congress. General Eisenhower was primarily the representative of the Eastern financial wing of his party, which had gradually come to believe in a cautious internationalism and in broader trade relations with the outside world. There was therefore a sharp division within the ranks of the Republicans over what their tariff policy should be. While the party was trying to make up its mind, two one-year extensions of the Reciprocal Trade Act were passed. The Republican Party was marking time. In 1955, with the return to a slight Democratic majority in Congress, President Eisenhower asked for a three-year extension of the Act but with the amount of any reduction strictly limited to five percent in any one year. Thus, if a tariff amounted to twenty-five percent, it could not be cut in a given year by more than one-twentieth of this figure, or by one and a quarter percent. The possible cuts were, therefore, to be only nominal and were not to be cumulated.

It is noteworthy that even this extremely weak act, advanced by a Republican President and supported by the Democratic leadership, passed the House by an extraordinarily narrow margin. On some roll calls this amounted to only one vote (i.e., 193 to 191 and 193 to 192), while on the motion to recommit, the margin was also very slight (i.e., 206 to 199). Two features of these roll calls were very revealing. Only about one-third of the Republicans voted for the bill as compared with approximately two-thirds of the Democrats. Secondly, every Congressman from the textile-dominated Piedmont regions of the South voted for crippling amendments and against the bill.*

A further struggle was waged in 1958. Little progress had been made in the meantime in negotiating additional reductions and President Eisenhower had appointed a highly protectionist Tariff Commission, one of whose members had been a paid lobbyist for protectionist interests. In addition to the usual powerful high-tariff forces, the coal industry and the independent oil producers were now anxious to limit the importation from Venezuela of the rival fuel of residual oil. At one time it appeared as though a very unsatisfactory bill would be passed which

---

* Thus, the motion by Congressman Reed (R) of New York to recommit the bill (which would have killed it) received 119 Republican votes, or 64.4 percent of the Republican votes cast. There were 80 Democratic votes for the Reed motion, or 36.4 percent of the Democratic votes cast. The party proportions to defeat the motion and save the bill were, of course, almost precisely the opposite. 63.6 percent of the Democrats voting, or 140, were against the motion to recommit as compared with only 66, or 35.6 percent of the Republicans.

would have been modeled on the 1955 Act. Finally, however, the Act was extended for four years with the provision that the reductions of five percent a year could be cumulated. This permitted an ultimate total reduction of twenty percent or by one-fifth in the level of the existing tariffs.

The way in which this more liberal act was obtained can now be told. The bill came from the Senate Finance Committee in the form of only a three-year extension with a maximum reduction of only five percent in any one year. I threatened to make an open and prolonged fight upon the floor against both these limitations and to denounce the leadership of both parties for agreeing to them. The bipartisan leadership was anxious to avoid this open debate and proposed as an alternative that the prospective Senate members of the conference would privately pledge to me that they would agree to a longer extension with the allowed decreases to be cumulated. I agreed to this. The pledges were given and were carried out.

When we finally went to conference in Geneva in 1960 under the auspices of GATT to negotiate further reductions under the 1958 law, the weighted average of our tariffs was approximately thirteen percent. This was only about one-quarter of the level which had prevailed a quarter of a century before at the start of the Hull program when it had been around fifty-three percent.* This great decrease had been effected in two ways: First, by the increase in the price level which had dimin-

---

* I recognize, of course, the inadequacies in the computation of any average and the difficulty of computing a properly weighted average. The Tariff Commission has estimated the pre-Hull average at fifty-three percent. See *Operation of Trade Agreements Program*, 1934–48, p. 19. Weighted averages of fifty-three percent for 1934 and thirteen percent in 1960 seem, however, to be as close as possible to reality.

ished the proportional importance of most of the "specific" duties. Thus, if the normal price of an imported article in this country had been twenty cents, a specific duty of ten cents a pound would have been the equivalent of a fifty percent tariff. But, if the price had risen over the years to forty cents, (without the specific duty being changed) the tariff would now amount to only twenty-five percent. The doubling in price would, in fact, have halved the relative tariff.

The relative size of the reduction through a failure to increase specific duties seems to have been by about this degree.

The second form of reduction came from cuts in both the specific and *ad valorem* duties. These seemed to have amounted, over the span of a quarter of a century, to an unweighted average of about fifty percent and, hence, to have accounted for the second halving in the rates.

In other words, about equal relative parts were played by both the increases in the price level and reductions in rates so that the combined effect was to cut tariffs from around fifty-three percent to approximately thirteen percent. In thirty years we had moved from being perhaps the highest tariff country in the world to one of the lowest. Cordell Hull had largely obtained his objective.

GATT had been founded in 1947 by agreement between twenty-three allied countries and friendly neutrals. The most important of these nations were, of course, the United States, Great Britain, France, the Benelux countries (i.e., Belgium, the Netherlands, and Luxembourg) together with such members of the British Commonwealth as Canada, Australia, New Zealand, South Africa, India, and Pakistan, and a few Latin American countries such as Chile and Brazil, and Norway among the Scandinavian countries. Russia and its satellites held themselves aloof and refused to participate. But Czechoslovakia, China, and Cuba, which were then outside the Communist orbit, did take part and signed the final agreement. The countries represented probably included between sixty-five and seventy percent of the world's trade and the reductions and concessions which were granted on approximately 45,000 items covered somewhere around forty-five percent of the world's imports.

The GATT group was enlarged in 1949 at Annecy by the addition of the three Baltic countries of Sweden, Denmark, and Finland, together with three more Latin American states. This conference contented itself with extending the Geneva reductions over more countries rather than initiating any movement for widespread further cuts. The same general policy was also carried out at Torquay in 1951. Here the former enemy states of Germany and Austria were admitted as was the hostile "neutral," Turkey, and the new state of Indonesia. The previous enemy and occupied countries were therefore gradually joining the alliance as were some of the neutrals. By 1953, probably not far from three-quarters of the foreign trade of the world was being handled by the member countries and the items upon which reductions had been agreed upon came to about forty billion dollars.

In 1955, the largest Far Eastern power, Japan, also joined although a number of Western European states such as Great Britain, France, Austria, and Benelux refused to grant her the "most favored nation" treatment in its unconditional form. In the following year, a further agreement was concluded. Finally, in the Geneva Conference of 1960, the two dictatorial countries of Spain and Portugal were admitted, as was Israel. Even the Communist bloc began to melt slightly along the edges. Czechoslovakia had maintained a nominal membership and, in 1960–1961, Yugoslavia and Poland asserted a certain degree of independence and became associate members of GATT. Today GATT members probably account for about eighty percent of world trade and the items upon which concessions have been granted probably come to about half the world's imports. Mexico and most of the new African states are not, however, members of GATT.

There has been a great deal of discussion about the extent of the concessions which we have granted and obtained at these conferences. They fall into three classes: first, tariff schedules which have been reduced; second, tariffs where an agreement is reached that they will not be increased—these are called "duty bindings"; and third, goods which are now admitted without duty and where an agreement is reached that no future tariff will be imposed—these are called "free bindings."

First, let us see the extent to which we granted concessions at the various conferences on goods which we imported into this country.

GATT Conference	Year for which Value of Imports is Computed	Value of U.S. Imports from All Countries in millions of dollars		Percent of U.S. Imports of Given Categories on which Concessions were granted		
		Dutiable	Free	Duty Reductions	Duty Bindings	Free Bindings
Geneva 1947 and prior agreements	1939	906	1,341	56	14	84
Annecy 1949	1948	2,918	4,174	7	11	8
Torquay 1950–1951	1949	2,708	3,883	15	1	1
Geneva 1955	1954	4,572	5,688	2	1	1
Geneva 1956	1954	4,572	5,688	20	—	—

It will thus be seen that the major volume of reductions came prior to and at the initial GATT conference in 1947. We reduced tariffs on fifty-six percent of the dollar volume of our imports in 1939 and "bound" our tariffs against future increases on fourteen percent more. We also agreed not to impose tariffs on eighty-four percent of our imports which were already duty free. At Annecy in 1940, where the three Scandinavian and three Latin American countries were admitted, the reductions amounted to only seven percent of our 1948 imports, the "duty bindings" to eleven, and the "free bindings" to eight percent.

The admission of Germany, Austria, Turkey, and Indonesia in 1951 led to a further reduction of about fifteen percent in our dutiable imports of 1949 but with very slight "bindings" whether free or dutiable. Reductions for Japan were carried out at the 1955 conference itself, but in the following year when the members really got down to business, reductions were effected on twenty percent, or one-fifth of our dutiable imports. There were virtually no "bindings" at this conference whether dutiable or free.

It will be noticed that little progress was made in the field of reciprocal trade during the years 1953–1960 except for the reductions of 1955–1956 which were connected with the Japanese entry.

One charge which has been made against our conduct of the GATT negotiations has been that we have conceded more than we have received in return. I have tried to get at the facts behind this allegation and believe that the following statistical summary is the best that can be obtained. The dollar figures certainly are not strictly comparable from year to year, and may involve double counting, but the total picture is at least a first approximation to reality as to how we fared comparatively.

Conference and Year	Duty Reductions Millions of Dollars VOLUME OF IMPORTS		Duty Bindings Millions of Dollars VOLUME OF IMPORTS		Duty-Free Bindings Millions of Dollars VOLUME OF IMPORTS	
	In U.S.	In All Other Countries	In U.S.	In All Other Countries	In U.S.	In All Other Countries
Geneva 1947 and prior agreements	508	500	128	519	1,130	303
Annecy 1949	215	277	314	159	322	50
Torquay 1950–1951	419	324	24	397	34	363
Geneva 1955	81	61	53	140	45	195
Geneva 1956	911	260	—	62	—	85
TOTAL	2,134	1,422	519	1,277	1,531	896

A study of these overall figures indicates that we gave tariff reductions on 712 million dollars more in imports than we received from other countries. Almost all of this was in the 1956 negotiations. We "bound" 635 million dollars more of duty-free goods than did the other nations, and all of this and then some occurred either at the initial GATT conference or before. On the other hand, in the "binding" of dutiable goods, we received 758 million dollars more than we gave. On the whole, the evidence seems to suggest that, up until the "Dillon Round" of 1960–1962, we probably gave more than we gained. But this is more an inference than a definite proof since we do not have comparable figures of the relative depths of the cuts which we gave and received. When it is remembered, however, that during this period we consented to the imposition of quotas by the European governments upon our exports, it can certainly be concluded that the designation of "Uncle Shylock" which many Europeans like to apply to us is both untrue and unfair in trade as in other financial matters.

8

The
Dillon Round of
1960 - 1962

Taking advantage of the possibility of further tariff cuts
of twenty percent which had been authorized by the
Tariff Extension Act of 1958, we entered into a further
round of negotiations under GATT in 1960. These negotiations were called "The Dillon Round" after Mr. C. Douglas Dillon, who was then Undersecretary of State in the
Eisenhower Administration and who later became the
Secretary of the Treasury under Presidents Kennedy and
Johnson.

In the first phase of the negotiations, which began on
September 1, 1960, we dealt chiefly with the six nations
of the Common Market, i.e., the three Benelux countries,
France, West Germany, and Italy. Here the problems
dealt primarily with the peculiar difficulties which had
been created by the process of averaging tariff rates
within the Common Market. Since the low-tariff Benelux
countries (Belgium, the Netherlands, and Luxembourg)
had to increase their tariffs in order to come up to the
common average and, in the process, breached the maintenance of duties which had been negotiated in earlier

conferences, the United States exercised its right to negotiate for compensatory tariff reductions so as to maintain the general balance of concessions.

Then, in the latter part of May, 1961, we began the second phase of the round by negotiating with both the Common Market and the seventeen countries outside it, most of which were British oriented, as being either members of the European Free Trade Association (EFTA) or of the British Commonwealth. In this second phase, the parties concerned got down to the real business of negotiating mutual reductions in the tariff schedules on a multitude of specific commodities.

The Common Market started by offering to reduce its external tariffs by twenty percent on most industrial items and it actually made initial adjustments towards this new target. We could not make any similar offer because our Tariff Commission, which was then protectionist in its membership, reported under its "peril point" procedures that no duty reductions could be made on many items without causing or threatening serious injury to domestic industry. In some cases, such as flat glass, this led, under the escape clause, to actual increases in the duties. The American delegation was at first instructed to hold fast to these peril points. When the Common Market found out that we could not make offers which were comparable to theirs, they partly withdrew their original offers and seemed ready to let the conference break up.

President Kennedy then came to the rescue. Acting under the residual authority held by the President, he gave permission for our negotiators to go below the peril points on imports from the Common Market which were valued in 1958 at 76 million dollars. This offer broke the deadlock and we reached an agreement with the Common Market.

Under this agreement, the Common Market made somewhat greater concessions than we. While it reduced its common external tariffs by appreciably less than its original offer of twenty percent, it made greater net cuts. The common external tariff of the Common Market on industrial goods was reduced by eleven percent, or by one-ninth. Only minor cuts were made on farm products so that the combined reduction was approximately six percent. This reduction was not only carried into effect by the high-tariff nations, but also by the low-tariff countries of West Germany and Benelux.

On the other hand, we cut our tariffs by about twenty percent on articles which, however, formed only one-fifth of our imports. Our overall reduction was about four percent in comparison with the Common Market cut of six percent. Since our former tariffs had averaged between twelve and thirteen percent, this meant a net reduction in our tariffs of only about half of one percentage point. This brought the average overall rate to a little less than twelve percent.

The final results, while not discouraging to believers in freer trade, were nothing to become elated about. But a little progress had been made and, for once, we received more concessions from the European democracies than we granted.

The concessions which we made during the Dillon Round to the Common Market on a fifth of our imports were, of course, automatically extended to the EFTA nations and other negotiating countries. In the same way, the concessions granted to the British-oriented countries were extended to the Common Market countries. The reductions given to both were then also granted under the most favored nation principles to those countries which did not formally participate in the Dillon Round.

The final result was that we granted tariff reductions on imports which had amounted in 1960 to just short of 1.7 billion dollars, and we agreed not to increase duties on 24 million dollars of imports, and kept a further duty-free status on 66 million dollars more.

But trouble loomed ahead on farm products. No basic agreement about them could be reached either within the Common Market itself or in their negotiations with us or any of the other countries outside their ranks. Both General de Gaulle and Chancellor Adenauer relied on the farmers of their countries for political support and both wanted to keep grain and other farm prices high in order to placate their followers. This meant that they wanted to restrict and, if possible, to exclude lower cost American grains and foods. Since German agriculture was less efficient and produced under higher costs than French farming, there was also a conflict between these two nations over the level of farm prices which should prevail within the Common Market. The Germans wanted a high price which would permit their high-cost foods to come on the market. The French wanted a lower price which would enable them to dominate the market. Both wanted to reduce the quantity of American foods to be imported, and they maintained this position despite all the efforts of the Kennedy administration and Secretary of Agriculture Freeman. It was clear that, since we were exporting two and a third billion dollars of our farm products to Europe, the loss or curtailment of this market would cause our total trade to contract rather than to expand. Because of a complex of reasons, the Common Market could not agree on a unified agricultural program and the issue was postponed until 1963. The sources of cleavage remained but were temporarily covered up by the agreement on the industrial products.

9

The Common Market:
The Burgeoning of Hope,
1957 - 1962

The development of the European Economic Community, known as the Common Market, is one of the most important economic events of the last decade. It has also deep political implications both for good and evil.

During the nine years of its operation, it has lowered tariffs by eighty percent on industrial products and by from sixty to sixty-five percent on most agricultural goods among the 180 million people of the six member countries of Western Europe, namely, France, West Germany, Italy, Holland, Belgium, and Luxembourg. In so doing, it has realized the economic advantages which a broadening market always brings. It has made it easier for an area or a concern to specialize in those lines of activity which it can do best, and to realize the economies of large-scale production. It has promoted the geographical division of labor between areas of Western Europe and it has also permitted a much greater division of labor within individual concerns.

During the century and a half from 1793 to 1945, two attempts were made at the forceable unification of

Europe. The first was by Napoleon, who, in his more lucid moments, saw the economic and political advantages of a united Europe and tried to attain them through French domination. The second was by the modern Attila, Adolf Hitler, whose military might and iron reign of terror nearly conquered most of Europe, and, indeed, the world.

The two military efforts at unification properly failed, but many Europeans saw the advantages of a voluntary economic federation. The prelude to such a federation came in 1944 when the three small countries of north-western Europe, Belgium, the Netherlands, and Luxembourg formed a customs union. This brought free trade in industrial goods between these countries and their twenty million inhabitants and a low common tariff to the outside world. The Benelux countries therefore furnished the model upon which the movement for the projected economic federation of Europe began to take shape.

Meanwhile, the United States had paved the way for further economic co-operation through our reciprocal trade program and by the 17 billion dollars of aid given to Europe under the Marshall Plan. This sum had been freely granted as a gift and not a loan, and this generosity probably prevented the Western European countries from being taken over by the Communists and helped to lead to the economic recovery of free Europe. To give direction to the Marshall Plan of economic aid, an Organization for European Economic Cooperation (OEEC) was set up and the countries of Western Europe began to work together through this body. An internationally minded Senator, J. William Fulbright of Arkansas, and others then proposed that the Marshall Plan itself should reward efforts at the political and economic integration of Europe. While this idea was at first squelched by the members of the Foreign Service, it found a response among forward-looking Europeans, notably on the part of two remarkable men, Jean Monnet of France and Paul Spaak of Belgium. The State Department finally came around not only to support the idea but, characteristically, even to claim it as its very own.

A second prototype was created in 1952 in the form of the European Coal and Steel Community. This provided for the ultimate abolition of the tariffs on coal, iron, and steel between West Germany, France, Italy, and the Benelux countries. A central fund was set up to indemnify workers who were displaced by the development of lower-cost and more efficiently produced coal and steel, and also to help firms which were similarly injured. The headquarters of the community were located in Luxembourg and, by the middle 1950's, an international civil service was evolving with the start of an international commercial court and an embryonic legislative body. Unfortunately, Luxembourg was also the headquarters of the European Steel cartel and suspicions grew that the new community would be largely a "front" for the cartel which continued to ration output and to fix prices.

But the coal and steel community proved to be a success and, despite the complaints from the displaced and inefficient plants, it won widespread popular support. In 1954, the creation of an integrated European Defense Community was proposed. This plan was however torpedoed on the eve of its adoption by Premier Mendès-France, who, after withdrawing his troops from French Indochina, felt he could not further reduce French national sovereignty.

Monnet and Spaak then decided to push for further economic integration by the six members of the Coal and Steel Community. They were confident that economic integration would lead rapidly and inevitably to political integration as well, as had happened in Germany during the nineteenth century. The State Department at this point fully and loyally co-operated in the program of European economic integration.

Amidst many doubts as to its ultimate survival, the European Common Market was set up in the early part of 1957 through the medium of the Treaty of Rome and it began operations in January, 1958. In its purely trade aspects, the treaty was to end all internal tariffs which each of the six states imposed against each other by 1970 at the latest. This elimination was to be gradually carried into effect by cuts of at least twenty and fifteen percent in the first two periods of four years each, respectively, and by the elimination of the remaining duties during the final phase. There was to be a common external tariff which, in the case of most industrial goods and some farm products, was to be the unweighted arithmetical average of the tariffs levied for a given commodity by the four jurisdictions, namely, Benelux, France, Italy, and West Germany. Since Benelux was a low-tariff area while France and Italy were high-tariff nations, this process of averaging would increase the absolute duties on exports to the first group while lowering them for the next two with the final average rather closely approximating that of West Germany. The members decided to postpone any final decision about such crucial agricultural products as wheat, feed grains, dairy products, and meat until after the end of the first period, or 1963.

As in the coal and steel community, workers were to be compensated for losses suffered from displacement by the widening of the market. This compensation was to be at full wages for up to two years and during this time the workers were to be trained for the expanding industries. But the treaty went further. A completely free migration of labor between countries was ultimately to be allowed, and each of the migrants was to be given social security protection in the country where he was working.

The executive, legislative, and judicial branches of the Common Market were to be virtually the same as those for the Coal and Steel Community and for the Atomic Energy Authority. The main executive body was to be the Council of Ministers representing the cabinets of the various countries which would meet periodically and make the basic decisions. For the first eight years, unanimity was required. But, beginning in 1966, decisions on many matters were to be taken by a majority vote which was to be binding upon all members. This was not to apply, however, to the admission of new members.

The day-to-day conduct of affairs was confided to a commission of nine members consisting of two members from each of the three major powers (France, West Germany, and Italy), and one each from the three members of Benelux. The seat of this administration was placed in Brussels although the administration for the Coal and Steel Community still remained in Luxembourg. A large body of civil servants were trained and Brussels soon began to hum with their activity. These civil servants, as well as members of the commission itself, were supposed to represent the European community instead of the conflicting interests of their own nations.

The judicial branch consisted of the Court of Justice with seven judges appointed for six-year terms by the member governments acting together. The court was to adjudicate commercial and internal disputes and was also located in Luxembourg. A common body of commercial law is now being built up under this tribunal on such matters as contracts, negotiable instruments, and the like.

A quasi-legislative body of one hundred forty-two members was set up with thirty-six members from each of the three major countries, and fourteen from Holland, fourteen from Belgium, and six from Luxembourg. This body meets in Strasbourg on the French side of the Rhine. In this legislature, in which all political parties are represented except the Communists, the parliamentarians vote not by countries but as members of similarly oriented groupings common to all member countries. Thus, the Social Democrats from the various countries sit together on the left, the Christian Democrats in the center, and the conservatives and laissez-faire liberals on the right. This parliament considers questions of basic policy although its recommendations are not yet binding. In practice, it has not been very effective.

The founders of the Common Market had, however, political as well as economic aims. They looked forward to a future in which the European Economic Community would have a common system of social security together with a single currency and postal system. From this it was but a step, also, to prevision a common banking and clearance system. Many of the founders, such as Monnet and Spaak, also hoped that this would ultimately lead to a United States of Europe with a common military force and an integrated foreign policy.

These were the inspiring and idealistic features of the Treaty of Rome, but material interests were also present and furnished a substantial and necessary underpinning to the idealistic superstructure. It has been well said that the Common Market had both its lofty watchtower and its bargain basement. Its watchtower is the Treaty of Rome with its encouragement to a hitherto divided Europe to bury its past quarrels and join in the peaceful task of increasing productivity and improving the common lot. Its bargain basement, so it is said, was an implicit understanding which was never put in writing that West Germany was to be permitted to become relatively supreme in the manufacture and sale of most industrial products while France was to dominate the market for farm products. This latter consideration helps to explain some of the quarrels and conflicts of the past few years.

If Great Britain had applied for membership while the Common Market was forming and if it had taken part in drawing up the Treaty of Rome, or had even tried to join shortly afterwards, she would probably have been gladly welcomed as a member, for France and Germany were then in a comparatively co-operative mood. This would have increased the total population within the Common Market from 170 to 260 million, for, in addition to the 53 million in Great Britain, it would undoubtedly have also brought the affiliation of most of the minor European states with populations of about 40 million more. This would have been a great forward step.

But the forward step was not taken. The conservative government in Great Britain under Macmillan feared the economic competition of a united and efficient continent. It was also afraid that the Common Market would seriously reduce the imports of farm products such as wheat, meat, and butter from Canada, Australia, and New Zealand, together with the tropical products of the colonial African states not only into Europe but even into Britain itself. Such a development, they believed, would hasten the dissolution of the British Commonwealth and weaken the political power of what the British still regarded as the Empire.

Britain's previous policy toward Europe also encouraged her refusal. She had always supported a balance of power under which no European nation was allowed to grow so powerful as to predominate over Great Britain. Traditionally, therefore, Great Britain had wanted a divided Europe over which she could reign supreme. This helps to explain Britain's diplomatic policy during the nineteenth century, before and after World War I, and even for the period immediately after World War II. It still remained as a dominant motive in the fifties. In actual fact, Great Britain tried hard to prevent the other countries of the Common Market from coming to an agreement at Rome and finally withdrew its own observers.

Britain therefore decided to keep out of the Common Market and to set up instead a separate organization known as the European Free Trade Association (EFTA). This second economic solar system consisted of Great Britain as the sun with six subsidiary planets associated with it, namely, the three Scandinavian countries of Norway, Sweden, and Denmark, plus Switzerland, Portugal, and Austria. Of these, Britain had traditionally enjoyed close commercial relations with the Scandinavian countries and with Portugal. In all, the constellation comprised a population of 90 million, or a little over one-half that of the Common Market. EFTA, or the "Outer Seven" as it was called, was to do away with tariffs among member countries but, instead of imposing a common external tariff, each nation was to maintain its own separate tariff.

The British statesmen probably expected the Common Market to fall apart and to founder upon the jealousies and conflicts of interest of its members. But this hope proved initially false and EFTA itself was ineffective for the first few years. When later Britain did apply for membership in the Common Market, it thereby created great uncertainty about the future of EFTA and brought a standstill to its evolution. Moreover, trade among the

EFTA countries grew far more slowly than among the countries of the Common Market.

Results speak louder than words and the prosperity which Western Europe enjoyed under the Coal and Steel Community and the Common Market was an eloquent tribute to their effects. From 1950 to 1956, the real gross national product of the EEC countries increased at a geometrical rate of almost six percent a year. Part of this increase came from the great pressure of demand following the destruction of wartime, but part was due to the Coal and Steel Community. From 1957 through 1961 the growth rate of the Common Market was five percent a year on a geometrical basis. This was still a high rate of increase.

Unemployment in France, West Germany, and the Benelux countries now became almost nonexistent except in isolated areas. The industrial expansion of these countries, together with that of Northern Italy, provided jobs for what were formerly the large idle labor reserves of Sicily and South Italy. As a result, Italian unemployment which once ran between two and two and a half million went down to less than 1.4 million of whom perhaps two-thirds to three-quarters of a million were close to being unemployable because of their former prolonged idleness and for other reasons. Workers were also drawn into Northern Europe from Spain and Portugal as well as from Greece, Turkey and Algeria.

In contrast, the average growth rate in the United States from 1955 to 1960 was two and a half percent, or about half the rate of the Common Market. On a per capita basis, the difference was even greater. We had a population increase of not far from one and seven-tenths percent a year for the years 1950–1960. Our annual increase in output per person during the five years from 1955 to 1960 was therefore only about eight-tenths of one percent. This was only about one-fifth of the per capita growth rate inside the Common Market. While our absolute level of production was still appreciably higher than that of the Common Market, there was no doubt that during this period the Western European growth rate vastly exceeded ours. This disparity along with Russia's greater growth rate was a central issue in the 1960 Presidential election and played a part in the victory of President Kennedy.

Meanwhile, all of Western Europe prospered and in this industrial renaissance the Common Market had a major, although not an exclusive, role. The prosperity occurred partly because of the inherent advantages of broader areas of trade which we have already discussed.

During the next four years the growth rates in Germany, Austria and Holland declined markedly. Thus, in Germany from 1960 to 1964, the yearly rate of growth declined from 6 to 4.8 percent. In France, however, the rate rose from 4.2 to 5.4 percent, while in Italy the annual rise was from 4.8 to 5.4 percent.* Meanwhile in the United States, the total Gross National Product in terms of 1958 dollars of constant purchasing power advanced from 488 billion dollars to approximately 585 billion dollars in the last quarter of 1964 † and to 613 billion dollars in the fourth quarter of 1965. This rise in real purchasing power of about 128 billion dollars amounted to a total rise of twenty-eight percent, or a compounded yearly growth rate of around 4.7 percent. The United States had reached the growth rate of Germany but was still somewhat behind the rates of France and Italy. Great Britain, however, was unfortu-

---

* *OECD Policies for Economic Growth*, 1962, p. 16. *Bank for International Settlements*, 34th Annual Report, p. 6.

† *Economic Indicators*, December 1964, p. 2. (The increase continued in the first quarter of 1966 to 634 billion, in 1958 dollars.)

nately still lagging behind the rest of the Western World, since their yearly rate for the years 1960–1964 was only three and a half percent.

The extended market also permitted greater geographical specialization. For example, Italy found a larger market for its tropical fruits, as Germany for its beer, and France for its wines. The French silk industry expanded, as did tourism in all of the countries.

The broader market also encouraged specialization within factories and companies and led to increased internal rationalization. Many companies concentrated on products in which they had either an absolute or comparative advantage. In particular, the German chemical and auto industries flourished because the broader market increased their total volume of sales.

A third advantage came with the increased outside competition which weakened private price controls and restrictions. In their zeal for maximum profits, national cartels and monopolies had held back both production and employment by their price and output policies. Outside competition somewhat weakened their hold and, by forcing price reductions, increased total effective demand and, therefore, production. The Brussels commission seemed determined not to allow international cartels and monopolies to replace the national ones, although the future is still uncertain.

The labor surplus in southern Italy, Spain, Portugal, Turkey, and Greece helped to furnish the needed manpower for the great expansion in the north.

Partly as cause and partly as a result of the successful working of the Common Market, the rate of the original tariff reductions was greatly speeded up. Internal tariffs on industrial goods dropped in seven years by seventy percent. It was then hoped that all internal industrial tariffs would be removed by 1967, or soon thereafter. The commercial policy achievements which were expected to take twelve years were therefore to be fulfilled within nine.

As we have pointed out the Common Market had shown a willingness to lower its external tariff on industrial goods and on certain noncompetitive farm products. It is always hard to judge the average tariffs of a country because of the difficulties of weighting and taking into account the so-called free list. Our average, excluding the so-called free list, is somewhere around twelve percent. This is about the same as the average of the Common Market rates, but whether the respective tariffs are in fact at the same level is disputed. The Europeans claim ours is higher. Our experts say it is lower. Probably the most accurate statement is that, on the average, the differences on industrial goods between the two are small. For this reason, there should not be any prolonged and bitter arguments about the general level from which the two parties will start in any future negotiations over industrial tariffs. But, while this is true on the average, tariffs on similar items are frequently different and this creates the problem of reconciling the disparities. The farm tariffs are another matter, and it is there that the greatest frictions have developed. It is certainly true that on these goods the European tariffs are much higher than ours.

There is no doubt that the Common Market has been of great benefit to its member countries, but what has been and will be its effect on the United States?

We must recognize that the Common Market, like any customs union, places all outside countries at a comparative disadvantage. Whereas American products formerly entered Germany on the same terms as those from France and also entered France and Italy on the same terms as did

German goods, when the Common Market comes fully into effect, there will be a tariff on imports from America while Common Market goods will move freely across the national boundaries of the member states. This in itself will discourage imports into the Common Market and will increase the self-sufficiency of the European community. The higher the external tariff set up by the Common Market, the greater, of course, will be our own disadvantage.

This creates an attraction for small neighboring countries either to join or associate with the Common Market. It encourages us, for whom formal membership or association is a political impossibility, to try to bargain down the external tariffs of the European Community. In fact, this was one of the forces behind the United States' Trade Expansion bill of 1962.

But it is also important to recognize another principle which is basic. In the long run, both as individuals and as a community, we profit from the prosperity of our neighbors. A poor community is one which cannot buy much from others. A prosperous community can and will buy much more. To this degree, and it is an important one, the economic interests of mankind run parallel.

This is the tie which should bind the United States and the Common Market together. Just as American productivity helped to rebuild Europe after World War II, so the increasing productivity of Europe increases their peoples' demand for American products, such as farm and electrical machinery, earth-moving machinery, soybean oil and meal, powdered milk, and others. The closer the co-operation and the greater the mutual reduction of tariffs, the more each can prosper. In the long run, this mutuality of interests may be greater than the disadvantages created for us by the formation of the Common Market.

The experience so far has been reassuring. Our exports

to the Common Market countries have grown from 2.4 billion dollars in 1958, the first year of the Market's existence, to 3.9 billion dollars in 1963, an increase of sixty-three percent. In contrast, our exports to all countries in the same period rose by only thirty percent.

There was an allied political advantage which we believed that the European Community could bring to the Free World. Europe has been convulsed three times during the last century by wars between Germany and France. Almost inevitably and against our will, we have been involved in the last two of these wars at great loss to ourselves in lives and resources. We now face a third power, Soviet Russia, which has expressed hostile designs upon us and upon the whole Free World. If France and Germany were to remain divided and embittered, the Russian chances of splitting the Free World and of winning either a cold or a hot war would increase. It was to our interest therefore to help develop friendship and co-operation between a democratic France and a democratic Germany.

Our State Department and the Presidents of both parties realized this truth and showed foresight in furthering it. A strong and democratic Western Europe we believed, would not only be a peaceful complement to us, but also a bulwark in defense of freedom. Such were our high hopes.

10

The American
Trade Expansion Act of 1962
and Its Operation

President Kennedy made the reduction of tariffs and the expansion of foreign trade one of the main features of his legislative program. He wanted to have the United States co-operate with the Common Market in a further and mutual lowering of tariffs and hoped that by such reductions American trade with the Common Market would grow and the political alliance between ourselves and the free nations of Western Europe would be strengthened. To help give impetus to this purpose, he appointed George Ball, the American attorney for the Common Market, as Undersecretary of State for Economic Affairs. A Trade Expansion Act was drafted early in his administration for which the President marshaled widespread industrial support. This bill allowed us to lower tariffs on any commodity by as much as fifty percent in return for similar concessions made to us. On groups of commodities where eighty percent of the total world's trade was conducted by the nations of the Common Market and the United States, all tariffs could be removed. Where our tariffs were less than five percent, they could similarly be eliminated. President Kennedy intended, therefore, to open the way for the future integration of the American economy with that of the nations of Western Europe.

The bill allowed financial aid to be given to those concerns which had actually suffered or were threatened with serious injury as a direct result of increased imports created by lowering specific tariffs. And they were also to be helped to expand into other lines of production by low interest loans. The bill had parallel provisions for paying liberal unemployment benefits to workers who were displaced by increased imports, and provided retraining for them. This principle of compensation for losses suffered has long been proposed by the advocates of freer trade and low tariffs. Since the nation, as a whole, benefits from the gains effected by lower tariffs, the free-trade forces had always urged that the nation should also meet the incidental costs inflicted by the stepped-up foreign competition upon workers and specific industries. The staff of President Eisenhower's Commission on Foreign Economic Policy had tentatively suggested such a proposal in 1954. But it had been later repudiated by all but one of the members of that commission and by the leaders of the dominant Republican Party. It was strongly opposed by the protectionist forces led by O.R. Strackbein. This opposition of the protectionists to compensatory assistance for specific groups of owners and workers was probably due to their correct belief that, if such a provision were included, it would weaken their arguments against any real reduction in tariff rates. They preferred, therefore, to retain a grievance in order to defeat a principle. The assistance included in the bill for displaced workers was, in turn, the consideration which enabled the leaders of the American labor movement to support the bill, which otherwise promised to injure many of their number.*

The bill was reported out by the House Ways and Means Committee in June of 1962 with only minor changes and, after being passed by the House, came over to the Senate for final action. In the meantime, the Administration had been making concessions to specific American industries in order to reduce or eliminate their opposition to the bill itself. It negotiated an agreement with Japan, Hong Kong, and other countries under which these countries agreed to restrict their exports of textiles to the United States. The Administration also gave informal assurances to the domestic cotton mills that it would offset the eight-cent-a-pound export subsidy which was given under the farm program on cotton shipped overseas and which, consequently, gave foreign mills a differential advantage over our domestic manufacturers. The oil industry was, in turn, appeased by promises of added protection against the increased import of oil and residual fuel from Venezuela. The President also issued an order restricting the entrance of carpets and flat glass. It may be remembered that the Tariff Commission had recommended a higher tariff on the latter product. These latter increases, however, primarily hurt Belgium which is, by and large, a low-tariff country. This unwise concession spurred Belgium and others in the Benelux bloc to demand and obtain from GATT compensatory tariff increases on commodities which we exported to them. All these concessions were hurtful from the international standpoint although they reduced the immediate opposition to the bill.

Sweetened by these arrangements, the Act was ap-

* But the final result of this provision was highly unsatisfactory. As of March 7, 1966, not a single American worker had ever received any compensation for damages suffered by reductions in the tariff.

proved by the Finance Committee and passed in September by the Senate by the overwhelming vote of seventy-eight to eight.

As a result of several trips to study the Common Market and its effects upon the United States, I had become convinced that at least three amendments to the Trade Expansion Act were needed: First, to give the President more power to retaliate if Europe imposed high tariffs against our products. To begin with, the only weapon which was proposed to be given to the President was the authority to deny tariff reductions to the nations which discriminated against us. This weapon was not adequate and, over the opposition of the State Department, I proposed an amendment to permit us to raise tariffs up to the Smoot-Hawley level of 1930 if our exports were penalized by foreign action. This amendment was adopted in an even more severe form and armed the President with a retaliatory stick as well as with an olive branch.

The free-trade purists have disapproved of this action, but since the farming interests of France and Germany were clearly planning either to reduce or to eliminate the exports of American farm products to the European market, and since the European nations still refused to make an adequate contribution toward the defense of their countries in the form of either men or money, it seemed wise to arm our negotiators as they entered the tariff conferences. I hoped that these weapons might never be used. I did not want them to be loosely brandished about, but I did want them to be in reserve for use if necessary. And I believed that their presence might encourage a more co-operative spirit on the part of the nations in the Common Market.

My second amendment, which was also adopted, was to make our chief negotiator directly responsible to the President rather than to the Department of State. The

members of the Foreign Service have often been unjustly
criticized and are certainly patriotic, but, as a whole, they
possess certain built-in disqualifications which prevent
many from fully representing American interests. Since
they spend so much time abroad and in Washington, they
commonly get out of touch with the problems of the average American. For many years, moreover, the Foreign
Service was primarily drawn from members of the American Establishment and, hence, tended to favor European
culture and institutions. By the very nature of their jobs,
moreover, they are thrown into close and intimate relationships with the diplomats who represent foreign nations. Since it is a natural tendency for people to desire
their associates to approve of them, this creates a further
tendency on the part of many members of the Foreign
Service (although, of course, not all) to be overly solici-
tous of the interests and claims of foreign states. Sometimes, in unguarded moments, they even speak of foreign
nations as their "clients." Lacking a domestic constituency,
many representatives of the State Department would be
more than human if they resisted the desire to seek agreement and promote peace by yielding. It is well to have
some such voices raised in the determination of our policies lest we become unduly jingoistic, but it is also true
that our legitimate trade interests are not likely to be adequately represented by conventional diplomats.

There was little opposition to this amendment and the
President appointed a prominent Republican, Christian
A. Herter, to the post of chief negotiator. Mr. Herter had
been a Congressman from Massachusetts, the Governor
of his state, and, finally, had been both Undersecretary of
State, and, upon the death of John Foster Dulles, the Secretary under President Eisenhower. Mr. Herter engaged a
competent staff and, although handicapped by illness, has
represented us adequately.

My third amendment failed. It was meant to help the Administration carry through its program for the complete removal of tariffs even if Great Britain did not enter the Common Market. The administration bill allowed tariffs to be completely removed on commodities where eighty percent of the world's trade was conducted by the United States and the Common Market. If Great Britain had become a member of the Common Market, this provision would have applied to no less than twenty-three important groups of commodities. But, without British membership, there would be only two groups so covered—one of which would be airplanes.

This provision, which was drafted by the State Department, was based on the premise that Great Britain not only should but would enter the Common Market. We all desired this, for it would have not only brought Great Britain into the Common Market, but also most of the Outer Seven. This would have raised the total population within the Common Market to over a quarter of a billion. With the 190 million citizens of the United States, this would have meant a more or less unified trading area of nearly 450 million. This would have been still further increased by any co-operative relationships which might have been worked out with the English-speaking Commonwealths. A mighty trading area could then have been developed among the nations of the Free World, which would also have provided ample markets for the nations of Latin America were they to be admitted to the full privileges of the broadened alliance. Not only would such a step have created material benefits to all, but it would also have undergirded the loose military and political alliances of the Free World.

While I desired such an economic alliance as much as did the State Department, I did not want it to depend solely upon the formal entrance of Great Britain and the EFTA countries into the Common Market. I was personally doubtful that Great Britain would actually apply for membership in the European Economic Community, or, if she did, that she would actually be admitted. Not only was the right wing of the British Conservative Party opposed to applying for admission, but also large sections of the Labour Party as well. Moreover, there were obvious signs of opposition within France to the admission of Britain. If Britain and its allies did not enter, there would be only two instead of twenty-three groups of commodities on which we could eliminate all tariffs. In this event, there would be almost no possibility of doing away with tariffs. I, therefore, proposed, in collaboration with Congressman Henry Reuss of Wisconsin, that the eighty percent requirement be satisfied if the foreign trade of Great Britain and EFTA were also included regardless of whether or not they were members of the Common Market.

To my surprise, the State Department strongly opposed this proposal. They argued that they had already made commitments to consider only the members of the Common Market. I reminded them that the United States was not Great Britain and that Congress had the right to modify proposals advanced by the executive branch and should not be confined merely to ratifying everything that the State Department had previously proposed.

The Department then argued that, by giving Great Britain free access to our markets if she were to stay out of the Common Market, we would weaken her desire to ask for such an entrance and, hence, would help to make up her mind in the negative. I replied that the existing provisions certainly put some affirmative pressure upon Great Britain to enter and that, therefore, the State Department was not in fact neutral but was really seeking to influence her probable decision. While I hoped that Great Britain would ask for admission, I wanted her decision to be made without American influence. I did not want the full benefits of broader trade to be denied to the world because of any possible slip in her admission.

The State Department continued to oppose this amendment up until the very eve of the final vote by the Senate Finance Commitee. It then gave a somewhat grudging acquiescence and the amendment was then adopted both by the committee and by the Senate. It was, however, later eliminated in conference between the Houses. In the meantime, the protectionist forces had taken alarm, and I am informed that the State Department did not make any real effort in conference to retain it.

As a result of General de Gaulle's veto of British membership in January, 1963, the grand design of our State Department was shattered. In order to help repair the damage, I again introduced, along with Senator Javits, the same amendment to the Trade Expansion Act which I had previously prepared.

However, since the State Department has refused to admit that it had originally miscalculated the ultimate turn of events, it has steadfastly refused to support this amendment. It remains in the limbo of lost opportunities. Its fate illustrates, I believe, a further weakness in the bureaucracy of the State Department and perhaps of all administrative agencies, namely, an almost inveterate unwillingness to admit that legislators may at times have knowledge and foresight at least equal or superior to their own. Since then, Congressman Reuss, in an eloquent book, has urged that we hold the doors of free trade open to the whole Free World. But no sign of agreement has come from the State Department. The iron tongue of midnight has apparently tolled on the proposal.

11

The Common Market Goes
into Decline and Then Revives

Although Great Britain had refused to enter the Common Market when she could have done so and had instead tried to build up the Outer Seven as a competing organization, she had begun to develop qualms about her actions by 1960–1961. The Common Market was going ahead rapidly while Britain was moving very slowly with an annual increase in the gross national product of only about two and a half percent. Thoughtful Britons recognized that their ties were far stronger with the 170 million people of the Common Market than with the 40 million members of the English-speaking Commonwealths. If Britain were to remain aloof from the rapidly expanding prosperity of Western Europe, she was in danger of becoming another Venice, which was left high and dry as world trade shifted from the Mediterranean to the Atlantic. The Common Market was, therefore, exerting a strong, gravitational pull upon Great Britain.

In the summer of 1961, the leaders of the Conservative government, therefore, announced their intention to apply for membership in the Common Market. After much opposition, this policy was approved at the Conservative Party conference and the top-heavy government majority then gave it general approval in the House of Commons. The little Liberal Party warmly supported the move, but the right-wing Tories, along with the left-wing Labourites, were strongly opposed.

Negotiations with the Common Market went on during 1962 and, although there were many problems, they seemed to be on the way to solution. The Labour Party opposition, however, hardened and its leader, Hugh Gaitskell, finally threw his influence against membership under the then existing terms. Labour was afraid that political democracy was not firmly established in either France or Western Germany and also distrusted the unknown future successors to the aged Adenauer and De Gaulle.

Nevertheless, the Conservative government thought that if they asked for and received membership, Parliament would then approve this before the next general election. They were jolted on January 14, 1963, when President de Gaulle announced his opposition to the admission of Great Britain. Furthermore, he opposed having either Great Britain or the United States assume a leading role in the economic or political affairs of Europe. The Constitution of the Common Market had provided that, up until 1966, any one of the major parties had the right of individual veto on the admission of new members. The French veto was therefore decisive. Germany and France had just concluded a treaty of agreement and Chancellor Adenauer did not wish to disturb this relationship by objecting too vehemently to the French action.

This refusal by France was a heavy blow to those who had hoped that Britain and other nations of EFTA would enter the Common Market and thus create a trading area of more than a quarter of a billion people. But it was precisely this which most aroused the ire of President de

Gaulle. He believed that the entry of Great Britain into the Common Market would be quickly followed by that of the other members of EFTA, and then of still other minor European states. And there loomed beyond all this what was to him the dire prospect of some affiliation with the United States, as we had envisaged a few months before when we passed the Trade Expansion Act. Under such conditions, sonorously declared the General, "the cohesion of all its members, who would be very numerous and very diverse, would not hold for long and that in the end there would appear a colossal Atlantic Community under American dependence and leadership which would soon completely swallow up the European community." De Gaulle therefore had decided to maintain a more restricted customs union for Western Europe in which France was to be the dominant figure.

The French veto cast a pall over the proceedings of the Common Market and an air of pessimism succeeded the buoyant optimism of the preceding years. The movement toward wider economic and political co-operation had been at least temporarily balked.

For the three years following the rejection of Great Britain, the affairs of the Common Market continued to go from bad to worse. By November, 1964, it had apparently overcome the crisis of deciding upon a common price for grain by effecting a compromise between the lower French and the higher German prices with flexible tariff rates designed to equal the difference between this Common Market price and the much lower world market price as evidenced by the Liverpool market. A preferential price was to be added on top of this. The money from this tariff was, under a previous agreement, to be used to help indemnify those farmers who would be injured or put out of business by the lower prices. Under this 1962 agreement, this money was to be contributed by the member nations to the Common Market fund.

The Council of Ministers in December, 1964, then proposed that the Commission develop a new agricultural subsidy plan under which the revenues from the common external tariff would be collected by the Common Market itself, and then be distributed by it to the various nations. The European Parliament meeting in Strasbourg was also to take over partial responsibility for the budget of the Common Market.

This plan, advocated by Dr. Hallstein, the German Chairman of the Council, was then strongly opposed by the French, acting under instructions from President de Gaulle. At first, they ostensibly objected to making the member countries dependent upon the European Parliament for the budgeting of the external receipts on grain and other products. President de Gaulle obviously did not want the Common Market to develop into a supranational political body which had financial independence. The other five members of the Council supported the proposals of the Commission and France thereupon walked out on July 1, 1965. The French boycott of the Council continued for over six months and, during this time, it became evident that France and President de Gaulle had still further purposes in mind. First, they wanted a formal guarantee that majority voting, which was scheduled to replace unanimity on January 1, 1966, would never be applied to them on a number of crucial issues. France, in other words, wanted to have a continuing veto over the important decisions of the Common Market. Second, France also wanted to restrict the scope and powers of the Commission and, finally, to dismiss some of the so-called "supranationalists" on the Commission, notably, Dr. Hallstein, when the Common Market was merged with Euratom and the Coal and Steel Community.

Through the summer and fall of 1965, a tug of war ensued behind the scenes with the Common Market itself being rendered almost completely ineffective.

Finally, the Ministers of the six countries met in Luxembourg on January 17, 1966, and struggled for two weeks to reach an agreement.

On January 30, the press announced that a compromise had been reached and that the crisis was over. The majority principle was not formally revoked, but there was apparently an informal agreement that in the immediate future the majority would not impose an important decision over the objection of one of its members. As the New York *Times* said, "France reserved the right to walk out again." On the other hand, the other five countries, in the words of the *Times*, while "agreeing with France that a consensus is highly desirable on major matters" would "not renounce the possibility that a prolonged and inconclusive search for an agreed position must eventually end in an exercise of majority rule."

What the ultimate results of this compromise will be, no one can say. While the five will probably not seek in the near future to impose majority rule over French opposition, this may happen when De Gaulle has passed from the scene. In any event, there has been no final agreement on majority voting, the functions of the Parliament and Commission, and the basic issue of supranationalism.

The agreement provided that within three weeks negotiations were to be resumed on those matters which had been shunted aside by the French walkout. The most important issue from their point of view is the completion of the common agricultural policy including the financial regulations under it, while we are primarily interested in completing the Kennedy Round on mutually beneficial terms.

Some progress was, however, made within the Common Market at the opening of the year. The member countries, for example, agreed to reduce their internal tariffs against each other by a further ten percent. This brought them to only one-fifth of their 1957 rates. They also agreed to continue for an indefinite period the twenty percent "temporary reduction" in the common external tariff which otherwise would have expired on January 1, 1966. It is possible that the Common Market may encourage Great Britain to apply again for membership. But Britain will assuredly not do so until she has a firm commitment that, if she does so, she will be accepted. And that still depends on President Charles de Gaulle. He may be softening as the result of the large opposition vote in the French elections when he polled only forty-five percent of the total on the first ballot and fifty-five percent on the second. Within Great Britain, sentiment in favor of affiliation seems to be rising. During the electoral campaign of March 1966, the leaders of the British Labour Party adopted a somewhat negative attitude toward entrance. But after their smashing victory which gave them an overall majority of 97 seats and of slightly over 120 on those matters in which the Liberal Party was in agreement, there were signs that Britain, if encouraged, might move cautiously and slowly toward entrance.

While the Common Market was declining in vigor, or, at best, marking time, the European Free Trade Association (EFTA) or the Outer Eight, namely, Austria, Denmark, Finland, Norway, Portugal, Sweden, Switzerland, and Great Britain, was moving forward. Although somewhat damaged by Great Britain's emergency increase of fifteen percent in its tariffs in the fall of 1964, it has also pushed ahead in its reduction of its internal tariffs.

At the end of December, 1965, it cut its internal tariffs by ten percent. This brought their internal rates down to twenty percent of their 1960 level and thus kept pace with the Common Market. By the end of 1966, this final twenty percent will be removed and there will then be complete internal free trade in non-agricultural goods within the EFTA countries. The Association then intends to try to reduce the so-called nontariff barriers to trade between its members and, subsequently, to negotiate for some merging with the Common Market itself. For as its Secretary, Sir John Coulson, has remarked, the presence of two customs unions in Western Europe with tariffs against each other is "absolute nonsense."

During 1965, the trade between the EFTA countries increased markedly showing a gain during the first nine months of ten percent over the preceding year. The exports to the Common Market rose by only four percent, but in total volume were still slightly greater, namely, 597 million dollars, as compared with 555 million dollars.

There is little doubt that EFTA would like to join the Common Market if it could be sure that it would be welcomed. Here again the immediate decision is in the hands of President de Gaulle.*

* On May 11, the Common Market agreed that by July 1, 1968 all internal tariffs would be abolished and a common external tariff adopted. An annual joint farm fund of $1.5 billion for financing farm exports, price supports and structural improvements in agriculture is to go into effect July 1, 1967.

12
The
Kennedy
Round

President Kennedy signed the Trade Expansion Act on October 11, 1962. Hopes were then high that a further sweeping reduction in tariffs would soon be concluded.

But soon it was not to be. Both the Common Market and the United States had to decide upon and to formulate the proposals upon which bargaining was to be conducted. In this country, we had to schedule a long drawn-out series of public hearings under the Tariff Commission to determine what commodities we wanted to have exempted from the bargaining process. The countries of the Common Market had to make similar time-consuming, if less publicized, soundings and decisions. In addition, the Western European countries, and, to some degree we, ourselves, were thrown into a temporary trauma by President de Gaulle's brutal refusal to admit Great Britain to the Common Market and by his increasing hostility to any closer ties of economic co-operation between the United States and France.

The situation was made worse by a series of decisions of the Common Market which, by August 1963, tripled

140

import charges on frozen chickens from 4.8 to 13.4 cents a pound. The Europeans had never developed this industry and American shipments of such delectables found ready customers there in the late fifties and early sixties. The German and other Western European farmers cast covetous eyes upon this potential market which had been developed by American ingenuity and insisted upon restrictive measures to displace American chickens and substitute their own. After a series of administrative discriminations, and, despite American protests, the Common Market, under German and French pressure, put the increase into effect.

If, in the interests of Allied harmony, we had meekly submitted to these acts, the French and Germans would probably have pushed us still further. In decent self-respect and as a protective measure, we therefore invoked our rights to retaliate commensurately under the provisions of GATT. An adjudicative commission was set up. We claimed that the damages we had suffered amounted to 46 million dollars. The commission fixed them at 26 million dollars. We thereupon withdrew tariff concessions on potato starch and dextrines, luxury brandies, and small foreign trucks. The latter withdrawal was designed in such a way as to injure Germany primarily since she had been the prime mover in the restrictive actions which had been taken.

The Common Market also had to compose its major differences on the price of wheat and other farm products before it felt it could negotiate with the United States. In December, 1964, the price of wheat in France was approximately $2.50 a bushel, or nearly a dollar more than the free market price in Liverpool. German agriculture, never efficient at best, had been rendered still less effective by its loss of the farmlands of East Prussia to the

Poles and the Soviet Union. Its agriculture is chiefly based upon the small farm units all over Germany, but primarily in Bavaria, where yields per unit of labor and capital are relatively low and production costs consequently high. German wheat was therefore selling in Cologne for approximately $3.24 a bushel, or seventy-five cents more than in France, and $1.75 more than in England. Under the Treaty of Rome, a common price for wheat was to be fixed not later than 1970. The German grain farmers, fearing a reduction in their prices, did not want to help establish a common price. But, if this could not be prevented, then they wanted the Common Market price to be as high as possible to permit some of their lower cost grain to find a market. These farmers, moreover, had a powerful influence inside the dominant Christian Democratic Party. For, in addition to being opposed to the Social Democratic Party of the left, the farmers are strong Catholics as are most of the other active members of the Christion Center. They, moreover, form a semi-independent and highly conservative faction within the Christian Democratic Party, with a consequent danger that, if offended too deeply, they might secede to form a separate party of their own or that they might withdraw from active participation in policies, thereby penalizing the Christian Democrats who need their support. In either event, they would seriously threaten or perhaps completely overthrow the dominance of the Christian Party which, in 1961, lost its outright majority and governed only through a somewhat shaky coalition with the Free Democrats. As a result, the two successive German Chancellors, Adenauer and Erhard, have been partial prisoners of the German peasants and have felt compelled to struggle for as high farm prices as possible and to get for Germany the maximum share in filling Europe's need for foods.

The desires of the French farmers were no more unselfish than those of Bavarians. They, too, wanted to keep out cheaper American wheat which with an export subsidy was selling at Liverpool for as little as $1.58 a bushel. But they also wanted a lower Common Market price than their German cousins and would have liked to have it set at their national price of around $2.50. Such a price would have forced much of the German wheat off the German Market and have permitted the French grain to enter. This they believed to have been the implicit agreement which lay behind the Treaty of Rome. But this was also before De Gaulle came to power.

Like wary wrestlers, France and Germany skirmished with each other over these issues for some years. Instead of agreeing upon a common agricultural price in 1963, the decisions were successively postponed not only then but again in early 1964. While these postponements were partially an effort to prevent the sharp differences between Germany and France from breaking up the Common Market, they were also probably due to an effort to put the United States at a bargaining disadvantage when negotiations with us began.

In October 1964, however, France brought the grain price issue to a showdown. She stated that she might cease to participate in the Common Market unless a settlement was reached by the end of the year. After round-the-clock bargaining, the Common Market's negotiators announced on December 15, 1964, that they had come to an agreement on grain prices, thus providing the foundation for further progress toward a common agricultural policy for the Community. The newly agreed-upon target price for wheat was $106.25 per metric ton, or approximately $2.87 per bushel. This was much closer to France's domestic target of $100.22 (i.e., $2.71) than to Germany's

$118.22 (i.e., $3.19). Feed grain target prices were also agreed upon. These prices are all to become effective on July 1, 1967. General de Gaulle also insisted that common prices be set on all other farm products by July, 1965.

The German farmers, who now faced the prospect of lower prices, were to be compensated both by the Common Market's Agricultural Fund and by the German Government. The Agricultural Fund was to pay German agriculture 180 million dollars over the years 1967–1969, while the German Government has promised payments of 210 million dollars in 1965 and 275 million dollars per year thereafter. The supporters of the Common Market thought the main hurdle had been taken and breathed a sigh of relief. The rest, they believed, would be easy. They were sadly mistaken.

Nearly a third of our exports to the Common Market countries consist of agricultural products such as wheat, feed grains, cotton, tobacco, and soybeans, while farm articles form only one-tenth of their exports to us. Common Market exports to the United States are overwhelmingly in manufactured goods. From the standpoint of national interest, Europe would be more interested in obtaining concessions on manufactured goods from us while we would be more interested in getting tariff concessions on farm commodities from them. By spinning out the time during which the two European powers haggled over a common agricultural price, they helped to throw the American negotiators off balance and increased the pressure upon them to take up first the question of reductions in the industrial tariffs and to postpone until later the consideration of the farm tariffs. By that time, presumably, the Europeans would have obtained concessions in the field which mattered most to them and would be under little pressure to sacrifice their agriculture to obtain concessions for their industry.

Some of us in the Congress perceived this stratagem early and warned against it as did our Department of Agriculture. Our negotiators were certainly aware of the trap, and they early declared that both agricultural and industrial tariffs should be considered together. But they were anxious to arrive at some kind of agreement and to effect a reciprocal reduction in tariffs even though it might be partial. In the face of a refusal by the Common Market to show its cards and confronted with the prospect of further interminable delays and the possible collapse of the Kennedy Round, our negotiators finally gave way and agreed to separate the submission of offers on farm tariffs from the industrial offers, and to take up the latter first and postpone the former. Whether by accident or design, we had been outwitted in the preliminary sparring for position. Once again the generous desire of the Americans to co-operate had been turned by the Europeans to their own advantage.

The next showdown came when the respective offers of reductions on industrial goods were finally unveiled. We had shown great restraint in beating off the demands of our protectionists that they be exempted from the bargaining process and permitted to continue with their existing tariffs. We then offered cuts of a full fifty percent on about seventy percent of all our dutiable industrial imports, and on ninety percent of the goods specifically imported from the Common Market. If we deduct the ten percent of our imports from the Common Market which are agricultural, this would be equivalent to reductions on a total of eighty percent of our EEC imports. On the remaining thirty percent of industrial imports upon which exemptions were asked, mandatory and technical exceptions came to one-third and economic exceptions to the remaining two-thirds.

The Common Market proved, upon analysis, to be much less generous. Allowing for some statistical legerdemain in the case of steel and oil, their proposed cuts of fifty percent applied to only eighty percent of their imports of nonagricultural goods. Deducting the thirty percent of their imports from us which are agricultural and about which they have not yet made a proposal, this amounted to a proposed cut of fifty percent on only one-half of their imports from us while we were willing to make cuts of one-half on four-fifths of our total imports from them.

Since we were pledged to get as much as we gave, it is obvious that if such an equality was to be obtained, one or more of the following three adjustments would have to be made: First, either we would have to restrict or withdraw some of our offers on industrial goods. This would diminish the importance of the Kennedy Round; or second, persuade the Common Market to offer further cuts on industrial products; or third, get the Common Market to grant a truly important liberalization of trade in farm products which would increase rather than diminish our exports of such commodities as wheat, cotton, tobacco, and soybeans to the continent of Europe.

The determination of these issues was put over until 1965. But President de Gaulle's withdrawal in June from the activities of the Common Market delayed action still further.

As bargaining was resumed in 1965, it was apparent that political as well as economic considerations were at work in determining the policies of the Common Market. Taking their program from President de Gaulle, the

French negotiators seemed determined to minimize any economic reliance of Europe upon the United States, in the same way as its foreign ministers were resolved to minimize European reliance upon our nuclear weapons. What De Gaulle seemed to be seeking was an independent Europe, which, under French leadership, would not be closely tied economically, politically, or militarily with either Great Britain or the United States. It was to be a Europe which would be primarily self-sufficient in all these matters but one in which there was not to be a close federation of the existing nations as Monnet and Spaak had planned, but rather a somewhat loose confederation of sovereign powers which would draw their inspiration from France. And in the planned-for symphony, the French President saw himself as its magisterial conductor —restoring once again to France the power, glory, and pomp which, in happier times, had once been hers.

The walkout from the Common Market by France on July 1, 1965 however put the negotiations over the Kennedy Round into the economic and political deep freeze. Previously, the countries had exchanged lists of their industrial commodities which they wanted to have exempted from their fifty-percent tariff cuts. The lists of exemptions filed by the Common Market were, as we have said, much longer than those proposed by the United States and the EFTA countries, and some strong tendencies for the Common Market to become a relatively closed trading area were obvious.

In May of 1965, in the discussion on grains, the Common Market, largely at French insistence, would not reveal their specific offers and thus prevented meaningful negotiations. In September, when other countries presented their general programs for agricultural products other than grains, the Common Market because of its internal conflicts, did not do so and, as a result, the United States very properly declined to make offers which might have been of interest to the Common Market and made it clear we could not go forward unless the Common Market also came forward with meaningful offers.

Negotiations were at a standstill for much of 1966. One ray of hope injected into a hitherto somewhat gloomy situation has been the action of Germany in which it linked progress toward a common farm program (which is of most interest to France) to progress in other phases of economic integration, such as the Kennedy Round. In early March an agreement was reached for a common set of prices for the major farm products other than wheat. But, meanwhile, time is slipping by and it is not neutral in its effects. The longer the delay, the stronger the forces of protectionism become in all nations. Our own Trade Expansion Act of 1962 will expire on July 1, 1967, and if no action is taken before then, it is possible that it will not be renewed by Congress and that the whole program will lapse. The General is becoming more and more openly anti-American and no one can tell what the future will bring. The next move is clearly up to Europe and in particular to France. Although a speed up in the negotiations seems to have occurred, the issue is still in the balance.

Part Three

Special Problems

13

East-West Trade

The ordinary practices of trade have never applied for Communist Russia and its Eastern satellites. When the Bolsheviks assumed power in November, 1917, they took Russia out of the war by concluding a separate peace with Germany. This was a heavy blow to the Allies, since the peace released German combat divisions for the Western Front. Almost at once, the Bolsheviks and the Western democracies squared away for armed combat. The Communists, believing that the change to socialism could not be effected either peacefully or gradually, encouraged revolutionary movements in the West while the Allies helped the anti-Bolshevik forces which were staging civil war inside Russia itself.

It is probably futile to try to apportion the relative blame for these hostilities or to try to judge their cause. The acts of each side provoked and intensified those of the other. The Communists wanted a world-wide revolution which would overthrow the existing political and economic order and they believed that their own revolution would not be safe until at least Continental Europe was also communized. In order to avert this danger, the Western Allies hoped to eliminate it at its very source. But their interventions confirmed and deepened the fears of the Russian Communists who thereupon redoubled their efforts at world revolution. A vicious and cumulative cycle of hostility was set in motion which, from the very start, poisoned relationships between the East and West. By the spring of 1920, the Communists had defeated the last of the so-called white armies and were militarily supreme inside Russia. Their own armies, however, had been unable to carry the revolution westward, and they were driven back by the Poles at the very gates of Warsaw. This brought a military truce and stalemate.

But there was no psychological truce. The Russians were still bent on world revolution. The wholesale feeding of millions of starving Russians by Herbert Hoover and the Quakers was a humane act, but it had no effect on Russian policy. The Bolshevik leaders set up revolutionary Communist parties under Russian control in all of the Western nations. These made war not only upon the established order, but also upon the reformist trade unions and the democratic socialists. Trade between the East and West almost ceased. In order to feed its armies and city population, the Communists requisitioned from the peasants almost all of their farm surplus above a bare minimum. This destroyed the economic incentives of the peasants and made them cut back on production. Russia ceased to be an exporter of wheat and could only offer timber, furs, and gold for the manufactured goods which they badly needed.

But with their collectivist beliefs the Communists did not want foreign trade to be carried on in the usual capitalistic way. Instead, they created state-controlled corporations which monopolized their foreign trade in the various countries. These would deal directly with the individual corporations with which they traded. At the same time, they held their foreign suppliers at arm's length from the ultimate purchasers and played them off against each other.

As Russia began to recover from the famine, its rulers decided to make their country as self-sufficient as possible. They centered their efforts upon heavy industry which could be used, either directly or indirectly, to turn out military equipment. They imported machines to use as prototypes from which they could construct their own machines. They also brought in foreign engineers and technicians for limited periods of time to help direct their production. They even sent some of their young engineers for training abroad in such companies as Henry Ford's. While the American government, under Harding, Coolidge, and Hoover, would not recognize Russia politically, it did permit these private arrangements, as did France, Great Britain, and Germany.

The world-wide depression which began in the autumn of 1929 largely paralyzed the relatively minute trade between the East and West. Nevertheless, we granted diplomatic recognition to Russia in 1933. This was the very time that Stalin, who had become dictator, staged cruel and widespread purges of many varying groups. While the Communists protested that they wanted a united front with the democracies against the fascist dictatorships of Hitler and Mussolini, the Kremlin itself was secretly considering a possible alliance with its fellow dictators.

Finally, in the latter part of August, 1939, as France and Britain screwed up their courage to resist Hitler's war against Poland, Stalin made his infamous pact with Hitler to join in dismembering both that country and the Baltic States.

This ended the economic relations of the democracies with Russia. The American Communists who had tried to get us to intervene against Hitler suddenly switched to a virulent campaign against any such intervention. Across the country they flashed their slogan: "The Yanks are not coming."

Hitler reversed all this in June of 1941, when he suddenly invaded Russia. Churchill and Roosevelt promptly changed their tactics. Since Russia was now the enemy of our enemies, they decided we should strengthen Russian resistance against the sweep of the Nazi armies. In the swift-paced action of that year, the Japanese attacked us at Pearl Harbor and when Hitler then declared war against us, we speeded and enlarged our supply efforts to help the Russians.

For three years we were loyal and unstinting Allies. Thirteen million Americans served in the armed forces during the common struggle, and at the same time we sent the Russians eleven billion dollars in supplies and equipment. While the Russian troops fought with great bravery, and their efforts in the East helped us on the Western Front, their leaders were both sour and surly.

Even before the Japanese had surrendered and the war brought to a victorious close, the French Communist leader, Duclos, issued orders to the American Communists to stop co-operating with the American government and, instead, return to open opposition. The wartime hopes that Russia and the United States could co-operate in peace as in war were being dashed. We still tried to co-operate, but the Russians went back on the Yalta pledges and set up not democratic governments as they had promised, but Communist dictatorships in the Eastern European countries. Having grudgingly joined in the United Nations, they sabotaged efforts to negotiate peace treaties dealing with Germany and Eastern Europe. They tried to take over Iran, and then, successively, Greece and Turkey. Finally, in 1948, they tried to force the West out of Berlin and, by means of a blockade, to take over all of that stricken city. Having resisted all the former attacks, we then broke the Berlin Blockade by a Herculean airlift. By this time, American public opinion had come to recognize Russia as our enemy, and opposed furnishing her with supplies and equipment which she might later use against us.

In 1949, because of the hostile acts and the propaganda campaign of the Russians and their Eastern European satellites, Congress began to restrict trade with the Soviet bloc. The Act passed in that year was primarily designed to shut off military equipment and supplies from Russia and her allies, and gave to the President the power to "prohibit or curtail the exportation of any articles" to any nation if in his judgment this would be harmful to our national security. The President was also directed to plan a unified trade policy which the non-Communist nations might observe in their dealings with the Communist bloc.

In 1950 Communists invaded South Korea. Although this was staged by the North Koreans, it was, in reality, inspired and aided by the Chinese Communists who had taken over that country in early 1949, and by Russia. We rallied to the defense of the South Koreans and the United Nations not only declared the attack an act of aggression, but urged resistance to it. However, the aid given by all but a few other nations was minimal, and the overwhelming share of the burden fell upon us.

In 1951, Congress tightened our export controls by the Battle Act which placed an embargo on all material which could be of a strategic economic as well as of a military nature. The first embargo required the preparation of an agreed list of strategic items for direct military purposes upon which all nations would declare and enforce an embargo. Some years later, Secretary of Commerce Hodges, in charge of the administration of the Act, stated that our allies had observed this requirement with comparative fidelity.

But the second part of the Battle Act created grave difficulties. This section gave the President power to embargo the export of vital economic goods to Soviet dominated countries and it directed the administrator of the Act to seek the co-operation of other nations in the preparation and enforcement of such a list. It also gave the President discretionary power to shut off all American aid to countries which did not co-operate. Our list of such embargoed items is lengthy and detailed.* However, food and agricultural products were specifically exempted from any mandatory embargo by the 1950 Act.†

Co-operation with our European allies has been primarily through a consultative committee of fifteen industrial nations which has prepared a common list of both strategic and other materials. As time has passed, the European nations have felt less in danger of attack. This has been particularly the case since the death of Stalin. There has been a growing pressure, therefore, to reduce the number of embargoed items and to soften the enforcement of the controls. We have tried to withstand these pressures, but our ability to do so has become progressively more limited as the European powers have increased their industrial strength and as we have discontinued our direct military and economic aid to them. We have therefore lost a great

* By 1962 it included many specific items under such general headings as 1. metal working machinery, 2. chemical and petroleum equipment, 3. electrical and power generating equipment, 4. industrial equipment, 5. transportation equipment, 6. metals, minerals, and alloys and their manufactures, 7. chemicals, petroleum, and rubber products, 8. miscellaneous items which, while not directly military equipment, could be of military use.

† For a full discussion of the present operation of both the 1950 and the 1951 Acts, see *Sixteenth Report to Congress on the Battle Act,* 1963, and *Export Control, 69th Quarterly Report,* 1964. Also Secretary Hodges' and Secretary Rusk's testimony before the Senate Foreign Relations Committee, Hearings on East-West Trade, 1964, pp. 53–111; pp. 2–52.

deal of the leverage we formerly possessed. As a result, the European countries are increasingly trading with the Soviet bloc on so-called nonstrategic items. In 1963, we sold Russia only 23 million dollars of nonessential goods while the rest of the free world sold them nearly a billion dollars' worth. Thus the British sales amounted to 179 million dollars, while those of West Germany came to 154 million dollars, France to 64 million dollars, Austria to 62 million dollars, and Sweden to 54 million dollars. Australia and Canada, as we shall see, sold Russia large quantities of wheat with total exports amounting to 53 and 139 million dollars respectively. Such countries as India, Japan and Malaysia were also huge exporters to Russia.* A great deal of machinery and capital equipment was also included in these sales by our allies.

There is no compulsory or statutory embargo on wheat or other farm products, although the President can impose one should he believe it to be in the national interest. Some small quantities of wheat, cotton, oils and fats had been exported over the years to Poland, but very little to Russia.

Prior to World War I, Russia was a big exporter of wheat to Western Europe. As a result of that war, and of the civil war which followed, Russia as we have said, ceased to export wheat.

In 1963, because of bad weather, there were poor crops all over Europe. This failure was especially severe in Russia where, in spite of forty years' effort to make their collectivized system work, the Communists had met with severe setbacks. Khrushchev, who was then the Russian

* Exports of Free World Countries to Sino-Soviet Countries, January to December, 1963. International Trade Analysis Division, U.S. Department of Commerce, 1963.

premier, had been trying to get grain from Rumania, Bulgaria, Poland, and East Germany. These countries had also been hard hit by the weather and they did not want to give their needed food to their Communist overlords.

To avert widespread hunger and possible starvation, Russia was forced to import substantial quantities of wheat. She obtained large shipments from Canada and Australia, both countries with ample reserves which they had been unable to sell on the world market at satisfactory prices. West Germany also sold Russia flour milled from wheat which had been imported from us and from other countries.

Russia needed still more wheat, and in the early fall of 1963, approached American traders. Secretary of Agriculture, Orville Freeman, himself a war hero and man of unquestioned patriotism, made an inspection trip in Eastern Europe and studied the Russian situation. He came back to advocate such a wheat sale. This position was supported by the farm groups in the Middle West and especially by those in the wheat belt. Congress approved such a sale, although some of us, who felt the policy was ultimately unwise, voted against it. At first it was thought that some 150 million bushels could be sold, or one-sixth of our reserve of 900 million bushels.

The program was slowed down, however, because President Kennedy attached the provision that half of all such exports had to be carried in American ships whose shipping rates were appreciably above the world level. Ultimately we sold only 63 million bushels.* The trade was handled by private firms and was paid for in dollars, although Congress had given its consent to have the sale financed on short-term credits by the Export-Import Bank.

* *East-West Trade,* Hearings before the Senate Committee on Foreign Relations, 1964, Part I, p. 132.

The Russian wheat crop apparently improved in 1964, since specific proposals of this type were not renewed. A widespread demand grew for relaxing the trade barriers with Russia and the Soviet bloc. Bankers and businessmen visited the Soviet Union in 1964 and came back advocating more trade with the Soviet Union.

In 1965, Russia had another crop failure and sought wheat in the West. Canada and Australia were again only too happy to fulfill this request, and were paid in gold. But the previous Presidential requirement that half of any American shipments had to be on high-cost American ships, and the threatened boycott of any such shipments by the Longshoremen's Union, discouraged any corresponding American response.

The discussion continued as to what our own trade policy should be toward the Soviet Union. The Senate Committee on Foreign Relations held extended hearings on this general issue and, on soliciting the opinions of business leaders, found them to be generally favorable to increased trade.

The fundamental question would seem to be whether Russia really wants to live on peaceful terms with the democracies of the West, or whether this is merely a false pretense. Believers in the former assumption urge that in return for such a Russian pledge we should trade with her in nonmilitary items and recognize her dominance over Eastern Europe.

But if Russia's ultimate aim is to overthrow our system of government and of economics, it would be the height of folly for us to build them up by trade, since this would merely strengthen them in their ultimately hostile purposes. Nor would the two common excuses for our co-operating in this manner be valid. For while our capitalists would reap a temporary profit, they would risk an ultimately greater loss and we should not allow their short-run gains to weaken our long-run interests. Nor should we forget that it was Lenin himself who said that the capitalists would ultimately be hung by the rope which they had sold to the Communists for a profit.

Similarly, the argument that if we do not trade relatively freely with the Russians other democracies will, and that consequently we cannot afford to hold back, misses the whole point. If Russia is, indeed, not only our enemy but also the enemy of the Free World, we should seek to get others to join us in the embargo rather than abandon the ship because the others are leaving it. For resolution and courage are as contagious as fear and flight.

Judgment as to which of these policies should be followed will hinge on which assumption turns out to be more nearly correct. If Russia is indeed seeking some reconciliation with the West, then some loosening of trade relations would be justifiable. If this is not the case, and if Russia is, instead, a relatively implacable enemy, it would seem both unwise and improper for us to strengthen them even if we made a short-run profit from the transaction.

In view of the basic Communist philosophy and of the way in which they have frequently switched overnight from co-operation to overt hostility, probably the safest course would be to practice caution and to require protracted and convincing proof that the Russian government has, in fact, turned over a new leaf. Even then, any beginning should be tentative and should not involve commodities which could be of any appreciable military significance, and should be balanced by Russia's sending us articles of similar value.

Furthermore, we might well seek political concessions for any economic benefit which Russia might receive. Foremost among such concessions would be the practical cessation of aid to the North Vietnamese government in its aggressions against South Vietnam, Laos, and Southeastern Asia in general. Further reciprocal concessions would be the withdrawal of Russian troops from Hungary and other satellites, and the granting of religious freedom in certain of the countries under Russian control. These need not be included in the same document as that on trade, but could be by parallel and preferably prior action by Russia itself. In other words, we need to be hard bargainers for freedom, and not succumb to excessive naïveté and false trustfulness.

Moreover, the argument that trade promotes friendship is not as strong an argument as its advocates believe. For Russia does not permit foreign suppliers to come into close contact with their ultimate purchasers, but handles all such matters through its foreign trade bureaucracy. Russian trade missions to this country, moreover, always have secret police attached to them to prevent the others from becoming too friendly. On the whole, a policy of genuine caution would seem to be wisest until a clear and continuing protracted change of policy has become evident.

With the exception of Poland, we have applied many of the same embargoes against Russia's satellites as against Russia itself.* Our European allies have traded very freely with these nations, selling in 1961 no less than 1.4 billion dollars' worth of goods.

With Poland, however, we have permitted a much larger volume of trade in nonmilitary items which has amounted to around 100 million dollars a year. In return we have primarily taken the justly celebrated Polish hams and sausage.

* During the Eisenhower Administration, however, defensive fighter planes were furnished to Yugoslavia.

We have tended to regard Yugoslavia, although communistic, to be relatively independent of Russia and, except for sporadic acts of Congress, have not applied rigid embargoes on economic goods. This was done in order to increase the already large economic dependence of Yugoslavia on the West and, hence, to decrease Russian influence on its policies. There are sections of the State Department which desire a similar policy to be followed in the case of Rumania, which has shown some signs of independence. But it is almost impossible to tell whether this would work. Some years ago Rumania was one of the most ruthless of the Russian satellites.

Communist China and Cuba are openly hostile to the United States. The Chinese Communists conquered the mainland of China in early 1949, forcing Chiang Kai-shek and about two million of his Kuomintang forces to the neighboring island of Formosa. We then threw a naval and air shield around the island to protect them, and gave liberal military and economic aid to enable its people to progress. At the same time, we restrained Chiang Kai-shek from attempting to invade the mainland.

Communist China concentrated its anger upon us. With the aid of Russia, it prodded the North Koreans into an attack on South Korea in the early summer of 1950. The United States and the United Nations rallied to the defense of South Korea. Finally, in the early winter of that year, Red China sent troops into North Korea. The Chinese attacked us before we attacked them, although President Truman had flatly refused to expand the war into China. A stalemate peace was negotiated by President Eisenhower in 1953 along the lines of the 1945 boundary. However, Communist China continued to stir up trouble not only along the Korean border, but in Southeast Asia, as well. It conquered Tibet by force, attacked India, and has incited North Vietnam to infiltrate and attack South Vietnam.

Because of Red China's many aggressions, we have refused to recognize their government and have placed an outright embargo and boycott on all trade and intercourse with it. This boycott has been strictly enforced so that our trade with that country is virtually nonexistent.* We have also opposed the admission of the Red Chinese to the United Nations on the grounds that its charter limits membership to "peace-loving" states. This policy has not been followed by many of our allies. Great Britain and France, for example, have not only recognized China diplomatically, but are trading with her. In 1963, for example, Great Britain sold China 37 million dollars' worth of goods while France sold 58 million dollars' worth. But China's poverty, together with the bad economic effects of communism, has prevented her from offering much besides raw materials in exchange. Australia and Canada have, however, sold large quantities of wheat to China, and in so doing have helped to protect the Chinese Communists, as they have the Russians, from feeling the political effects of their own farm policies. In 1963, Canada indeed sold 167 million dollars' and Australia, 200 million dollars' worth of grain and in 1965 they sold another 400 million dollars' worth.

In 1964, China became a potential nuclear power when it touched off its first atomic explosion. After this the Red Chinese grew even more militant. They denounced the counseled restraints from Khrushchev and attacked the Russian-announced policy of "peaceful coexistence." China instead advocated the early Trotskyan doctrine of "perma-

* There is probably a great deal of "bootlegging" of goods through the British port of Hong Kong and our trade with Hong Kong has risen to over 200 million dollars a year.

nent revolution" and of undying hostility between the communist and the predominantly capitalistic and democratic worlds. Mao Tse-tung, the Chinese leader, is reliably reported to have said that he would welcome nuclear war. Although 300 million Chinese might be killed, an equal number would survive while the relative damage to the Western World would be irreparable.

The Cuban revolution followed that of China by a decade. Cuba was cursed by several corrupt governments and, from 1953 to 1959, by the Batista dictatorship which was notoriously corrupt and cruel. Unfortunately, American policy until 1958 had supported Batista. In that year, however, an arms embargo was imposed. Some form of rebellion was inevitable. The great mass of the Cuban people and most of the outside world, therefore welcomed the successful overthrow of Batista by Fidel Castro on New Year's Day of 1959.

The United States hoped for friendship with the new administration, but this was not Castro's wish. On an early trip to Washington, he denied wanting any economic aid although he later said that the Americans had refused to grant it. He then claimed that this refusal justified Cuba in adopting a hostile policy towards the United States. Throughout 1959 and 1960, the situation became steadily worse. Castro moved Communists into the government, the army, and the trade unions and displaced those noncommunists who had been his earliest supporters. He constantly used terror to crush opposition. Finally, in 1960, he seized all American properties in Cuba and nationalized them without compensation. These included utilities and hotels, a big nickel mine and bauxite properties, three-sevenths of the sugar acreage, and a wide range of other properties.

The United States replied by shutting off all trade with Cuba except for a limited amount of medicines and food. This hit the Cubans in their most vulnerable spot. Cuba's soil surpasses all others and she depends almost entirely on the production of sugar. Far from exploiting Cuba, we had been paying its producers two cents a pound or forty dollars a ton more than the world price.

Our shutting off the American market deprived Cuba of well over 300 million dollars of foreign exchange a year which she had formerly used to import food, consumer goods, autos, trucks, machinery, spare parts, and gasoline.

Cuba called on Russia to fill the breach and soon became dependent on the Russians for military and economic help. Russia raised the paper price of the sugar which she bought to 6.5 cents a pound although the world free market price fell to 2.5 cents by the fall of 1964 and to 2.1 cents by October 1965. In addition, Russia sent Cuba large amounts of aid to prevent her economic collapse. The total of this aid is thought to be at least a million dollars a day, or over 350 million dollars a year. Cuba has thus been an expensive satellite for the Russians.

We have severely crippled Cuba's economy by shutting off most of her needed machinery and spare parts, and by reducing her consumer goods. In so doing, we have added to the domestic pressures against Castro, although it is improbable that these alone can overthrow such a strongly entrenched dictatorship. They could, however, be a contributing factor.

While Cuba grew more dependent upon Russia for economic aid, for some time it also moved away from peaceful coexistence and toward Red China in both its political tactics and foreign policy. It is seeking to export revolution into other countries, notably Venezuela and

Colombia. However, there also have recently been clear signs of a split between Cuba and China.

There is obviously a growing desire amongst the people of other countries for an economic and political truce not only with Russia, but with China as well. This was evidenced by the very narrow margin by which we defeated the motions to admit mainland China into the United Nations, as well as by the desire on the part of nearly all countries for greater trade with China. If this movement should continue to grow despite the Vietnamese war, it is not certain how long we can successfully oppose it. But much as we want peace and great as the destruction of a nuclear war would be, we should practice great caution in dealing with these proposals. For such economic co-operation with Russia and China would at once discourage popular movements from within the Communist bloc and would increase the danger that the resulting economic advantages to them would ultimately be turned against us militarily. If this applies to Russia, as I believe it does, it applies in even greater measure to China and Cuba. They are open in their hostility and we have seen so many instances of broken faith that we should not be seduced by fair hopes and pleasant words.

14

Trade Between Developed and Undeveloped Areas

Thus far we have been dealing primarily with trade relations among the nations of the Northern Temperate Zone. For it is here that modern industry has developed and thrived and it is here that the economic power of the world is largely concentrated. Over the millennia, there has indeed been something of a northern and westward march of industrial progress. More recently, Temperate Zone areas in the southern latitudes such as Australia, New Zealand, and Argentina have come forward. But industrial progress is still primarily confined to the Northern Temperate Zone. Here are the developed countries.

These areas, however, comprise only a minority of the people of the world. Nearly two-thirds live in or near the tropics—in the forty-six degrees of latitude or approximately 2,700 miles which stretch between the Tropics of Cancer and Capricorn.

One of the most striking contrasts between the economic life of the people in the Northern Temperate Zone and those in the tropics is the great difference in productivity and the standard of living. The best measure which we have of this at present is the arithmetic average of the Gross National Product per person. This has obvious disadvantages in that it does not allow for inequalities in the distribution of income. In all countries the position of the average man who stands at the midpoint (median) of incomes because of inequality is not as high as that shown by the arithmetic average. Differences in the degree of inequality, therefore, affect the comparative standing of the various countries. Thus in countries like Australia, New Zealand, and Sweden, where there is a much greater equality of incomes than elsewhere, the average man would fare better comparatively than in a country with the same arithmetic average, but with a larger share of the total income received by a few. Similarly, marked inequalities in the distribution of income would mean that the average man fares not only absolutely but comparatively even worse than indicated. A second weakness of the index is that in the case of the less advanced societies it does not make allowance for the unpaid services of the women within the households nor give adequate weight to the vegetables and fruit raised in small plots around the house.

But despite all these weaknesses the following table of the average per capita Gross National Product does give a rough picture of the comparative well-being of the people of the various nations and areas.*

The contrasts between these areas are striking. The American average is from fifty to one hundred percent higher than that of the major countries of Western Europe and from two to three times higher than that of the minor European countries. It is from four to five times higher than that of most people in the semitropical and Southern Temperate zones.†

* There is also a difficulty in classifying countries by climatic differences. Nations such as Costa Rica and Bolivia may be tropical at the seacoast but temperate in the plateaus and uplands. A country may also extend north and south to cover both temperate and semitropical areas or as is more often the case, the tropics and semitropics.

† Except, of course, for Australia and New Zealand.

Average Annual Gross National Product Per Capita (1962 and 1964) as Between People of Developed and Undeveloped Areas or Temperate and Tropical Zones

Average Annual Gross National Product per Person	Northern Temperate Zone
Over $3,000	United States
$2,000–$3,000	Canada
$1,500–$2,000	Sweden, Switzerland, Denmark, France, West Germany, Great Britain
$1,000–$1,500	Norway, Belgium, Netherlands, Austria
$750–$1,000	Italy
$500–$750	Spain
$200–$300	Portugal

	Semitropical and Southern Temperate Zones
$750–$1,000	Israel
$500–$750	Uruguay
$400–$500	Argentina, Chile, Jamaica, South Africa, Lebanon, Greece, Cyprus
$300–$400	Mexico

	Tropics
$750–$1,000	Venezuela
$500–$750	Trinidad
$300–$400	Costa Rica, British Honduras
$200–$300	Colombia, Dominican Republic, Peru, El Salvador, Honduras, Nicaragua, British Guiana, Jordan, Algeria, Ghana, Libya, Southern Rhodesia, Iran, Turkey, Malaysia
$100–$200	Brazil, Bolivia, Ecuador, Guatemala, Paraguay, Liberia, Tunisia, Northern Rhodesia, Senegal, Morocco, Ivory Coast, Philippines, Thailand, Iraq, Saudi Arabia, United Arab Republic, Syria, Ceylon, Cambodia, Taiwan
Under $100	Haiti, Burundi, Cameroons, Congo, Dahomey, Ethiopia, Kenya, Mali Republic, Nigeria, Nyasaland, Raundee, Sierra Leone, Somali, Tanganyika, Togo, Uganda, Upper Volta, Yemen, Afghanistan, India, Pakistan, Burma, Indonesia, South Korea, Laos, South Vietnam

The real contrast, however, is between the north and the tropics. Except for Venezuela and Trinidad, which are special cases because of their natural resources of oil and asphalt respectively, the differences are enormous. The average American income is from ten to thirty times that of the people of the tropics while that of the Europeans runs from six to twenty times as much. It is the people in the tropical belts of Asia, Africa, and Latin America who are in abject poverty. Their condition is actually worse than it seems, since the arithmetic average is raised by the large incomes of the wealthy, who in some countries own most of the land and natural resources and who control the industries.

It is natural, therefore, that as the people of the tropics become aware of their poverty in comparison with the relative affluence of the northern peoples, they should resent and dislike the latter. It is inevitable that many should come to believe that our affluence has been largely obtained at their expense and is a major cause of their poverty. There are two other factors contributing to added bitterness. The north and the industrialized countries have on the whole been progressing rapidly during the last ten years. The tropics have made little or no progress and in some cases, because of rapid population growth, have actually lost ground. The northern countries, moreover, up until recently have either held the tropics as colonial possessions or exercised almost complete political and economic domination over them. This has inevitably aroused dislike and opposition which continues long after political independence has been gained.

The record of the colonial powers in the tropics has indeed been a mixed one. On the one hand, they brought greater internal order and added capital to these countries; on the other, they were frequently brutal in their treatment of the conquered people and their cruelties were more resented than were those by fellow-countrymen. The colonial interests, moreover, commonly took most of the gains from the opening up of the natural resources and the operation of industry.

But whatever the economic balance sheet might be of colonialism and imperialism, it was domination by outsiders. This inevitably bred arrogance on the part of the rulers and resentment on the part of the subjects.

Added to all this were differences in color. The foreign rulers were white; the subject people were black, brown, and yellow. This deepened and embittered the hostility between those of the north and of the tropics. Out of the mélange of these antagonisms, the Communists, led by the Chinese, seek to forge a militant alliance of the darker-skinned and poverty-stricken peoples of the world. They hope that this alliance will ultimately surround and engulf the capitalistic, democratic nations of the world so that totalitarian communism will inherit the earth.

Any such danger is not as immediate as many fear. But it is an ultimate possibility and it could lead to a bloody series of wars which in many places would degenerate into race conflicts. It is prudent, as well as ethical, therefore, for the relatively affluent nations to try to improve the economic and political position of these people and to do so in a nonpatronizing manner.

At the same time, while we of the north should admit and seek to atone for such errors and sins as we have actually committed, we should not magnify them unduly nor develop any false inferiority complex. For the major part of the poverty of the tropics is due not to exploitation, but to climate, geography, social institutions, and the absence of science and adequate education.

The social institutions of the tropical peoples have not

encouraged effort and initiative. The heat of the tropics discouraged effort. Slavery prevailed for many centuries, schools were nonexistent, and political democracy was absent. Disease was rampant and medicine lacking. A feeling of fatalism permeated the population, largely caused by absolutism in government, widespread diseases which struck overnight and over which man had no control, and religions which emphasized a passive acceptance of life's hardships and evils rather than an effort to overcome and to transform them. It has been primarily opposite influences which have helped to get modern industry started in the northern temperate zone.

The people of the tropics have, moreover, always had a very high birth rate and during the last thirty years the coming of modern medicine and sanitation has so reduced the death rate that the rate of population growth has markedly increased over much of Latin America and indeed over the whole tropical and undeveloped world. This now amounts in Latin America to between two and two and a half percent a year and in Mexico to a full three percent. Over half of the population of Latin America for example is now under the age of twenty-one. This has held back improvements in the standard of living and in some instances even caused a decrease.

The people of the developed countries certainly cannot be blamed for the high birth rate in the tropics, which is one of the most important causes of tropical poverty. Nor can even their most bitter critics castigate them for helping to reduce the death rate by medicine and sanitation, although this has brought a much greater rate of population increase. Nor are they responsible for the high temperatures which impede hard work.

But since it is not so much the truth which determines history as what people believe to be the truth, the resentments of the people of the tropics, both justified and unjustified, are powerful forces which are helping to shape the economic, as well as the political, demands of the southern peoples and governments.

As trade opened up between the countries of the temperate north and the peoples of the southern tropics, an obvious division of functions developed which persists to this day. This was for the northern countries to obtain raw materials from the south and, in return, to sell manufactured products and to invest capital. From the tropics have come such fruits as oranges, bananas, figs, and dates, together with sugar, tea, coffee and cocoa, copra and cocoanut oil. Silver has come primarily from Mexico and gold from South Africa, asphalt from Trinidad, tin from Malaysia and Bolivia, rubber from Malaysia and Indonesia, and spices from the islands lying between Java and the Philippines. More recently the oil deposits of Venezuela, the Persian Gulf countries, and North Africa have been tapped and are flowing into the north.

The countries from the Northern Temperate Zone in return have sent manufactured goods to the south. These began with textiles, primarily in the form of cotton cloth. Woolens were added later. Then came hardware and tools, and finally, power engines and machinery.

Investments were also made in forms of social overhead capital, or what modern economists call "the infrastructure," such as railroads, street railways, highways, docks, warehouses, water and sewer systems, telephones, together with generating plants and distribution systems for gas and electricity. Originally, this capital was principally furnished by Great Britain and later in part by Germany. But recently the United States has been the big exporter of such capital. This flow began after World War

I and it has continued in greater volume since World War II.

Moreover, northern capital has, as we have seen, moved in to develop and indeed to take over the natural resources of many of these countries. Illustrations of this are the British control over the rubber plantations and tin of Malaysia, and the copra plantings of the South Seas, Belgian ownership of the Congo copper mines, and American control over the banana industry of Central America, the copper of Chile, the oil of Venezuela, and at one time of nearly half of Cuba's sugar. American and British interests, moreover, control nearly all the fabulously rich oil wells around the Persian Gulf.

These developments have helped to open up the natural resources of the tropics and to give employment to large numbers of the local populations. They have been resented because they siphoned off most of the profits from these developments into alien hands. Moreover, since economic power inevitably becomes interwoven with political power, the citizens of the less developed countries have felt deeply injured by foreign influences upon their governments and policies. It is natural, therefore, that all these forces should feed the fires of nationalism and make the mass of the people anxious to win economic as well as political independence.

This economic nationalism takes many forms and uses many weapons. Its most radical form is the outright nationalization of key foreign holdings. This was first seen in Mexico, where the big foreign-owned estates, the railways, and oil wells were confiscated by the Mexican government. In 1956, Egypt seized the Suez Canal, hitherto owned by a consortium of British and French capital. In South America we have witnessed the nationalization of the tin mines of Bolivia and the American holdings in

Cuba. In most of these cases compensation has ultimately been agreed upon. But this is not always true, as witness what has happened in Cuba.

The next step, for which there is a considerable degree of justification, is to levy large and increasing severance taxes or royalties upon the natural resources which are taken out of the countries. Illustration of this practice is found in the fifty-percent charge upon gross oil yields first levied by Venezuela. This quickly spread into the countries of the Persian Gulf and is now being increased to two-thirds or three-quarters over most of the world. The mildest expression of this economic nationalism is to insist that local capital be permitted to share in the ownership and local talent admitted to middle and top managerial posts. This movement is particularly strong in Mexico.

Still another conflict between the tropics and the northern industrial countries has been created by the nature of the demand curves for most of the tropical products, such as tea, coffee, cocoa, sugar, bananas, and the like. These demand curves tend to be highly inelastic. This means that slight changes in the quantities produced and marketed will, if other things remain constant, cause a much greater relative change in the price per unit. Thus, an increase of five percent in the production of sugar will, if other things remain the same, cause a decrease of ten percent or more in the price per pound. The producers and sellers of sugar will, therefore, suffer a reduction in total income from an increase in the crop, and this will be true whether the increase is due to favorable weather or to an improvement in technology.

Even where local people own the resources, therefore, they will suffer from such an expansion of output unless it is accompanied by a corresponding or greater increase in demand. The workers will also suffer, for if an enterprise encounters a loss, it will naturally try to retrench on its costs.

Conversely, if total supply is curtailed from any cause, whether natural or human, the producers as a whole will tend to gain more from the increase in unit price than they will lose by the decrease in volume sold. It is, therefore, in the interest of most tropical countries to curtail the output of their raw materials, if they can, in order to increase their total net income. They are therefore restrictionist in their output policies and try to control output and sales. This begins in the form of national cartels, as in the case of Brazilian coffee, but where the product is produced by two or more countries these efforts are inevitably widened to make them international and to take in as many major producing nations as possible.

However, individual countries will often want to operate as lone wolves outside of any international cartel. For if other tropical nations will reduce their production, then any one country can reap a gain. It can allow the others to send up the price per unit and, at the same time, by expanding its own output, have more units upon which such profits can be made. Jockeying for national advantage, therefore, lessens the cohesion of a tropical-output cartel. This is intensified if the various nations are jealous political rivals.

A further consequence of inelastic demand is the tendency towards great fluctuations in prices. Thus, good harvests will send prices down markedly, and poor harvests will send them up sharply. Fluctuations in the weather will have a heightened effect upon the national incomes of tropical people so that their economic life will resemble a roller coaster.

This effect not only unsettles the economics of the tropics but it also makes it easy for the people to blame the decreases in prices and incomes on the commodity traders either at home or in far-off markets. Sometimes these speculators do make large speculative profits, buying low and selling high.

This feeling of unfair treatment has been intensified by the fall in raw material prices during the last decade. World War II and the Korean War sent up the prices of rubber, tin, sugar, and other tropical commodities to a very marked degree. The subsequent peace and recession caused them to tumble. Traders and speculators had made the chief gains out of the price advances on their accumulated stocks, but the general public in the tropical countries bore a large share of the subsequent fall.

It is natural for people in the tropics to develop a growing dislike for the countries of the temperate zone and to feel that they are being unfairly exploited at almost every turn. It is small wonder that, as they have moved out from political domination by the Western colonial powers and into the sunlight of independent nationhood, they should make a series of economic and political demands upon the nations of the North.

This sentiment finally found coherent expression in the United Nations Conference on Trade and Development held in Geneva during the spring of 1964. The less developed tropical nations had felt for a long time that the conference and rules of GATT did not meet their needs or desires. The aim of GATT was to reduce tariffs and trade impediments and to produce a substantial economic equality of treatment between countries. Concessions given to one country were to be universalized and those receiving reductions were expected to reciprocate. However, the less developed countries were not satisfied with this system. They frankly wanted special favors in order to compensate for the handicaps from which they believed they unjustly suffered. Some countries, such as Mexico, would not join GATT, others gave it only nominal support.

Under pressure from these less developed countries a United Nations Conference was called to see if a common policy could be agreed upon. At the huge conference, where more than a thousand delegates assembled, the Secretary-General of the Conference, Dr. Raul Prebisch of Argentina, threw down the gauntlet to the industrialized nations of the north. In his preliminary report,* Dr. Prebisch advocated a sweeping series of trade and financial changes which were frankly designed to provide special advantages for the so-called emerging nations. The main planks in Dr. Prebisch's platform were:

1. Commodity agreements between nations which would materially raise the prices of the raw materials exported by the less developed and impoverished countries and which would be recognized and enforced by the importing or developed countries.

2. Lower tariffs on goods imported by the affluent nations from the less developed countries than are imposed on goods from the relatively more advanced countries. A considerable proportion of these goods, it was urged, should indeed be admitted duty-free.

3. The less developed nations should foster greater trade between themselves by means of custom unions and should impose higher tariffs on goods coming from the advanced countries.

In these last two ways, it was planned to develop more manufacturing within the relatively retarded nations by excluding some of the northern mass-production goods.

* *Towards a New Trade Policy for Development,* Report by the Secretary-General of the United States Conference on Trade and Development.

The tropical nations, in effect, wanted the north to give special favors to the tropics while accepting trade discriminations against them.

4. In addition, the developed countries of the north were expected to invest large additional funds in the developing countries which would rapidly reach the goal of one percent of their total national income. For the United States this would amount to approximately seven billion dollars a year and a similar investment by other advanced nations would raise the total to approximately fifteen billion.

5. The northern world also was expected to provide outright grants which were to be free from both interest and amortization payments as an indemnity to the less developed countries for any losses they had suffered in the terms of trade on specific commodities. It was not quite clear just what years were to be taken as the base unit. It was implied that these were the years of the highest relative prices of either World War II or the Korean War.

It would have been impossible for the more advanced nations to have agreed with all of this program. For, in effect, they were being held personally responsible for the impersonal workings of the market system and were being asked to indemnify the tropics for the failure of the latter's products to maintain the high prices which they had enjoyed during the Korean War. And special tariff favors would violate the GATT principle of nondiscrimination.*

Throughout the long spring of 1964, the less developed nations continued their pleas for special treatment. Finally, a compromise was agreed upon. A more or less generalized statement of principles was issued under which the devel-

---

* But curiously enough we are in effect carrying out this policy by extending the GATT negotiated tariff reductions to those undeveloped countries which are not members of GATT, such as Mexico.

oped countries agreed to help the undeveloped countries
to increase their income. Perhaps more important was the
establishment of the conference on a permanent basis. It
was now to meet every three years and to be provided with
a secretariat and a fifty-five-member governing board.

The issues raised by this conference will be permanent
and will probably be a continuing source of cleavage between the peoples of the north and south.

Let us now see to what degree the grievances of the
tropical countries are being met in the fields of regional
customs unions, the investment of capital and commodity
agreements or cartels.

Definite steps have been taken recently in Latin America
to obtain the advantages of a wider market through a
regional customs union.

The five small republics of Central America * began in
1960 when they formed a common market for the thirteen
million inhabitants of their countries, based upon the
European model. It became fully operative in 1963 and
provided that all import duties among the five would be
eliminated within five years and a common outer tariff
established. Very rapid progress has been made under this
agreement. The duties on about ninety-eight percent of
the some 1,276 products which have been classified have
been swept away, while all the remainder, except on coffee, will be shortly removed. It has also established uniform external rates on all but about thirty commodities
and tax favors are being granted by the various countries
to new business. This common market is governed by a
council consisting of the economics ministers of the member countries.

* Namely, Guatemala, El Salvador, Honduras, Nicaragua, and Costa
Rica.

The advantages of such an arrangement are obvious. Instead of the relatively minute markets which each of these countries could previously afford, a much larger one of approximately thirteen million people has now become possible. Consequently, a number of new manufacturing plants producing such consumer goods as shoes, clothes, drugs, toilet articles, chemicals, and the like have been established. Many of these have been set up in El Salvador and Guatemala, but all of the countries have obtained some.

In addition, a Central American Bank of Economic Integration has been created with four million dollars of capital from each of the five countries, together with ten million dollars more from the Inter-American Development Bank. This, in turn, is largely financed by the United States. An additional three million dollars for research has also been granted by the United States. Numerous long-term loans have been made by the bank to help finance new industries in all of the five countries. A Central American clearinghouse has also been set up to handle checks between the countries.

Largely as the result of these efforts, the total volume of trade between these Central American countries increased from 33 million dollars in 1960 to 50 million in 1962, and 130 million dollars in 1965. All this has opened up a considerable volume of new employment, chiefly in factories owned by American firms, in these relatively impoverished countries whose populations hitherto have depended for their scanty living upon the cultivation of tropical products such as coffee, bananas, and sugar and which, with the possible exception of Costa Rica, have been controlled by a relatively small number of large plantation owners and exporters.

This common market should, therefore, help to build up

in these sharply divided countries a much-needed middle class which, in its upper reaches, would include entrepreneurs and managers and, in its middle and lower layers, foremen, skilled workers, and factory employees. Moreover, as the general standard of living rises, there will be a further increase within the common market in the production of consumer goods and services. There will thus be a cumulative spin-off which, in turn, will lay the basis for a further advance. This is already evident in Mexico and may be expected within Central America.

The effects upon the United States will be much the same as those of the European Common Market. We will gain from the increased prosperity of the people which will enable them to buy more comforts and luxuries, tools, and machinery from the United States. We will lose, however, to the degree that the increased volume of consumer goods manufactured within Central America displaces purchases which would otherwise have been made from us. This loss will be more acute if the Central American market should raise its external tariffs above its previous average. It is hard to weigh these two contrary forces against each other, but it is clear that the experiment should help Central America itself both economically and politically. It will diminish the danger of war which a few years ago threatened to break out between Nicaragua and Costa Rica. It may, in the long run, even lead to a much needed political federation which would also be to the advantage of the United States.

But we should not pitch our hopes too high. Most of the people of these countries live in abject poverty and their chief trade is not with each other, but with the countries of the Temperate Zone, notably, the United States. They tend, moreover, to be one-crop countries. Until recently coffee formed over seventy percent of the exports of El Sal-

vador and Guatemala and over fifty percent of the exports
of Honduras while cotton constituted about forty percent
of Nicaragua's exports. These countries are, therefore, more
interested in the comparative prices of these products than
in the volume of trade with their sister nations.

Faced with many obstacles, a much larger proposal is
struggling to come into being in South America. This is the
Latin American Free Trade Association formed in 1961,
which includes nine of the twelve countries of that continent.* It is based, as its name implies, upon the principles
of the Outer Seven in Europe, rather than those of the
Inner Six. Like its European prototype, its aims are to
eliminate all internal tariffs within its ranks but to allow
each country to maintain its separate tariff to the world
outside the Association.

Such an association, if fully carried out, would have
great possibilities, since the countries include 180 million
people who have a combined gross national product of
nearly 50 billion dollars and an estimated import capacity of about six billion dollars. The aim of the Association
is to obtain a completely unified internal market by 1973.
It intends to do this by average yearly cuts in tariffs of
eight percent.

These pledged reductions are, however, surrounded by
so many qualifications that the actual progress has been
relatively slow. Each nation, for example, can choose those
products on which it is willing to reduce its rates. There
is a natural tendency, therefore, for each country to reduce
rates on those commodities which are not produced within
its borders and for which there is no immediate prospect
that they will be. Previous concessions can be cancelled by
a country provided it makes an equivalent concession on

* That is, all except Bolivia, Panama and Paraguay.

other goods. The Association also has been handicapped by not having a council of the responsible cabinet ministers which would authorize the basic agreements.

In spite of the obvious weaknesses in negotiating these "national" lists, a little progress has been made. During the first two years, no less than 7,600 tariff concessions were agreed upon of which 2,300 were in the form of a complete removal of duties. There has also been an appreciable increase in the internal trade between the members from 299 million dollars in 1961 to 354 million dollars in 1962, and to 558 million dollars in 1964.

In addition to the "national" lists which are negotiated each year, there is to be a "common" list which is to be agreed upon every three years and which is to cover at least a quarter of the trade within the Association. The inclusion of a commodity on this common list does not mean that its tariffs would be reduced immediately but merely that the member countries promised that by 1973 all such duties were to be abolished. The first of these triennial conferences was held at Bogotá in the autumn of 1964. It was not a marked success and, in general, the program has not been able to get off the ground.

National jealousies are all too real; land transportation between the countries almost nonexistent; and ocean transportation slow and costly. The countries tend to specialize in one or two commodities such as coffee, tin, copper, wool, and beef and to depend upon the European and American markets rather than on each other.

The device which is being pushed most vigorously by the raw material and tropical countries is that of commodity agreements, or international raw material cartels. These are agreements between the producers or governments of exporting countries to control and restrict the quantities to be sold on the world market in order to raise the prices of their raw materials and hence the incomes of their producers and owners. Formerly, these cartels were privately directed, as in tin, which was run from London and which controlled the export of that metal from both Malaysia and Bolivia. This was based both on the control of the mines and on the ownership of the smelters. The control by the De Beers interests over the diamonds of South Africa was another case of a commodity cartel. Still another was the Stevenson plan in the 1920's to cartelize and restrict the production of rubber in Malaysia and Indonesia (though this later broke down).

In later years the governments of the exporting countries have tended to become the managers of these commodity cartels. They have also been expanded to become international rather than purely national in scope. The producers are also putting pressure on the governments of the consuming countries to join these compacts and to become enforcing agents for the cartel in return for some voice in determining the quantities which are to be exported and sold.

Commodities where such international export and price agreements have been developed include coffee, sugar, and tea. The workings of these cartels illustrate some of the problems, methods, and costs which are inevitably involved.

The major portion of the world's coffee was formerly grown in Brazil. In efforts to raise the price, first the state of Sao Paulo and later the central government of Brazil tried to control the total amount which could be exported. This was done by restrictions upon output, by controlling the amounts to be stored and upon occasion by the outright destruction of part of the crop. These efforts led to temporary increases in price which could not permanently be maintained because of the stimulus which they gave to increased production both inside Brazil itself and, perhaps even more, in other Latin American countries and ultimately in Africa. In a sense, therefore, Brazil held a price umbrella over the heads of other countries which encouraged them to increase their plantings. The relative ineffectiveness of these national efforts inevitably created demands for an international cartel. This was finally brought into being in 1962 when twenty-four countries concluded such an agreement. They included virtually all of the coffee producing and exporting countries, such as Brazil, Colombia, Mexico, and the five republics of Central America, together with a number of African countries. The main consuming countries which signed the agreement were the United States, France, Italy, Japan, and Great Britain. By the spring of 1964, West Germany, Canada, the Netherlands, and the three Scandinavian countries had also signed.

Under this agreement, a total annual basic export quota of 45.6 million bags was set of which 18 million bags was allotted to Brazil, 6 million to Colombia, 1.4 million to El Salvador, 1.3 million to Guatemala, 1.5 million to Mexico, while a little over 10 million bags were assigned to the various African countries. It will be remembered that under the Common Market special rights of free entrance were granted to all the farm products of the ten former colonies of the French and Belgians.

It is sometimes contended that these "basic export quotas" were not actual quotas but merely prescribed the relative proportions which the various countries were allotted of the total, namely, that Brazil was to have $18\%_{456}$ths of the total amounts which could be exported in any year. This is a very deceptive half-truth. The actual volume of exports permitted in the initial year was ninety-nine percent of the "basic quotas" so that countries agreed that they would not exceed their quotas. To enforce the quota each nation was to give certificates of origin for each authorized shipment. This, in turn, would be reported to the international organization for verification.

But export control over the supplies of coffee was not the only control. The importing countries, too, were expected to help. In the implementing legislation which was presented to our Congress * we were asked to give to the President the power to deny entrance into the United States of any shipment of coffee from a member of the International Coffee Organization which was not accompanied by a certificate of origin. We were similarly to prohibit the admission of coffee from any nonmember country and thus were to be an enforcing arm for the coffee organization or cartel.

Within the governing council of the coffee organization, two separate panels were set up for the exporting and importing countries, each with a total of 1,000 votes. These votes were apportioned between the exporting countries in proportion to their quotas and for the importing nations according to the relative volume of their imports during the preceding three years. No state, however, is to have more than 400 votes. In practice, this gave Brazil thirty-nine percent of the votes on the exporting panel. While the United States imports came to fifty-two percent of the world trade, our representation on the council was, therefore, scaled down to 400.

The quotas, once fixed, can only be changed by a two-thirds vote of each panel. This would seem to mean that we can veto any decrease in the total quotas. But this is not wholly true because, if we were the one country voting

* H.R. 8864, 88th Congress, 2nd Session.

negatively, the proposal would be considered to have been adopted. Furthermore, if only two countries object but have more than one-third of the vote, another polling could take place within twenty-four hours and, if three countries comprised the group, a second vote could be scheduled within forty-eight hours. The provision also means that either Brazil or a coalition of countries which can muster more than a third of the votes can veto any increase.

The demand for coffee is steadily increasing, since population is rising rapidly all over the world, and new groups are adopting coffee as a drink. Coffee itself, moreover, is in a sense habit forming. It is estimated that this increase in the quantity demanded at the same price is somewhere around three percent a year. If the quotas are not increased proportionately, therefore, this will inevitably mean an increase in the price of coffee.

Each increase of one cent a pound means an added cost to the American consumer of from 30 to 35 million dollars, and about an equal loss to the consumers in foreign countries. The import price of coffee has gone up very markedly since the Agreement was signed. In March of 1963 the import price of Brazilian coffee was 34 cents a pound. On March 2, of 1964 it was 51 cents a pound, or an increase of 17 cents a pound. On May 10, the price was 47.75 cents. The immediate loss to the American consumer was therefore between 400 and 500 million dollars a year. More recently, however, the price has been relatively stabilized.

After two years of discussion the coffee agreement was finally approved by Congress. Inside the international coffee organization, continuing struggles have been waged over the size of the total quota. Brazil and the exporting nations have urged that it be reduced. This, of course, would have raised both the price per pound and their total revenues. The United States and other consuming countries have wanted to increase the quota by at least the estimated annual increase in total demand or by around three percent. In 1964, influenced in part by fear of adverse action by the United States Senate, an agreement was reached to leave the quota untouched. In 1965, after another battle it was actually increased by 115 million bags, or by a little over three percent. This, however, was the first increase authorized since the intergovernmental cartel was formed. The price of Brazilian coffee on the New York market on March 25, 1966 was 42 cents a pound.

It is urged in support of this agreement that it is necessary both to raise the standard of living of the poverty-stricken peasant who raises the coffee and give greater stability to hard pressed governments such as that of Brazil. Those are both desirable purposes and it is probable that the previous price of 34 cents a pound was altogether too low. But it is questionable whether the peasants who do the physical labor would get much of any increase in price. They did not in the previous periods of high prices. The profits were instead largely intercepted by the relatively small group of wealthy planters and traders. In El Salvador, for example, the well known fourteen families largely control the land and with their associates reaped the major share of the benefits from the high prices of the early 1950's. It was much the same way in Brazil and Colombia. It must be granted, however, that an increased price does increase the revenues which producing countries can raise through export taxes and that, to this extent, it amounts to an indirect subsidy to the governments and wealthy planters with some crumbs falling from the table into the mouths of the hungry peasants at the bottom of the Latin-American social structure.

Some of us contended that it would be better to give this

aid directly to governments and peasants through the Alliance for Progress. This would not only reach those who needed it but it would remove the repressive effect of an increase in the price of coffee. Since no more coffee is consumed by the well-to-do than by those of lower incomes, an increase in the price per pound forms a larger fraction of the income of the poor than of the well-to-do. What a price increase of this type does, therefore, is to compel the poor and those of moderate means in the United States and in other consuming countries to subsidize among others, the rich planters in the producing countries. There is a real question as to whether this is the best form of aid.

But dealing with what they believed to be the practical and administrative realities of the situation, the State Department insisted upon approval of this agreement and, over the objections of some of us, Congress gave its consent. It is still uncertain what the future will be. Up to date the results have not been as bad as some of us had feared but, if the producing nations can hold together, further increases may come. There are powerful groups inside these nations demanding an increase of at least ten cents a pound. This would cost the American consumers approximately 300 million dollars and the consumers abroad an equal sum. But historically the State Department has not been robust in defending the American consumer, except when under pressure from Congress.

Whether the producing nations can stay united is doubtful. It would be difficult enough within Latin-America itself, but there is even greater doubt whether the African countries will be satisfied with their quota of approximately twenty-two percent. If they withdraw and start exporting more, the cartel is likely to fall apart and the ultimate state will be worse for the producing nations than the first.

Much the same situation is true in the case of sugar, although here there is no one international sugar cartel but instead no less than four markets. Three of these are nationally controlled, namely, the American, British, and Russian, while the fourth or so-called "free" market comprises the rest of the world.

Since the American market is the most important and concerns us most intimately, a brief discussion of it is in order. In a rational world devoid of selfish interests and national rivalries, it would be economical for us to get our sugar from the islands of the Caribbean and the immediately adjacent countries. For here the soil is extraordinarily fertile and the climate favorable. Historically however the cane-sugar interests of Louisiana and the beet-sugar interests of Michigan and the West, which produced sugar at higher than Caribbean costs, have demanded and attained a tariff on imported sugar which raised the price to the consumer by from one to two cents a pound.* In 1933, a new agreement was worked out under the general guidance of a humane Senator, Edward Costigan of Colorado, a big beet-sugar state. In return for obtaining the elimination of child labor and securing better working conditions in the beet fields, both the domestic and foreign producing interests were granted total quotas of production which were designed to raise and then stabilize the price. Then, the foreign producers whose price on the free market was much less, were guaranteed the higher American price at New York. Puerto Rico was given a liberal quota, as were the Philippines. Cuba was allotted virtually all the rest and hence received, over ten years, bonuses of hundreds of millions of dollars over the world price. About three-sevenths of this went to American companies which owned

---

* Wright, Phillip, *Sugar in Relation to the Tariff,* Brookings, 1924, footnote p. 47.

sugar plantations and grinding mills. But there was a large margin for Cuban producers, some of which may have seeped downward, but even more spread outward to other groups in the Cuban economy. While Castro and his followers have denounced this arrangement as an exploitation of Cuba, it was in reality nothing of the sort. It was on the whole a huge bonus to the Cuban economy, although its benefits went largely to those on top of the social structure.

When we were forced by Castro's hostility to break with Cuba, the Cuban quota had to be reassigned. Some was given to the American beet and cane interests while a host of other countries swarmed in to get as large a slice as possible. The lobbying became widespread and Americans with presumed influence were paid large fees for their efforts. All of the foreign sugar was paid the domestic price which came by 1963 to amount to about two cents a pound or 40 dollars a ton above the free world price. On the three million tons assigned to countries other than the Philippines and Puerto Rico, this came to a total of approximately 120 million dollars. Quotas were assigned without too great logic to the separate countries.

In 1963 I was successful in getting the Senate to agree to paying the foreign producers the world, rather than the American, price and to levying a recapture fee equal to the difference. This revenue would go to the Treasury, and would offer some relief to the taxpayers. The system of individual quotas by countries was to be abandoned and in its place a world, or global, quota was substituted under which producers and shippers would be treated on the basis of first come, first served. This proposal met with intense opposition from the favored nations and their representatives and finally a compromise was found under which only a part of the foreign quota was assigned on a global basis to which the recapture fee would be applied. The remainder was to be assigned by individual quotas to favored countries which would receive the full American price. Some 41 millions were collected by countervailing duties in 1962–1964 and then the free market price of sugar took, for a brief time, an almost unprecedented leap above the American price, only to fall later to an even lower level. Open market prices in the Caribbean were about 2.1 cents a pound, and adding shipping and insurance costs, this would amount to about 3.25 cents delivered in New York. The American price was about 6.25 cents.

I renewed my fight to eliminate this bonus of about three cents a pound or 60 dollars a ton to foreign producers and to have it transferred to the Treasury. But this time the forces against this proposal were stronger; for the State Department, which had hitherto given quiet support to the proposal, now switched its position under the direction of Thomas C. Mann, who was in charge of Latin-American affairs. Mr. Mann emphasized the political desirability of keeping governments in the tropics friendly. He said the peasants did get a big share of the bonus, and finally urged that we must pay as much or slightly more than did the Russians and British. His arguments prevailed and even a modest proposal I advanced to eliminate all quotas outside of the Western Hemisphere and use the recapture fees for the benefit of the Latin-American peasants through the Alliance for Progress was defeated. The State Department opposed even this proposal, making it clear that they preferred the commodity agreement to additional appropriations for foreign aid and the Alliance for Progress.

The State Department has now agreed to a commodity cartel for tin which they claim is designed to stabilize rather than to raise prices permanently. Once again the need to strengthen the governments of Malaysia and Bolivia is being urged as a dominant reason for our membership.

Thus far, the State Department has resisted efforts to form an international cartel for cocoa which is much desired by the African nations. It is now apparent that our State Department will support the formation of commodity cartels designed to raise the prices received by producers in the less developed and tropical countries but will seek thereafter to stabilize them at a level which it does not regard as excessive. The undeveloped or less developed nations therefore seem to have won acceptance for one of the major planks in their platform.

But whether these agreements, which will primarily raise the cost of living for the consumers of low and moderate incomes in the more advanced countries, are in the general interest as a long-run policy is very doubtful. The lack of cohesion between the producing countries is, moreover, liable to make them fall apart after a few years.

On the whole, I would prefer a more liberal policy of aid to girding the earth with a series of international commodity agreements. But it is true that the great poverty of the less developed areas of the world does demand sympathetic action on the part of the so-called "have" nations of which we are the most prominent. But in the aid which we give and the capital which we invest, it should be our primary purpose to help the poverty-stricken families at the bottom of the social structure of these nations rather than the more favored elite at the top.

Though the estimated annual capital needs of the undeveloped peoples has been set at from 15 to 20 billions of dollars, the actual amounts granted have been much less than that. The Paris-based Organization for Economic Cooperation and Development estimates that the net

actual amounts both public and private which have been
furnished from 1961 to 1963, inclusive, were as follows: *

Year	Total Net Flow, Public and Private (In billions of dollars)
1961	$9.2
1962	8.5
1963	8.5

From two-thirds to nearly seventy percent of these
amounts were extended bilaterally, and slightly less than
ten percent through multilateral agencies, such as the
World Bank. An average of slightly over two billion dollars a year came from long-term private investments and
around a half billion yearly in the form of longer term
private credits on exports.

The United States has consistently provided at least a
half of the total and furnished a larger proportion of its contributions in the form of outright grants than any nation.
When we did make loans, our interest rates were lower than
those of any other country. Thus, in 1963, two-thirds (or
over a billion dollars) of our official loans were either
interest free or had rates of less than one percent. Slightly
over half the German official loans were, however, between
three and four percent, and forty percent (200 million dollars) between five and seven percent. Two-thirds of the
British official loans were at rates between five and six
percent. Most of the Japanese loans in 1962 were at more
than six percent, and this was true of the Italian loans in
1963.

* See the OECD Study, "The Flow of Financial Resources to Less Developed Countries, 1956–1963." Paris, 1964, pp. 128–133.

On the whole, the United States emerges from these comparisons as by far the most generous of the industrial nations. It has also distributed its assistance over a much wider spectrum of countries and, having no colonial empire of its own, has made liberal grants and investments in countries over which it has had no political control. France and Great Britain, on the other hand, have tended to confine their assistance to affiliated countries or to former colonies. Only the United States has taken on the world. For many of these countries there was literally no other place for them to go.

There can be little doubt that the Western European nations should make larger contributions at more generous terms. An attempt by some groups within the Common Market to prove that its member countries were doing their full share has met with a strong statistical rebuttal by Messrs Pearson and Schmidt.* That the total should be increased is seen by the following breakdown on the totals of official capital invested in 1963 in the various undeveloped areas and what these come to on a per capita basis.

Undeveloped Areas in	Net Official Capital Flow	Amount per Capita
	(In millions of dollars)	
Asia	2,756	$3.03
Africa	1,650	5.87
Latin America	1,140	5.00
Europe	471	5.23

Even when loans from the multilateral agencies and from private capital are added, these sums are seen to be

---

* Pearson, S. R., and Schmidt, Wilson E., *Alms for Alms,* Journal of Common Market Studies, October 1964, pp. 74–82.

greatly inadequate. I would therefore recommend several approaches:

(1) Private investments should be especially encouraged, if possible, by a re-insurance fund.

(2) That the European countries assume a larger share of the burden at lower interest rates and that they extend this assistance to a wider range of countries.

(3) That when (and only when) the European countries take up their full obligations, we should then increase our own investments—working as far as possible through low interest loans.

(4) That multilateral agencies, such as the World Bank, the International Development Association, the Inter-American Bank, and the new Inter-Asian Bank, be encouraged to extend their activities and to seek a wider basis of support.

Part Four

The Balance of Payments and an International Monetary System

15

The Beginnings of an
International Currency

Thus far, we have primarily treated national and international trade in terms of barter. We have assumed that goods and services are exchanged for other goods and services. This is basically what constitutes trade, but it is not directly so. Instead, in all but the most primitive regions, the exchange of goods and services takes place through the intermediary of money—that is, anything which is generally accepted within a trading area for goods and services. Money removes the necessity that the exchangers hawk their goods to a wide range of customers and in return that they must want the specific goods which are offered to them in exchange. Such a practice would be bad enough within a village; it is impossible within a nation, and completely so in world-wide trade. The Nazis, under the tutelage of Dr. Schacht, tried to use the method of barter, but those who traded with them were seldom satisfied with what they received.

Money thus removes the difficulty of obtaining coincident demand by providing a common medium of exchange. The firm which produces textiles sells them for money. This is generalized purchasing power, and with this money the company will buy raw materials, pay out wages, salaries, taxes, and other claims as well. It then reinvests the money profits which it makes or distributes them to the owners. It would be impossible to handle this multitude of exchanges on a direct-barter basis.

Society also avoids a further difficulty by quoting the exchange ratios between goods in terms of the common denominator of money for great discrepancies in the exchange ratios are inevitably created under barter. For example, suppose one bushel of wheat could be bartered for three bushels of oats and two of corn. However, let us assume that oats could also be exchanged on even terms with corn. Then a farmer could directly exchange his wheat for the three bushels of oats and barter the oats for three bushels of corn—or get one more bushel than what his wheat would command by a direct exchange. Hopeless confusion would result in the exchange of thousands of commodities. Money, therefore, serves as a common denominator or standard of value as well as a medium of exchange.

Money is also suspended purchasing power which can be used in the future and, hence, is not subject to the physical deterioration which most commodities obtained under barter would experience. In textbook language, it is therefore both a "store of value" and a "standard of deferred payments." This is, of course, subject to the qualification that if the prices of commodities and services increase in terms of money, then the exchange value of each unit of the currency itself falls, since it can purchase proportionately less. Or if prices fall, then the value of a unit of money rises correspondingly.

The extension of the market, the widening web of trade, and the myriad advantages of large-scale production, which lie at the base of our economic society could not, therefore, have been possible without the development of money.

But, invaluable as money is, it is not a purely passive factor. Its use indeed creates many special problems of its own and these are even greater in the field of international trade than in that of domestic trade.

In the early days of a society, all sorts of articles came to be used for money, such as shells, tobacco, cattle, and grain. Gradually, however, these were replaced by metals, such as copper, lead, silver, and gold. These were not only desired for their own sake and, hence, had an independent value of their own, but since they are relatively durable, they did not deteriorate with time. Over the centuries, silver and gold began to displace their more common rivals because of a greater preference for them combined with their relative scarcity. This gave them a greater value per ounce, therefore making them far less cumbersome to handle. These two metals continued for centuries to move together in double harness. They were freely coined into national currencies where they were appropriately stamped in various denominations as "pounds," "francs," "marks," "dollars," and so forth. When a pound of silver, minus a charge for coining, was returned as a coin called a "pound," this became the basic unit for the domestic currency of England. Ratios were established between the coin and gold in terms of the relative amount in "pounds" which would be returned for equal weights of gold and silver.

When goods were sold in international trade, this meant that articles produced under the currency of one country had to be sold under the currency of another. Ratios between the currencies had therefore to be established. The obvious measurement was the relative amount of the metals contained in the currency of each. If there was twenty-five times as much silver in the English pound as in the French franc, that became the ratio between them.

If a sovereign took an increasing profit in return for the privilege of coining, then, because of the decrease in the metallic content of the coin of that country, it exchanged for fewer units of the foreign currency than before. Bitter experience taught the dealers in foreign moneys to scrutinize and weigh these coins carefully in order to detect any short weights or adulteration.

With the passage of time, an ounce of gold became increasingly scarce relative to demand and, hence, much more valuable than silver. Its very scarcity and cost then gave gold added prestige value and gradually it began to displace silver as a national and, ultimately, as an international currency. England went to the gold bullion standard after the Napoleonic Wars by promoting the full and unlimited conversion of "pounds" into gold and vice-versa. This privilege was, however, denied to silver, the purchase of which was limited to quantities approved by the government.

Since England was the first to develop the factory system and the industrial revolution, it became the chief exporter and importer of the world. England's abandonment of silver and enthronement of gold exercised a pronounced gravitational pull upon other countries. Gradually they fell in line, as we did in 1873. By the end of the nineteenth century, the gold standard was virtually dominant in the two great trading areas of the world, namely, Europe and North America, while silver had retreated to Asia and Latin America.

But the gold standard itself has gone through an evolution of at least four stages, namely, the pure gold bullion standard, the fractional gold reserve standard, the international gold standard, and the international gold exchange standard.

The pure gold standard is what we commonly think of

when we speak of the historic gold standard, namely where gold, in the form of coins, circulates as part of the currency. In its second stage, it is also a reserve standard when, in addition to circulating itself, it acts as a reserve with which to redeem, upon demand and in gold coin, paper money and other types of currency. In this latter form it also becomes an international currency, for it is used to settle the deficits of a country in its net balance of payments with the outside world. In other words, both the internal currency and the external claims become convertible into gold.

Such was the gold standard up until World War I. Today it is not fully in effect anywhere. Its crucial weakness was that the amount of gold in the reserves came to be relatively slight in comparison with the increasing amount of currency and credit which it was legally obligated to redeem upon demand. It was therefore subject to the danger of both internal and external "runs." There was a constant danger that the claims for gold could not be met and that then the right of redemption would have to be suspended. This led to the ultimate transformation of the gold standard into the international gold and gold exchange standards.

In the beginning, the circulating medium, as we have seen, consisted of metallic coins. Then the gold and silver coins began a partial retreat from the market place. The goldsmiths and early bankers, both in England and on the continent, would be given gold for safekeeping and, in return, would give the holder receipts or notes entitling him to claim the gold which he had deposited. These notes, printed in various denominations, were obviously less cumbersome than the coins or metals themselves and were therefore more convenient to circulate. Then a cunning thought came to the goldsmiths and bankers. They observed that only a small fraction of the certificates which they issued were ever presented for redemption in gold. They concluded therefore that they could issue more certificates than the quantity of gold they held. The excess would be pure profit. This was done increasingly and the goldsmiths became rich. In the process, they created monetary purchasing power which they either spent themselves or, if thrifty, loaned out to others. In this very questionable manner, modern commercial banking originated.

As rumors began to circulate that these feats of legerdemain were actually going on, efforts were made to suppress the gossip. In some cities such talk (though not the practice) was made a criminal offense. For as long as the goldsmiths and bankers could keep the demands for redemption down to an appropriate fraction of the gold which they held, they were safe. If a minor run developed, their probity would be tested but apparently proved. Any gold withdrawn would soon be redeposited and the bankers could continue on their course.

But sometimes the goldsmiths and the bankers overreached themselves. In their zeal to make profits, they would issue many times more certificates than they held gold. Then, when a suspicious and frightened public went in large numbers to get the promised gold for their paper certificates, those toward the end of the line often found that the gold had been exhausted and that the cupboard was bare. Then, in revenge, the bilked certificate holders would frequently try to hang the goldsmiths and the bankers.

But, after a time, the public would forget; the incident would be glossed over and the lucrative practice would be resumed.

And yet the goldsmiths and bankers could always make a plea in defense of their profitable deceit. They could argue that the demands for money in a society where trade and exchange were expanding rapidly were far greater than could be satisfied by the actual amount of the precious metals which they held. The creation of additional purchasing power, it was claimed, fulfilled a social function and, even if it made them rich, amply justified putting both their bodies and their immortal souls in jeopardy. Their deceit was society's salvation and their moral martyrdom the redemption of the business world.

Without going too deeply into the apologetics for this practice, it can be said that the custom of issuing more bank notes than there was legal money with which to redeem them, became widely established among the banking fraternity. Such fractional reserves were silently assumed to be a sound and accepted practice. However, when it was used by governments, the financial world treated this variation as morally reprehensible and as clear evidence of unsound finance. What was standard and accepted procedure in the world of private finance became a heinous sin when practiced by the representatives of the public.

With the passage of time, the ratio between the quantity of notes and credit at the top and the amount of gold and silver in the reserve vaults, into which the credit claims were legally redeemable, steadily increased. Commercial banking was developing and here, when the banks made short-time loans, instead of giving the borrowers bank notes and currency for most or all of the loan, they created instead checking accounts against which the borrowers might later draw. In these cases, it was the loans which created the deposits, instead of, as is the case in investment banking, the deposits from prior individual savings creating the loans. Since the checks became widely accepted, the demand deposits became a rapidly increasing part of the money supply.

In a society with only one bank, this creation of monetary purchasing power could proceed rapidly. In a society with many banks, any individual bank would be restrained by the fact that most of its checks would find their way as deposits into other banks. They would then become claims on the first bank and these would ultimately have to be settled in gold. But, while only one bank by itself could not inflate the total stock of monetary purchasing power much above the general average, the banking system as a whole could do so and, as long as any given bank kept more or less in step with the others, the general supply of monetary purchasing power could be and was increased.

Professor Triffin has calculated that in 1815, in the three countries of Great Britain, the United States, and France, checks formed only six percent of the total money supply.* By 1848, however, they had increased to seventeen percent and then, by 1872, to as much as twenty-seven percent. During the next twenty years, the proportion of checks in the money supply doubled while, on the eve of World War I, it had risen to no less than sixty-eight percent or slightly over two-thirds.

The converse of this rise was, of course, the relative decrease in the proportion which the metallic coins formed of the total money supply. In 1815, they had comprised two-thirds of the total but this had decreased slightly by 1848 to a little over sixty percent while, by 1872, they formed only forty-one percent. This decline continued to twenty-five percent in 1892 and to thirteen percent in 1913.†

What was happening was that gold was moving from

* Triffin, Robert, *The Evolution of the International Monetary System,* 1964, pp. 58–59.

† The share of silver coins in the total monetary supply had decreased over the century from one-third to only three percent of the total.

everyday life into the reserve vaults to support the much greater volume of credit-money which was being created. The total demand deposits in the United States, Great Britain, and France rose indeed from sixty-five million dollars in 1815 to over thirteen billion dollars in 1913, or, in the course of a century, by over two hundred times. For every dollar in the metallic reserve, five to six dollars of checkbook dollars had been created.

By 1928, on the eve of the Great Depression, the eight billion dollars of gold in the monetary stores of the eleven major countries had almost entirely disappeared from circulation and were instead being used as a reserve for the 50 billion dollars of credit money of which 13 billion dollars was primarily in the form of paper currency and 37 billion dollars in the form of demand deposits. The gold reserve, therefore, amounted to only one-sixth of the total amount of credit money, both public and private, with which it was presumably interchangeable. The eyes of the medieval and renaissance goldsmiths would have turned green with envy had they been able to see the fruition of their experiment. The system had created and held title to over 40 billion dollars of purchasing power.

But the financiers of the twenties, like their renaissance predecessors, could have made a legitimate defense—namely, that if these demand deposits had not been created, the world would have suffered from a severe contraction of the circulating medium, a calamitous fall in the general level of prices, and prolonged depressions.

But, however necessary commercial banking had become, the arithmetic impossibility of redeeming six dollars of credit with one dollar of gold should a financial run develop, was a source of potential danger and upon occasion must have disturbed the sleep of the more thoughtful bankers. Some students of architecture as an expression of

civic emotions have sought to explain the overawing quality of most bank buildings and the interior air of hushed
solemnity as efforts by the bankers during this period to
convince themselves and their depositors of the basic
soundness of their institutions.

In 1933, this latent danger became a reality in this
country. We had gone through over three years of an ever
deepening depression, and the mistakes and misdeeds of
some members of the banking and industrial community
had begun to come to light. A crisis of confidence set in
like a thunderclap and depositors increasingly called at
banks and asked to have their deposits converted into legal
tender currency. Simultaneously, the Treasury and the
Federal Reserve Banks were being asked to redeem this
currency in gold. There just was not enough money and
gold to meet these claims. It then became necessary to
close all the banks in the country and when they were
reopened, we had gone off the internal gold standard.
Holders of our money could no longer have it redeemed
in gold, nor could they legally hoard gold. Instead they
were legally compelled to turn such gold as they held into
the Treasury and receive paper notes in return.* Gold was
thereby displaced as the ultimate money for internal purposes. Its sole function now was to provide a reserve with
which to meet international obligations.

But, while individuals could not get gold for their Federal Reserve Notes and member banks could not obtain
gold in return for withdrawing their deposits in the Federal Reserve Banks, the Administration did not request,
nor did Congress provide, any change in the previous legal
requirement that a reserve of twenty-five percent of these

---

* It is still not certain how much gold was hoarded in violation of
these provisions. It may have been a considerable sum.

notes and deposits in the Reserve must be kept in gold. No one inside the United States could get this gold, but it still had to be there. This requirement resembled the celebrated smile of the Cheshire Cat in Alice in Wonderland which continued long after the cat itself had faded from sight. The essential absurdity of this requirement was not realized at the time, but years later it arose to create real difficulties.

Our experience was not unique. In country after country during the 1930's the internal convertibility of currencies into gold which, after World War I, had been briefly restored was suspended. Nations moved into a situation where gold could only be used to settle international balances of payment. Dire predictions were made that this meant a complete collapse of faith in the currency and that people would refuse to accept the irredeemable paper notes which now circulated as money. But this did not happen. Though stripped of their convertibility, these notes were fully accepted everywhere and it was again proved that money is merely what people will generally accept as a medium of exchange.

Similarly, the banking system continued to create credit which, when drawn upon in the form of checks, became an increasing proportion of the circulating medium. Robert Triffin estimates that the total volume of demand deposits in the eleven major countries of the world rose from 31 billion dollars in 1933 to 40 billion dollars in 1937, and then soared to 113 billion dollars in 1949 and to 154 billion dollars in 1957. By 1963 the total had reached 194 billion dollars, which was over six times what it had been thirty years earlier and fifteen times its figure a half-century before in the years before the outbreak of World War I. Confidence in bank credit was obviously not shaken although the circulating money could not be redeemed in metallic coin.*

Two supplementary steps were taken in the United States: First, bank deposits were guaranteed up to the first five thousand dollars, and this amount was later doubled. A small assessment was levied to provide the necessary reserve and the danger of devastating bank runs was thereby reduced. Secondly, the price of gold which had been $20.67 an ounce was raised by almost seventy percent to $35.00. Other countries followed suit and the money value of the world's gold stocks was raised accordingly. Some treated this as a depreciation of the dollar in terms of gold. But it was also an appreciation of gold in terms of the dollar and it did provide an increased stock of monetary reserves with which to meet deficits in the international balance of payments. By abandoning gold as a reserve for domestic currencies, it was confined to the function of serving as an external world currency. The transition from an internal gold standard to an international gold standard had now become virtually complete.

It is perhaps appropriate that we retrace some of the other developments by which this materialized.

By the end of the nineteenth century, with the breakup of the Latin Monetary Union and the abandonment of the free coinage of silver by the United States in 1873, gold had become the international currency for the Western

* Once a year when the Secretary of the Treasury and the Chairman of the Federal Reserve Board appear before the Senate Banking Committee, of which I am a member, I hand them a Federal Reserve Note for ten or twenty dollars and ask that they redeem it for me in the pledged "lawful money." I ask for gold in return. They correctly reply they are prevented by law from giving me any. I then ask for whatever "lawful money" they can give me. They solemnly hand me another Federal Reserve Note. But all this has no effect on the confidence of the American public in the dollar. They continue to accept Federal Reserve Notes and bank checks.

World. When a country exported more than it imported, this balance was sooner or later to be paid in gold. Similarly, when its exports fell short of its imports, it was obligated to pay its balance in gold. Gold, therefore, moved across national lines to settle balances. An elaborate web of clearing claims and of crediting and of transmitting balances had to be created as the volume of international trade and investment multiplied.

In the two decades before World War I, the international gold standard was in virtually full operation. Not only were temporary balances in world trade settled primarily by gold transfers, but these gold movements in turn tended to bring each country's trade and investment accounts ultimately into balance. For, as we have repeatedly seen, a so-called "favorable" balance would result in the flow of gold which, in turn, would raise prices and dampen down exports. At the same time, the outflow of gold from the importing nations would lower their prices and, hence, at once restrict their further imports and increase their exports.

In practice, the operation of the international gold standard was effected with a relatively small quantity of gold. London was the heart of the international system of clearances and investment. The Bank of England, then a private institution and the center of the world's financial web, seldom had gold reserves which were in excess of a few hundred millions of dollars. It economized in the use and shipment of gold by its influence upon the interest rate. When the balance of payments turned against Britain, then instead of shipping out large quantities of gold, it would raise the interest rate in co-operation with the British government. This would induce fluid foreign capital to be invested in England, primarily in the form of short-term government obligations. This would counterbalance the debts owed abroad by British importers and either remove or lessen the need for shipping gold abroad.

But the higher interest rates which would be transmitted through the economic structure would also repress investment and, hence, also dampen down production and hence increase unemployment. This generally had the effect of reducing wages, labor costs, and prices. This reduction in costs and prices would in turn stimulate exports and ultimately help to restore a balance in international payments. Thus, while the actual international transfer of gold was minimized, the price system tended to produce an ultimate balance in the account.

This system operated at the expense of industry and labor in Great Britain. Moreover, by withdrawing purchasing power from other countries, a fall in prices was forced abroad, together with a dampening down of the trade and production in other countries. The much admired automatic functioning of the international monetary system was therefore effected at real human and economic cost. It was not as painless as its admirers represented it as being.

The international gold standard not only enabled the trade and investment accounts between nations to balance; with the aid of competition it helped to create an approximate equality of prices between countries in those commodities which were internationally traded. If wheat sold for more in Liverpool than its price here (plus shipping and other transportation costs), more wheat would be exported from the United States to Britain. This would lower prices in Liverpool and raise them here. This ultimate equality of prices also meant that, insofar as internationally traded commodities were concerned, a unit of gold tended to have substantially equal purchasing power in all countries. This did not apply of course to personal services where population pressures and differing productivities of labor created wide differences in real wages. Nor did it apply to bulky commodities, such as stone and gravel, which were too costly to transport.

The international gold standard, moreover, operated to restrain countries from inflating their own price levels by issuing large quantities of paper money. For to do so would drive up prices in the issuing country and, by decreasing exports and increasing imports, would lead inevitably to an outward flow of gold. If this turned into a hemorrhage, then the erring country would be forced to give up its membership in the gold standard club and would be relegated to a distinctly inferior position in the hierarchy of international finance. The preservation of the gold standard indeed became one of the most strongly held tenets of the financial world. It exercised a deep and pervasive influence over both the interest rates and the politics of the major countries. If inflation was either in process or was feared, then interest rates would be raised to dampen down economic activity, to check any flight of gold to other countries, and to attract short-time investments from abroad. If a government took any measures which greatly displeased the dominant financial powers, then the latter could always suggest that if this unsoundness were continued, they would be compelled to transfer some or all of their liquid balances to the banks of other countries. This carried with it the clear intimation that this would then be accompanied by a demand from abroad for gold.

An additional hammerlock could be placed on national policy by the international bankers selling stocks and bonds because of a real or alleged "lack of confidence" and then transferring the proceeds to some foreign country such as Switzerland. This would then create a further demand for gold and a consequent strain upon the ability of a government to maintain the foreign convertibility of its

216 PAUL H. DOUGLAS

currency at its previous figure. Thus, speculators in a currency, by demanding or threatening to demand gold, could generally strike terror into the hearts of governments and, hence, exercise a certain veto power over their policies.

There was a considerable degree of fraternal fellow-feeling between the dominant financial interests of the major industrial countries which, while it stopped short of being an international cartel, could multiply the effects of purely national movements. Those who exercised this power were in no sense ogres or sinister plotters, but they were not primarily concerned with the effect upon unemployment or the rate of economic growth or the condition of the people.

High interest rates would as a matter of fact tend to discourage investment and hence throw people out of work and plunge great numbers into severe distress. But this was regarded as an inevitable cost of conforming to natural law and of keeping the nations soundly orthodox in financial matters. Men were indeed regarded as economic commodities and reducing the demand for labor was deemed an essential means to attain the end of a fluid price system and of effecting an ultimate balance in international trade and payments. The heads of the various nationalized central banks which came into being after World War II, were either drawn from the ranks of private bankers or soon came to embrace both their psychology and their philosophy. Any idea that prices, interest, and exchange rates should or could be so managed as to promote human welfare was treated as an abhorrent violation of natural law.

The financial world spoke approvingly of the "discipline" which the international gold standard imposed on nations, but it was a discipline which applied to the families of laboring men and to the fate of small and marginal businesses. Those who imposed the "discipline" were themselves relatively secure and indeed, as lenders, directly profited from the higher interest rates which they prescribed as economic medicine. Like those well-to-do folks who favor poverty and adversity as stimulants to effort on the part of others, their own withers were unwrung by their prescribed remedies. And their intellectual followers in journalistic, academic, and governmental circles could always be depended upon to provide a patina of theoretical respectability for such policies as barriers to a price inflation.

Nor was the danger of inflation purely conjectural. Sometimes it actually did threaten and would in fact have greatly imperiled the fortunes of bondholders and of others upon fixed incomes, and have had an extremely bad effect on the economy as a whole. Such a restraining influence may therefore have been necessary, but it was frequently used in an excessive fashion and upon occasion to discredit and bring down popular governments which were disliked by the financial powers.

16
The International Gold Exchange Standard

Around the turn of the century, an important modification of the international gold standard crept, more or less unnoticed, into being. London was then both the financial and political capital of the world, and British capital was financing investments in many sections of the globe. The money thus invested was partially spent in the countries which were being developed. These amounts then constituted foreign claims against the British which were not wholly offset by the export of British goods. But, instead of demanding gold bullion to meet these claims, the countries in question—which were largely dominions and colonies of the British Crown—were persuaded to accept, instead, credits on London banks computed in terms of pounds sterling. Most of these credits were invested in short-time government obligations and some in commercial paper and hence earned interest.

A new form of international currency was, therefore, being created, namely, short-term claims by foreigners upon the currency of a world-trading country. The element of "exchange" had been silently added to that of gold. And these "exchange" claims, if in possession of the private and central banks, not only drew interest but could also be treated as part of their own currency and as bank reserves. They could thus be used to support a further internal expansion of their own bank loans and credit-created money. Credit in London was, therefore, being used to create added credit at home. Just as created bank deposits were swelling the internal money supplies, so created foreign credits served to increase both the internal and external currencies of the world.

There were other reasons why "sterling" came to be accepted as the world's currency of account. Just as one medium of exchange and standard of value is needed inside a country in order to reduce the infinite number of exchange relationships between commodities to a common measure so there was a similar need to have a common measure for the various national currencies. As more and more nations entered world trade and as more countries came into being, that need increased by a geometrical ratio. With fifty countries, there would be no less than 2,500 possible exchange relationships. By using the common measure of the pound sterling, these were reduced to one measure. This was a supreme merit of the international gold standard which made the relative value of a currency depend on the relative amount of gold which could be obtained for it. The dominance of British trade caused most national currencies to be translated internationally into their ratios to the pound. The addition of the exchange element to sterling did not change this fundamental relationship, so that promises to pay in gold at London when demanded came to be accepted in place of actual gold itself. Transfers of checking accounts in London banks came to be the way in which international balances were settled rather than by direct transfers of the metal itself. The world was being slowly weaned away from gold as an actual medium of exchange just as the

medieval traders were by the notes of the goldsmiths.

These claims upon "sterling" were regarded as being
"as good as gold," since the London banks were presumed
to be ready to redeem these claims in gold upon demand.
And so they could, as long as the claims were relatively
small in amount and not many of their holders actually
asked for gold. Many thought "sterling" was actually gold
itself and not merely claims on gold. The Bank of England
was able to keep "sterling" at full value despite the relatively small amounts of gold it actually held—which seldom exceeded 400 million dollars.

At first there was no trouble. The British pound sterling
seemed as solid as Gibraltar itself. But World War I greatly
weakened sterling as Britain was compelled to purchase
large quantities of supplies and munitions from overseas.
She paid for these in part by selling a large portion of the
British investments in these countries and borrowed the
rest. While these war debts were later, for all practical
purposes, largely forgiven, they hung over Britain during
the 1920's when it was obviously impossible for her to pay
either in gold or in goods.

In the meantime, foreign countries were accumulating
more and more claims against sterling. The rise of the
United States as a world trader and investor was also leading to the use of a similar dollar exchange by many Latin
American and Oriental countries. In 1922, therefore, the
Genoa Conference on International Monetary Matters endorsed the gold exchange standard as an international currency. Triffin estimates that by 1928, foreign exchange
amounted to about 2.25 billion dollars of international currency. This was nearly five percent of the total money
supply of the eleven principal trading countries of the
world.

But, just as had happened in the medieval cities, some investors and countries began to take fright. Winston Churchill, as Chancellor of the Exchequer, had brought England back to gold in 1926 by stabilizing the pound at its old figure of $4.867. But British costs and prices were high in comparison with those of the world and British exports now netted fewer pounds than when each pound was worth less. Britain now had more sterling exchange held against her than she could conveniently redeem in gold. Various industries, such as coal, textiles, shipbuilding, and steel, were suffering. Unemployment was high in the North, in the Midlands, and in Wales. The French financial authorities began to call in their sterling claims and to demand gold for them. The British had to resort to the humiliating device of asking that these claims not be further pushed. But a contraction of credit was nevertheless forced by these foreign claims and this deepened the depression.

Finally, in the late summer of 1931, the foreign, and especially the French, run on the pound was so great that Britain was forced to suspend redeeming its foreign claims in gold. The main support of the international gold exchange standard collapsed. The pound was then allowed and possibly even helped to depreciate from $4.867 to as low as $3.40. This gave Britain a temporary export advantage since the internal costs of her products did not rise proportionately to offset the basic fact that a given foreign price now netted her many more pounds.

But this devaluation of sterling inflicted heavy losses upon those faithful countries which had abstained from converting their exchange holdings into gold. Belgium, Holland, and the Scandinavian countries, as a consequence, suffered greatly, as did the British dominions of Canada, Australia, New Zealand, and India. France also lost in the lessened value of such sterling exchange as it still retained. All this helped to make the continental countries distrustful of sterling exchange and helps to account for the small proportion of sterling which they now hold as reserves and for their distinct preference for the solidity of gold.

The withdrawals of gold from Britain also helped to touch off a run on the American dollar, again largely initiated by France. With these runs, the exchange element in the international gold exchange standard more or less collapsed. The total volume of this exchange fell from 2⅓ billion dollars in 1928 to only 400 million dollars in 1933. This consequent international deflation intensified the world depression, helped to bring Hitler to power in Germany, and strengthened both the Fascist and Communist elements in all countries.

In this country, the Federal Reserve Board took fright and twice raised the rediscount rate. In a time of severe depression, the Board was so anxious to maintain the full redeemability of the dollar in gold that it further reduced economic activity and created more unemployment. Over a third of a century elapsed before a head of the Federal Reserve Board would admit that this had been an error, and even then he refused to state whether he would not follow a similar policy in the future were a comparable contingency to develop.*

The permanent structure of the gold exchange standard was severely damaged by these developments and by the competitive devaluations by various countries which followed. But the total volume of exchange increased slightly in the middle 1930's to a total of 700 million dollars.

During World War II, all normal dealings in foreign

* Testimony of William McChesney Martin before Senate Banking and Currency Committee in July, 1965.

trade were suspended. Britain sold most of her remaining American and foreign securities to purchase food, supplies, and munitions. Canada and the other dominions were generous and, in 1941, we gave Britain an ample line of credit disguised as "Lend-Lease."

From 1940 on, the farms and factories of America furnished the surplus goods which kept the free world going. Much of this economic life blood was given away; some, as in World War I, was made in the form of loans and some was paid for in the form of gold raising our gold reserve to nearly 25 billion dollars in 1949. In the process, the dollar inevitably began to replace the pound as the international unit of account. Most of the countries south of the border moved into the dollar area as did even Canada. Even in the Eastern Hemisphere, the dollar became increasingly the international unit. The fact that the dollar is based upon the metric system gave it an added convenience which "sterling" with its clumsy units of pounds, shillings, and pence does not have.

There were, however, three other monetary solar systems: first, the sterling area comprising the other British Commonwealths and colonies together with a group of closely associated nations such as Denmark, Portugal, and Norway; second, the area of the French franc, including the French colonies of Africa and, until lost, of Southeast Asia; and third, the mysterious area of the Russian ruble.

But more and more, the dollar tended to become the central point within the monetary constellations. As more nations, each with its own currency, were created the need for one measure of value became ever more important in international trade and finance. For otherwise there could be over ten thousand separate currency relationships. The total volume of American trade and the volume of our international investments were such as to multiply the world's dealings with us so that the dollar began to move into world dominance much as the pound had done a century before.

As victory neared, the representatives of the free nations gathered together at Bretton Woods in July, 1944, to approve a plan for financial reconstruction. The agreements reached there and at Savannah, in 1946, set up two international financial institutions, the World Bank and the International Monetary Fund.

The World Bank, or more properly the International Bank for Reconstruction and Development, was set up to provide long-term loans for capital investment in the countries which had been crippled by the war and, possibly, later in the undeveloped regions of the world. As the title of the new institution suggested, reconstruction was its first purpose, though development was to follow. America was to furnish the major amount of capital to the bank, and free Europe was to be the initial recipient.

The International Monetary Fund was established to help create a stable financial environment conducive to the movement of commodities between countries. The ultimate purpose was to help stabilize the foreign exchanges of the various member countries so that international trade could be conducted in terms of stable rather than fluctuating currencies. A number of crucial decisions, both explicit and implicit, were embodied in the final agreements.

The first was that the international gold exchange standard was to be revived and strengthened. The pure gold standard was rejected on the ground that there was an insufficient total supply of the metal, which was predominantly in American hands, and that there was no necessary coincidence between its rate of growth as an international currency and the needs of world trade. Similarly, the idea of freely fluctuating national exchange rates was rejected with horror as being too reminiscent of the five years following World War I and of the period of the middle 1930's. What was adopted, therefore, was a program intermediate between these two, namely, an attempt to establish a wider and stronger gold exchange standard. Short-term foreign claims held by state banks and governments were to be counted as part of the world currency along with gold.

The second decision, although not specifically mentioned in the Articles of Agreement, was that these short-term foreign claims could be, and indeed were expected to be, treated as internal reserves upon which further domestic credit within the various countries could be expanded.

Third, in practice, the claims upon only two currencies were recognized as constituting the exchange element in the international currency. These were the British pound and the American dollar. To these the American economist, John H. Williams, gave the term "key currencies." The choice of these currencies was both natural and inevitable. The United States and Great Britain were still the two strongest countries in the world and had suffered less material damage from the war than had other countries. France had been badly crippled by the German invasion of 1940, the Allied bombardments from 1941 to 1944, and the invasion and battles with the Germans from the summer of 1944 to the spring of 1945. The defeated countries, Germany, Italy, and Japan, were badly damaged and their political futures were uncertain.

Fourth, the promotion of "exchange stability" was declared to be one of the fundamental purposes of the Fund. And the resources of the Fund were indeed to be used primarily to maintain this stability. The existing exchange rates in terms of the American dollar were accepted by the

Fund as the norms to be maintained for an initial period of time. The British pound was thus valued at $4.03 and the French franc at five-sixths of a cent, while the Canadian and Cuban dollars were valued at par. It was realized that these were not precisely accurate reflections of the comparative national levels of prices and costs, and that some currencies enjoyed a higher exchange value than was justified on such a basis. But the founders of the Fund dreaded taking on the task of arbitrarily deciding what the proper exchange ratios were to be, and preferred to postpone the issue until the Fund was more firmly established as an institution and when time could effect some readjustments. Slight fluctuations in the exchange rates were to be permitted, but these were normally not to exceed one percent. This was the zone within which the exchange prices of the currencies could freely move.

If a country felt it must change the value of its currency because it was not in equilibrium with the international cost-price situation, it was required to notify the Fund in advance. If the proposed change amounted to less than ten percent of the initial par value, it could do so without obtaining the consent of the Fund. But, if the change were to be more than ten though less than twenty percent, the Fund was given seventy-two hours in which to register either agreement or objection. If the proposed change amounted to more than twenty percent, then the Fund was allowed a longer period in which to declare its position. If the Fund registered an objection to any change of more than ten percent but the member country nevertheless persisted in its course, then that country became ineligible for future loans or relief from the Fund, unless the Fund chose to grant it a special dispensation. If, after a reasonable period of time, the differences between the country and the Fund persisted then upon a majority vote of the governing board, the offending country could be expelled from membership.

But to lessen the danger that the Fund as an international body could attempt to dictate internal financial and economic policies to sovereign nations, it was specified that the Fund was not to object to changes of more than ten percent if these were adjudged necessary to correct a fundamental disequilibrium, and in making such a judgment the Fund was not to object because it differed with "the domestic, social, or political policies of the member proposing the change."

In other words, while stability of exchanges was made the goal, an escape hatch was left open for countries in those cases where their prices and costs were very high in comparison with those of the world.

The fifth decision was that the aid given to help member states maintain their exchange stability was to be in the form of loans from the Fund. This was primarily designed to meet emergency and short-term dislocations, and was not intended to maintain permanent international disparities in prices and costs. These were to be corrected either by internal action or by changes in the par value of the currencies. This, of course, in the vast majority of cases meant the devaluation of the external value of the currency in question.

Thus, England, in 1949, with the Fund's consent, devalued the pound from $4.03 by a full thirty percent to a new level of $2.80. This was no less than forty-two percent, or three-eighths below the historic value of the pound at $4.867 which had prevailed during the century from Waterloo to World War I and which had indeed prevailed in 1931 when Britain was forced off gold. This British devaluation was immediately followed by comparable action on the part of all the countries in the sterling bloc and by a number of other countries as well. Any export advantage which Great Britain gained was therefore at the expense of countries outside the sterling area, which did not devalue, most notably ourselves. Britain's exports to us were stimulated while our exports to them were repressed.

However, because of our desire to help the British, we did not object, though the British devaluation also weakened the gold exchange standard, since it meant another big loss in dollars to those faithful nations which had primarily kept their reserves in claims on sterling.

There were other changes in the exchange rates, of which one of the most notable was the appreciation of the German mark in March 1961 by five percent. This was done to repress inflation in Germany by slowing down the increase in the reserve component and, hence, in the expansion of credit. This was to be effected by a reduction in Germany's exports which would result from the same foreign price in dollars netting the German exporter fewer marks.

In 1960, France, under President de Gaulle, reformed its currency by restoring the franc to its old exchange value of twenty cents. Since the franc had fallen to two-tenths of one cent, this meant that each franc of the new currency replaced one hundred francs of the old. With these exceptions, the exchange rates of the major trading nations of the world, including Italy, Japan, the Scandinavian and the Low Countries, have been kept relatively steady during the last fifteen years. Those of many minor countries, however, have varied widely. Occasionally, as in Finland, a new currency has replaced the old. Here, following the example of France, the new markkas was substituted at one hundred times its former rate.

In the case of several Latin American nations, troubled by rapid inflation, political instability, and the sharp fall in the export prices of their chief crops such as coffee and sugar, the exchange rates have been lowered. Such have been the examples of Argentina, Brazil, Chile, Colombia, and Venezuela.

Sixth, the resources of the International Monetary Fund have been built up by the actual and pledged contributions of the member nations. The original subscription quotas fixed for the original members plus those subsequently admitted, such as West Germany, Italy, and Japan, came to approximately ten billion dollars.*

The United States' share was 2.75 billion dollars while that of Great Britain was almost one-half of this, or 1.3 billion dollars. Together, the two countries contributed a little over forty percent of the total. Because of the crippled condition of France, Germany, Italy, and Japan, their quotas were initially low. The French quota was fixed at 525 million dollars, Germany at 330 million dollars, Italy at 180 million dollars, and Japan at 250 million dollars. The combined subscription quotas of the four therefore came to a little less than 1.3 billion dollars. This was slightly less than the contribution of Great Britain alone and less than half that of the United States. The six big powers, however, contributed approximately fifty-three percent of the capital and therefore held that percentage of the votes.

With the virtual doubling of world trade between 1948 and 1958, it was felt that the resources of the Fund should be increased. A general increase of fifty percent in the

---

* The formula used in fixing the national quotas was substantially as follows: (a) the sum of two percent of the respective national incomes, plus (b) five percent of the gold and dollar balances, plus (c) ten percent of average imports, plus (d) ten percent of the maximum variation in exports, all this multiplied by (e) the percentage ratio of average exports to national income. See Rudolph Kroc, *The Financial Structure of the Fund.* Hearings, U.S. House Committee on Banking and Currency on H. R. 6497, 1965, pp. 36–43.

subscription quotas was therefore put into effect by the end of 1959. The share of the United States went up to 4.125 billion dollars, and that of Great Britain to 1.950 billion dollars. The rapid recovery of France and the three former enemy powers justified a much greater increase than fifty percent in their quotas. But this was not done. The French and Italian quotas were only raised by the general average of fifty percent to 787 million and 270 million dollars. The Japanese quota was doubled to 500 million dollars and the German figure raised to equal that of France. Proportionately, this was an increase of one hundred and thirty percent, but the totals were more than justified by the German share of world trade and the growth in its gross national product.

The admission of new members and the slight increases in the proportionate contributions of some of the original members raised the total resources of the Fund (or its pledged subscription quotas) by 1964 to a little less than 16 billion dollars.

The volume of international trade continued to rise and by the end of 1964 had gone up by an additional fifty percent, or to a total which was approximately three times that of 1948.

It was then decided to increase further the resources of the Fund. A general increase of twenty-five percent was recommended for all countries with additional increases for sixteen countries, including Germany, Japan, and Canada. This raised the total of pledged subscriptions by about five billion dollars or from 16 to 21 billions of dollars. It was estimated that had the original Bretton Woods formula been used, the total resources of the Fund would have been raised to twice this figure, or to over 40 billion dollars.

The share of the United States was raised by the standard proportion or from 4.125 billion dollars to 5.160 billion. While the shares of Germany and Japan were raised by more than the general increase of twenty-five percent, they were still below what they would have been, had only fifty percent of the Bretton Woods formula been applied. Thus, while the German quota was raised to 1,200 million dollars instead of to 985 million dollars, it was still 436 million dollars below what fifty percent of the Bretton Woods formula would have imposed. The deficiency in the case of Japan was seventy-five million dollars.* France was basically opposed to any increase in quotas but finally agreed to acquiesce in the twenty-five percent increase provided it was not to exceed this amount in her case.

The voting strength of the various countries is, as we have said, proportionate to their relative quotas or contributions to the Fund. Once the new total quotas of 21.0 billion dollars are in effect, the American share will amount to 24.6 percent, while that of Great Britain will come to another 11.6 percent. Canada will have 3.5 percent and Australia and New Zealand 2.4 and 0.75 percent, respectively. Altogether, the English-speaking Commonwealths will have eighteen and a half percent of the vote. An American-British bloc can therefore directly control approximately forty-three percent of the vote and, in conjunction with the votes of countries closely affiliated with them, can muster a comfortable working majority.†

* It should also be realized, however, that a strict application of fifty percent of the Bretton Woods formula would have required us to put up 1.2 billion dollars more. The nations which were over-assessed were the smaller countries.

† Thus, the combined quotas of EFTA countries of Sweden, Norway, Denmark, and Portugal come to 613 million dollars and, hence, these countries will have nearly three percent of the vote. British colonies and affiliates possess another two percent, while there are others who regard themselves as being economically attached to the United States.

This helps to account for some of the distaste felt for the IMF by the powerful countries of Western Europe, such as France. They would, of course, be able to increase their vote in the IMF by increasing their subscriptions. But in general they have been reluctant to do this.

Members of the Fund are required to pay into it twenty-five percent of their quota in gold or ten percent of their total international reserves whether in gold or U.S. dollars, whichever is smaller. We have always paid our full subscription in gold. Under the quotas prevailing at the end of 1964, our gold subscription was slightly over a billion dollars. Under the new quotas, we will subscribe 257 million dollars more in gold, thus bringing our total to just under 1.3 billion dollars.

The balance of the pledged subscription of a country, generally amounting to seventy-five percent, is to be paid in the currency of that country. At the end of May, 1965, these currency holdings came to a total of 11.75 billion dollars. If the exchange value of the currency of a country depreciates significantly, it must pay into the Fund a further amount to make good the loss.

A country can automatically draw from the Fund a sum to meet deficits in its balance of payments equal to its own gold subscription. It therefore does not completely surrender the use of the gold which it turns over to the IMF, but can still use it if needed.

The members may, of course, also borrow beyond their gold contributions from the Fund to meet deficits in their balances of payments, but such borrowings are conditional upon approval by the Fund. This will be almost always given as long as the Fund's holdings of a country's currency does not exceed one hundred twenty-five percent of its quota. In this way when approved it would draw upon the quotas of others to meet its obligations. If, however, the requests for loans of the foreign countries exceed this limit, they are subject to scrutiny by the Fund and to its consent. In practice, when the countries ask for foreign currencies, they generally ask for dollars. This was universally true in the earlier years, although much less so now. In practice, therefore, the American contributions have been drawn upon more freely than those of other countries and we have borne the major share of the expansion of this supplementary medium of international exchange.

Borrowings of more than twice a national quota are distinctly frowned upon. All borrowings should be repaid in from three to five years at the outside and are subject to service and interest charges. The latter start low but increase both with time and with the proportion of the quota borrowed.

The income from these charges, plus interest on the investment of gold, has enabled the Fund to meet its operating costs and accumulate a surplus of over 140 million dollars, nearly all of which has accrued in the last seven years.

It will be seen from this discussion that the Fund was designed to help a country bridge short-time deficits in its balance of payments. If the resources of a nation were insufficient, it could also meet seasonal deficits. More importantly, by its loans it could assist in overcoming cyclical deficits and thus lessen the danger of a depression in one or a few countries spreading to others.

But the Fund was not designed to support permanently the exchange rate of a country in which prices and costs were appreciably in excess of world levels. These were to be adjusted either by price and cost reductions within the country, or by a devaluation of the currency. In short, the IMF could help to protect exchange rates, but it could not permanently freeze them. Nor did it aim to do so.

The reserves of the IMF are, therefore, a secondary line of defense in time of national financial trouble. They are not international currency as such. Hence, they do not meet the specific needs of exporters, importers, and financial dealers. All that is left to national banking institutions. They are not "vehicle" or "transaction money" to provide added liquidity for the world's trade. They merely give added reassurance that the national currencies will in the future have a stable value.

During the first period, from 1947 to 1960, the IMF did not play an active part in world finance. It permitted the British devaluation of thirty percent in 1949 and the attendant devaluations of other members of the sterling bloc and of most European countries. It approved the German and French revaluations.

In 1961, however, it came actively to the support of the British pound by making available to the British 1.5 billion dollars in gold and large amounts of strong currencies. It again helped the British in the last quarter of 1964 and the first part of 1965, loaning that country no less than the enormous sum of 2.4 billion dollars. These debts were to be payable in from three to five years.

In addition, the Fund has come to the aid of numerous smaller countries, generally requiring in return a balanced budget and measures to stabilize the balance of payments and the exchange rates. It has proved to be a useful institution which has reduced the temptation to devalue currencies competitively and has provided a backing for countries whose basic position is sound but whose currencies are being subjected to temporary speculative raiding. Although American internal and international policy has probably been the major factor which has prevented the twenty years following World War II from being as calamitous both economically and politically as were the two decades after World War I, the International Monetary Fund has played an honorable part in helping to achieve this greater stability.

It should be realized that the obligation assumed by the United States to redeem in gold, foreign claims on dollar balances, applies only to official claims presented by foreign governments and central banks. We did not assume any such liability for the holdings of such exchange claims by private individuals or private banks. Britain, however, has assumed an obligation to redeem private claims but in practice does so in dollars rather than gold.

But, since such private claims can always be directly or indirectly deposited in the central governmental banks, they can rather quickly become transformed into official claims and, hence, be realized upon. The potential claims upon the gold reserves of the United States have therefore always been very much greater than those which are officially recognized. A good part of the gold exchange iceberg therefore lies underneath the surface of the financial ocean.

There is, indeed, a further element of danger. Investments in corporate bonds and stocks overlap national lines. Holders of these securities can always sell them and deposit the proceeds in their own private banks and these can be redeposited in the central banks. Claims can thus be created upon the gold reserves of the two key currency countries of Great Britain and the United States. Once a run starts on a country, therefore, foreign investors and banks, by taking fright, can create greater havoc.

Nor are all the possibilities as innocent in motive as those which have been suggested. There are speculators in international currencies just as there are domestic spec-

ulators in the field of industrial securities. These speculators perform some useful functions in helping to stabilize
short-term fluctuations in foreign exchange rates. But they
can, and sometimes do, exercise a malign influence. They
can decide that a given currency has elements of weakness
and then make it weaker by selling it short, thus making
it necessary for official institutions to increase their demands for conversions into gold. If this is sufficient to carry
a country off gold and force it to devalue its currency, the
speculators can then use their gold and other holdings to
buy up sterling or dollars at the lower rate and thus make
a profit just as the so-called "bears" can in the stock market.
Future sales can be similarly manipulated.

This is a very potent source of danger, since there are
such currency speculators who commonly operate out of
Switzerland and who are known as the "gnomes of Zurich."
These men are shielded by the cloak of secrecy which that
country throws around its depositors and, unrestrained by
patriotism, they can, in a cold-blooded fashion, engineer
raids upon a "key currency" and, by contributing to disas-
ter, subsequently profit from it.

Alvin Hansen has made the appropriate comment on
these dangers: "It would be ludicrous were it not so
serious that powerful nations tremble in fear of the petty,
greedy speculators. That great nations continue to protect
and even encourage this antisocial activity would be in-
credible were it not an obvious present fact."

All these factors contribute to the fundamental instability which is always inherent in any fractional reserve
system, namely, that the metallic reserve is always less
than the amount of monetary claims which can be presented for redemption. This is indeed the heel of the
monetary Achilles. We have escaped from this danger

domestically, but it is still present internationally. How to reduce or eliminate this danger is one of the most pressing of world monetary issues. But it is seldom openly acknowledged, lest in doing so we might add to the instability which we seek to reduce.

17

Gold, Reserves, and Loans within the International Monetary Fund

Up to this time, the system of world finance and economics has, on the whole, worked reasonably well. Europe has made an amazingly good recovery from World War II. We have gone forward with great strides, especially during the last five years. There has been no major depression. Unemployment, except in the United States, has been kept low and it is now low here. The standard of living of the people doing industrial work has risen. International trade has increased as tariff barriers have been lowered.

These facts have convinced many that no further action is needed and that we can continue to go forward with little or no change in the institutions which were set up at Bretton Woods. But, as we have indicated, distinct weaknesses are developing within the structure of international finance and may, within a few years, cause it to break down. Moreover, if either Great Britain or the United States were to become unable to redeem its foreign obligations, it would probably create a crisis of confidence. Nations would be likely to resort to competitive devaluations of their own currencies in order to gain temporary export advantages and another world-wide depression, similar to that which broke out in 1929, might set in.

It is vital, therefore, to determine just what these weaknesses are and how they may best be met. They seem to be basically two: First, the present system puts an ever-mounting strain upon the key currency countries of Great Britain and the United States by constantly increasing the ratio of foreign claims upon their gold to the actual amount of gold which they have available to meet them. We have dealt with some of these difficulties in the preceding chapters.

Second, there is no necessary coincidence between the amount of monetary purchasing power created by the international system and that required by the growing volume of international trade. Thus far, little trouble has been caused by this fact. But, as the United States greatly reduces or eliminates the deficit in its balance of payments, the reserves of the IMF will grow slowly. A real shortage of monetary purchasing power in relation to the volume of transactions will inevitably develop. This could lead to a world-wide decline in the prices of internationally traded commodities and, on the model of 1929, to a world-wide depression.

In 1948 the total volume of exports in the world amounted to 53.7 billion dollars. By 1953, they had risen to 74.3 billion dollars. This was an increase of over 20 billion dollars, or nineteen percent. By 1964 they amounted to 152 billions, or almost 100 billion dollars more than sixteen years earlier. This was an increase of 183 percent over 1948 and of 105 percent over 1953. For the period from 1948 to 1964, the annual geometrical rate of increase in the money volume of world trade amounted to 6.7 percent.

On the other hand, the total supply of the international reserve currency grew only from about 50 billion dollars in 1948 to 69 billion dollars in 1964. This was an increase of 19 billion dollars, or a rise of about thirty-eight percent and a yearly geometrical rate of increase of only about two percent. This was only about one-fifth the relative percentage increase in the volume of world trade over the period as a whole.

The following table shows the total reserves of the IMF countries from 1948 to September 1965, inclusive. The totals consist of gold holdings, official foreign exchange, and reserve positions in the Fund. The figures are roughly although not completely comparable from year to year and are therefore expressed only to the year and to the nearest billion.

Growth in World Reserves 1948–1965 *

Year	Total Reserves (In billions of dollars)	Year	Total Reserves (In billions of dollars)
1948	50	1957	59
1949	47	1958†	58
1950	50	1959	58
1951	51	1960	61
1952	51	1961	63
1953	53	1962	63
1954	55	1963	67
1955	56	1964	69
1956	58	1965	69

* IMF International Financial Statistics, January, 1966, pp. 14–15.
† There was a change in the method of computation at this point.

Probably a better time span because of more comparable statistics is that from 1958 on. Here the increase in total reserves amounted to 11 billion dollars, or nineteen percent, as compared with an increase of fifty percent in the dollar volume of world trade. This increase in reserves would seem on the surface to be markedly inadequate. And so, perhaps, it was.

But it should be remembered that these official reserves

were augmented by the unofficial "vehicle" or "transaction" money arising out of international transactions and deposited in private banks. By the summer of 1965, these sums probably ranged around 20 billions of dollars. Since there was little change in the volume of these deposits in British banks, the increase came almost entirely in private foreign deposits in American banks. This increase probably amounted to nearly ten billion dollars. If these were to be included, the total increase since 1958 would amount to around 18 billion dollars, or a percentage gain of more than one-quarter. On this basis, the relative inadequacy in the rate of increase in international currency would not have been as great.

If we examine the relative growth of the two main components of official international currency,* namely, gold and foreign exchange, we find that until 1965, gold increased slowly and exchange rapidly. Foreign exchange itself, therefore, came to form an increasing part of the currency.

The growth in the amount of monetary gold from 1948 to the end of 1964 was from 33 to 40.9 billion dollars. This was a little less than eight billion dollars, or about twenty-four percent, as compared with the 180 percent increase in world trade. The increase in official foreign exchange was from 15.6 billion to 23.9 billion or nearly eight billion dollars. Proportionately, this was an increase of approximately fifty percent.

From 1958 to the end of 1964, the increase in gold holdings amounted to only 3.6 billion dollars, or nine percent, while foreign exchange rose by 6.7 billion dollars to 23.9 billion, or by nearly forty percent. This caused the ratio of gold to foreign exchange to decrease from approximately two to one in 1948 to one of five to three at the end of 1964.

* And omitting reserve positions in the IMF.

In addition, there was the growth in "transaction" money by another seven to eight billion dollars, making the total increase which was nearly all in American obligations not far from 16 billion dollars.

It is thus apparent that it was the increase in short-time American obligations, both official and private, which furnished the major portion of the increased monetary lubrication for international trade up to the end of 1964. In 1965, however, the demands of France, Spain, Belgium, and the Netherlands that their official dollar claims be redeemed in gold, reduced the total volume of foreign exchange by 1.6 billion dollars to a total of 22.3 billion dollars at the end of the third quarter. This brought the proportion of foreign exchange in the national reserves back to thirty-five percent. During the early months of 1966, France continued to draw down our gold at the approximate rate of 33 million dollars per month.

If the American deficit in payments is brought under control, the increments to the total of the world's monetary stock will therefore begin to dry up and, if and when it is brought into balance, such growth will stop except through increases in the world's monetary gold supply. One factor alone could prevent this. That would be if countries such as Germany and France would be willing to run deficits in their balance of payments and step into the ranks of the official reserve currencies. But this they have specifically and firmly refused to do.

The bringing of our balance of payments under control will accentuate the need for adding to the world's monetary supply by other methods and will intensify the demand for international monetary reforms. It is likely, also, to lead to a reversal of Europe's complaints about the United States. The Europeans have already moved from their early demand that we run deficits so that they could ac-

cumulate dollars to their present complaint that we have
been "choking" them with dollars and "exporting inflation." They are now likely to object that, by bringing our
foreign exchange deficits under control, we are drying up
the world's supply of liquid funds. All this would be amus-
ingly ironical if it did not inhibit constructive international
action. By making the United States the whipping boy for
the financial difficulties of the world, the Europeans have
diverted their attention from the necessary task of making the international financial machinery work more adequately.

From 1948 to the end of 1964, the production of gold
in the free world amounted to approximately 17.5 billion
dollars. With gold at a fixed price of 35 dollars an ounce,
this amounted to 500 million ounces. But the additions to
the world's monetary supply of gold were only about 7.6
billion dollars, or only three-sevenths of the total production of gold. The remaining 10 billion dollars, or four-
sevenths, went elsewhere, namely, into hoarding, industry,
and the arts.* It is difficult to distinguish between these
divergent uses since a diversion of gold into ornaments
and jewelry is in many cases a form of hoarding. But what
is unquestionable is that there is a large non-monetary
overhang of gold which, under certain circumstances,
could flow back into monetary uses. This adds a perplexing
unknown element to the mapping of the world's monetary
policy.

This difficulty is accentuated by the fact that the statistics given are only for the Free World and do not include
the considerable but unknown amounts mined behind the
Iron Curtain. There is already some seepage of this gold

---

* This diversion was particularly marked in 1959 and 1960 when
rumors of devaluation were ripe and the entire free world production of
gold amounting to 2.3 billion dollars went into these non-monetary uses.

into the West through the secret and numbered accounts of the Swiss banks, as was evidenced by Russia's payment for wheat in 1963 and again in 1965. The Russians can also deal directly with London. How much Russian gold there is and what Russia would do with it under varying circumstances is an enigma wrapped within a mystery.

But if gold forms sixty-five percent of the over-all national currency reserves and foreign exchange approximately thirty-five percent, these proportions differ widely from country to country. They may be classified into five main groups: first, the key currency countries of the United States and Great Britain; second, the industrialized countries of Western Europe whose holdings are predominantly in the form of gold and only secondarily in foreign exchange; third, a miscellaneous group of nations whose holdings are about evenly divided between these two forms of reserves, ranging from sixty to forty percent; fourth, countries with a preponderance of their reserves in foreign exchange with the gold ratio ranging between forty and twenty percent; and fifth, a final group where the reserves are overwhelmingly in the form of exchange and where gold forms less than twenty percent of the total. This group, in turn, is subdivided between those in the sterling and those in the dollar bloc.

A brief summary of these groups may be in order. Of the two key currency countries, the American reserves are almost entirely in gold. At the end of September, 1965, we held 14.2 billion dollars in gold and slightly less than one billion in sterling. These were proportions of ninety-four and six percent, respectively. The British gold holdings amounted to 2.1 billion dollars in gold and 600 million in dollars. These amounted to ratios of seventy-eight and twenty-two percent. The partial dependence of the pound upon the dollar is indicated by these figures. The second group consists of those countries which, in September, 1965, held over sixty percent of their reserves in gold. The following are the figures for the main industrialized countries of Western Europe:

Country	Reserves in September, 1965 (In millions of dollars)		Percent of Reserves in	
	Gold	Exchange	Gold	Exchange
Belgium	1,554	464	77	23
France *	4,556	825	85	15
Germany	4,390	1,913	70	30
Italy	2,390	1,223	67	34
Netherlands	1,756	309	85	15
Switzerland	2,656	220	92	8

It will thus be seen that this is a strong gold bloc with every country having more than two-thirds of its reserves in gold. Italy has the lowest ratio of gold with sixty-seven percent, Switzerland the highest with ninety-two percent. France and the Netherlands have five-sixths of their reserves in gold while Germany and Belgium have seventy and seventy-seven percent, respectively. The six nations combined held 17.3 billion dollars in gold, or forty-two percent of the Free World's total and over three billion dollars more than that possessed by the United States.

Three other small countries on the periphera of Europe, Spain, Portugal, and Turkey, also maintain high gold reserves. Spain has increased its gold from 58 million dollars in 1958 to no less than 810 million dollars in September, 1965, when it formed sixty-two percent of its total reserve. This was over 230 million dollars more than during the corresponding period of the preceding year. At the same time, its exchange holdings were reduced by over 300 million

* By March 1966, the French gold reserves had risen to $4806 million.

dollars from 813 million to 494 million dollars. Just as Spain's balance had been largely built up by American military expenditures, so was she able to turn over 200 million dollars of this into gold by demanding that we redeem a large portion of her claims. Portugal, in September of 1965, had gold reserves of 560 million dollars and exchange holdings of 388 million dollars. She therefore just missed entering the 60 percent club with 59 percent of its reserves in gold. A large part of Portugal's gold has been obtained because of our expenditures in connection with our bases in the Azores. Turkey, with 116 million dollars in gold and only 16 million dollars in exchange, was another high gold ratio country. These holdings in turn have been largely built up by American military and economic aid.

South Africa, which produces about three-quarters of the gold in the Western World has of course a high gold ratio with 345 million dollars of gold to 114 million dollars of exchange, or a seventy-five percentage of gold. If these four countries are added to the preceding six the total gold held in this group amounted to $18.8 billion, or approximately forty-five percent of the total and nearly five billion dollars more than the American holdings. Two other small countries with high gold ratios are Uruguay and Lebanon. The former, in the fall of 1965 had 171 million in gold and only 33 million dollars in foreign exchange or a gold ratio of 84 percent. Lebanon had 182 million in gold and 56 million dollars in exchange. Here the ratios were seventy-six and twenty-four percent, respectively.

The third group of nations are those where the proportions of gold and of foreign exchange are approximately equal, ranging between sixty and forty percent. Among the most important countries in this group are the following:

Country	Reserves in September, 1965 (In millions of dollars)		Percent of Reserves in	
	Gold	Exchange	Gold	Exchange
India	281	225	56	44
Austria	700	567	55	45
Burma	84	70	55	45
Iran	141	120	54	46
Venezuela	401	351	53	47
China (Republic)	281	256	52	48
Kuwait	49	47	51	49
Iraq	122	127	49	51
Canada	1,112	1,511	42	58

It will be observed that four of these countries, where there was an approximately equal division between gold and foreign exchange, were so-called oil rich nations, namely, Iran, Iraq, Kuwait and Venezuela. While Canada is a part of the dollar bloc, she maintains a large degree of financial independence by keeping three-sevenths of her reserve in gold.

The fourth group are the countries where the gold reserves are only between twenty and forty percent and where they are predominantly invested in foreign exchange. The main countries in this group in September 1965 with the amounts and percentages of each are shown on page 248.

Four of these countries are in Latin America, one in southeastern Europe, and two in Asia.

The fifth and final group are the "gold poor" countries with less than twenty percent of their reserves in gold:

This is a miscellaneous group. Three, Japan, Australia, and New Zealand, are among the most rapidly developing nations of the world. The first is in the dollar, the latter two in the sterling bloc. There are some signs that Aus-

Country	Reserves in September, 1965 (In millions of dollars)		Percent of Reserves in	
	Gold	Exchange	Gold	Exchange
Chile	44	73	38	62
Peru	67	112	37	63
Mexico	161	301	34	66
Colombia	33	63	35	65
Greece	78	165	33	67
Pakistan	53	170	24	76
Philippines	34	126	21	79

Country	Reserves in September, 1965 (In millions of dollars)		Percent of Reserves in	
	Gold	Exchange	Gold	Exchange
Japan	327	1,432	19	81
Australia	231	1,189	16	84
Thailand*	96	579	14	86
African States (other than Egypt)	145	1,165	11	89
Israel	56	555	9	91
Costa Rica	2	18	10	90
Saudi Arabia	73	626	10	90
Brazil	63	538	10	90

* First quarter of 1965.

Country	Reserves in September, 1965 (In millions of dollars)		Percent of Reserves in	
	Gold	Exchange	Gold	Exchange
Ireland	20	378	5	95
Australia	231	1,189	16	84
Korea	3	119	2	98
New Zealand	1	126	1	99
Malaysia*	2	864	0.2	99.8
Honduras	—	29	—	100
Nicaragua	—	56	—	100

* Second quarter of 1965.

tralia might like to move into the dollar bloc since it has shifted its internal currency from the pound to the decimal system of the dollar. New Zealand, however, has virtually its entire reserves in sterling as has the British economic dependency of Malaysia. The three Central American Republics of Costa Rica, Honduras, and Nicaragua, which are closely tied economically with the United States, have a similar relationship to the dollar. Brazil, which has been in great financial difficulties has less than ten percent of its reserves in gold.

Summing up, it can be said that in the fall of 1965 the so-called "less developed" nations of the world held 7.5 billion dollars of exchange or nearly a billion dollars more than the nations of industrial Europe though they possessed less than one-sixth as much gold. There is little prospect that the undeveloped world will be able to acquire much more gold and its need for further loans and aid, if it is to develop, is therefore accentuated.

Thus far we have shown the proportion of the reserves of the various countries which are in gold and in foreign exchange claims on the dollar and pound. These statistics of the International Monetary Fund do not, however, in themselves inform us as to how much of the foreign exchange reserves are outstanding against the dollar as compared with the pound, or what are the ratios between these claims and the gold reserves of Great Britain and the United States. Nor do they tell us in themselves where these claims are held or how large are the private short-time claims which lie behind the official holdings which can alone be counted as reserves. All this is important since the possibility that the convertibility of the pound and the dollar into gold at the present ratios depends both on the strength of the gold reserves of Great Britain and the United States relative to the possible claims against them and on what countries actually hold these claims.

For possible runs on the dollar and pound will be influenced by political as well as by financial motives. Central banks are now universally owned by governments, and political considerations, never absent in decisions about international finance, are now even more powerful.

In the case of Great Britain, her gold reserve at the end of 1964 amounted, as we have seen, to 2.1 billion dollars. The total net claims against the pound were 8.6 billion dollars.

But the location of these claims is as important as their relative immediacy. There is little doubt that the British Commonwealths of Australia and New Zealand, which now hold about a fifth of the claims against the pound, will remain loyal. All but $200 million of Australia's $1.6 billion of exchange is in the form of pounds. So will the British colonies and protectorates be loyal as long as they are under imperial control. They now hold approximately 1.6 billion dollars of claims against the pound or one-fifth of the total. But the British Empire is a shrinking affair and, as countries such as India and Ghana acquire financial as well as political independence, they are guided by their own interests. Ghana and Nigeria have been using up their balances in expansion of one sort or another. The Scandinavian nations, which have been economically tied to Great Britain for at least a century and which hold close to a billion dollars of claims against the pound, will certainly not start any trouble. On the whole, therefore, the British reserves would seem to be fully adequate to meet present official claims and relatively sufficient even if the private holdings of pounds were to be converted into official claims.

But there would be great danger if private holdings of British stocks and bonds were to be sold and if the proceeds were then transferred to foreign banks which, in turn, would deposit these claims in their respective central banks and these would then ask for gold. In this way, speculators both inside and outside Great Britain could stage a run on the pound. As we shall see the chief immediate danger to the convertibility of the pound at its present figure probably lies in this direction.

While we in the United States do not have anything comparable to the British association of commonwealths and colonies, many of the countries with short-time deposits and holdings here would probably not take fright were a run on the dollar to be staged. Approximately 12 billion dollars of the official and unofficial claims, or half the total, are held by the European countries.

But, on the whole, our total gold reserve would seem to be ample to meet such claims even though it has been reduced from 16 billion dollars at the beginning of 1963 to a little less than 14 billion dollars. Formerly, no less than 12 billion dollars of our gold was legally locked up to maintain a twenty-five percent reserve against first, the some 17.5 billion dollars of deposits by member banks in the Federal Reserve system. This absorbed nearly 4.5 billion dollars of gold. And second, the same proportional gold reserve was required behind the 30 billion dollars of Federal Reserve Notes. This required approximately 7.5 billion dollars in gold. Since these claims could not be redeemed in gold, the required reserves served no real purpose. They did, however, cut down the supply of free gold which was available in 1964 to meet foreign claims to only a little over three billion dollars. Had they been rigidly maintained, we would have been vulnerable to a foreign run and the balance by the summer of 1965 would have been further reduced to only a little over two billion dollars.

Congress sensibly loosened these restrictions in the winter of 1965 by removing the twenty-five percent reserve requirement for member bank deposits in the Federal Reserve system. This raised the free gold reserve to around 7.5 billion dollars. But neither Congress nor the Administration wanted to go so far as to remove the reserve requirement for Federal Reserve Notes. If, however, the dollar were to be threatened by foreign withdrawals, this carryover from past times would doubtless be repealed, and the full force of our gold supply could be used to meet foreign claims.

We do not seem therefore to be vulnerable to a foreign run on our gold reserve. There is, of course, always the danger for us as for Great Britain that speculators may sell their holdings of stocks and bonds, convert the returns into deposits in foreign banks and that these claims would then find their way into central banks and be presented to us for redemption in gold.

Indeed the whole structure of international finance, as I have pointed out, contains within itself this danger. Balances can be shifted from one country to another and constitute claims upon the first. A general loss of confidence can indeed imperil virtually any national currency.

But if such a flight from the dollar is feared, it is appropriate to ask where would its frightened holders flee? On the whole, our price level has been the most stable of any of the major nations of the world. The wholesale price level since 1958 had risen by the late spring of 1965 by twenty-one percent in France, 7 percent in Germany, 11 percent in Italy, 10 percent in Canada, 4 percent in Japan, and 16 percent in Great Britain. The increase in the United States, however, had been only three percent. In the last year there has been a further increase here of over 2 percent.

Those who transfer their liquid purchasing power to

other countries are likely therefore to see it depreciate far more rapidly abroad than here.

And to those who reply that the flight will not be into any national currency as such, but into gold itself, there are several replies to be made.

1. That only in Switzerland can internal bank deposits and national currency be converted into gold.

2. That if the price of gold is not increased above its present level of 35 dollars an ounce, then the probable general rise in the price level will necessarily cause a depreciation in its value as in that of all monetary units. But it is precisely the opposite that speculators in gold are likely to rely on—namely, that the gold they hold will be worth more.

3. Finally, those obtaining gold for foreign exchange will receive no income from their holdings while they hoard gold, whereas the foreign exchange claims they now own earn interest as they are invested in short-time government or commercial paper.

As long as a high degree of co-operation in economic matters is maintained between nations, there would seem to be little reason to expect that we will be forced off gold. But there are, nevertheless, certain potential dangers which should not be ignored. One is that certain countries such as France might wish to weaken or destroy the predominant financial position of the United States and Great Britain and would then demand that its foreign exchange claims be redeemed in gold.

Secondly, that such countries would so influence their citizens and private institutions that they, too, would demand gold through the medium of their central banks.

Third, if a general belief should develop that the price of gold would be increased, then the speculators would try to hoard gold in anticipation of just such a development.

In short, the international gold exchange standard is subject to the same weaknesses and dangers as the internal gold standard, namely, of having a large volume of paper claims against it which, if all were called, either could not be met, or which, if met, would so shrink the total quantity of money as to cause great economic difficulties. It is also defective from a world standpoint in that there is no close relationship between the increase in world trade and in the world's money.

From a national standpoint, it is unfair to the key currency countries of the United States and Great Britain to tie a needed increase in the international currency so closely to their unfavorable balance of payments. It is not right that their national currencies are put into even greater jeopardy as they generate the needed increase in the exchange components of the international medium of exchange. Clearly, some reform is needed.

As we have said, the IMF was not very active during its first nine years from 1947 through 1955. During this period it only loaned 1.2 billion dollars of which 300 million was to help Britain in its currency troubles of the late 1940's. During this period also, India drew 100 million, France 125 million, and Brazil 168 million dollars. During the Suez crisis of 1956, the Fund gave a credit of no less than 562 million dollars to Great Britain and in the following year embarked on an even more vigorous period of lending. For in 1957, it loaned France, which was in monetary difficulties, 262 million dollars, India another 200 million, Japan 125 million, and large sums to Belgium, the Netherlands, and Brazil. The year 1961, when Great Britain experienced another exchange crisis, was also a year of large loans. The British received no less than 1.5 billion dollars,

India was given a credit of 250 million, and Australia 175 million. Chile, Colombia, Argentina and, once again, Brazil, each received loans ranging from 60 to 76 million dollars, while Communist Yugoslavia was granted an advance of 75 million dollars. The next big period of strain was 1964–65 when over 4.4 billion dollars were loaned out. The gigantic total of 2.4 billion dollars was advanced to Great Britain and 960 million to the United States. Italy received 225 million dollars and India 200 million dollars.

In all, up to December 1, 1965, the Fund had loaned out a total of 11.46 billion dollars, of which approximately 5.75 billion had been repaid by purchase and approximately a billion by other methods, leaving an outstanding indebtedness to the Fund of 4,354 million dollars. Of this total, Great Britain owed 2,370 million dollars and the United States 384 million. Other large debts were India, which owed 325 million dollars, Brazil 159 million, Argentina 146 million, Chile 125 million, and Colombia 84 million. The net indebtedness of New Zealand was 62 million dollars, of Pakistan 54 million, and of Yugoslavia 110 million.

There are certain general conclusions which can be drawn from this record. First, that the loans of the IMF have been relatively small in comparison with its resources. The amount outstanding was only about a quarter of its former total quota and a fifth of its new. Second, a reason for this has been the reluctance of most countries to take other currencies than the American dollar on their loans. Thus, ninety percent of the loans from 1947 to 1958, inclusive, were in dollars. During this period, the dollar was almost the exclusive support of the IMF and it should be remembered that, once these dollars passed into the possession of other countries, they became liable to redemption in gold. Large amounts were undoubtedly so presented thus adding to the gold drain.

Beginning in 1961, however, the currencies of other countries became acceptable, notably those of the major industrial countries such as Germany, France, Italy, Belgium, the Netherlands, and Japan. In 1961, the American dollar formed only about a third of the total loaned, while in 1964 it comprised only fifteen percent, and in 1965, but eleven percent. The other nations are, therefore, beginning to get under the load of supporting the IMF and this may increase the effectiveness of the Fund.

Third, in the main, the funds have gone overwhelmingly to the major industrial countries, notably, Great Britain, to which the total loans have amounted to nearly 4.8 billion dollars, or forty-two percent of the total. Our total borrowings have come to nearly a billion, while large sums have also gone to France and Italy. Germany, with a consistent surplus in its balance of payments, has never had to take recourse in the Fund. The Fund has also been of great aid to Brazil, Japan, Argentina, Colombia, and Chile. But its aid to the poverty-stricken nations of Africa and Asia has, with the exception of India, been relatively minute. This fact helps to explain some of the dissatisfaction with the IMF by the leaders of these countries.

18

Britain's Difficulties with Her
Balance of Payments

Great Britain has had serious difficulties with her balance
of payments. In relation to her gross national product,
Great Britain's recent deficits have been greater than ours.
Her gold reserves are proportionately much less and her
imports more important to her survival and comfort.

As the first country to develop the industrial revolution,
with its power-driven automatic machinery and its factory
system, Britain was the foremost industrial nation during
the century from Waterloo to World War I. During the
nineteenth century, Britain's exports greatly exceeded her
imports and she devoted a major share of the resultant
surplus to making capital investments overseas. Here she
played a leading part in the economic development, not
only of the dominions, but also of Latin America and even
of the United States.

In the field of trade, Britain furnished manufactured
goods and coal to other nations and drew from them food
and raw materials. Around the turn of the century, Britain's dominance in manufacturing began to be threatened
by the rise of industrial Germany and the United States,
but the income from her overseas investments was still
sufficient to continue her favorable balance of payments.

This, in turn, was largely used for further overseas investment.* As a result of all this, London early became the financial center of the world and the British pound was the keystone of the world's currencies for the full century between 1815 and 1914.

The First World War undermined this position. In order to finance her purchases abroad of munitions and supplies, Britain had to sell a large portion of her investments in the United States, thus decreasing her annual flow of interest and dividends. And when peace returned, the rise of nationalism in Asia and in the new states of Central Europe caused new tariff barriers to be erected which restricted the market for British textiles and machinery. Then, the coal mines, upon which British shipping had largely depended for outward-bound cargoes, began to be worked at increasing costs. The growth within Britain itself of cartels and monopolies also tended to restrict output and, hence, employment.†

As a result, and with an overvalued exchange rate throughout most of the 1920's, Britain was in a depressed economic state with high unemployment. This was in contrast to the rest of the world which went forward rapidly during the five years from 1924 to 1929.

The coming of the world-wide depression in the latter part of 1929 intensified Britain's difficulties. She obtained some relief by going off the gold standard and by allowing, and possibly even assisting, the pound to depreciate, thereby obtaining a temporary export advantage. But World War II, with its nearly five years of struggle, its loss in human life, its widespread destruction of plant and

* See Hobson, C. K., *The Export of Capital.* New York: Barnes & Noble, Inc., 1914.

† Much of Great Britain's difficulties, which J. M. Keynes ascribed to monetary and interest difficulties, were due in fact to these cartels, some of which he, himself, had promoted.

housing, and its huge costs, shook Britain to the very core. She was compelled to liquidate all but about seven billion dollars of her overseas investments of which one and a quarter billion dollars was held by the government. Her plant and equipment, already old in the twenties, became still further run down. Moreover, London had largely lost the huge Indian balances which the English colonial rulers had formerly kept there. The British reserves of gold were drawn down to an extremely low figure, not exceeding two billion dollars. This was relatively little for a country which was struggling to regain its position as the financial center of the world.

There remained the oil revenues from Kuwait and the Persian Gulf and the cocoa earnings of the Gold Coast (which was shortly to be renamed Ghana). But, as Ghana became independent and embarked on a development program of its own, and as British oil was dislodged from Iran and its royalties reduced elsewhere, the financial position of London was still further weakened. Added to this was the slow rate of economic growth which Britain experienced throughout the fifties and sixties of less than two and a half percent a year, which made it still more difficult to retool and re-equip British industry. Many people also believed that British exports failed to advance as rapidly as world trade in general largely because wages per hour rose more quickly in the fifties than productivity.

The last half century has, therefore, witnessed a marked erosion in Britain's relative economic position. And, as this has happened, it has become increasingly more difficult for London to maintain its former supremacy in financial matters.

For the twelve years from 1952 to 1963, inclusive, the volume of British imports, according to the British Central Statistical Office, exceeded her exports by a total of 1.7

billion pounds, or 4.8 billion dollars. On the invisible items however,* Britain had a surplus during this same period of 2.9 billion pounds (8.1 billion dollars). Nearly four-fifths of this, however, was accumulated prior to 1960. For the period as a whole, without regard to long-term capital movements, there was a surplus of 1.2 billion pounds (3.4 billion dollars) for the combined visible and invisible items. Most of this had been earned in the fifties. The record of the sixties was not as good. There was greater strength in the British economy than many of the pessimistic analysts were willing to grant. Britain was not losing ground in any absolute sense but, from a relative standpoint, it was not going forward as rapidly as other countries in the Western World.

When long-time capital investments are taken into consideration, the picture, as in the United States, is somewhat altered. The net exports of long-term capital over corresponding imports was approximately 1.8 billion pounds for the period, making a net deficit on current and long-term capital accounts for the twelve-year period of 600 million pounds (1.7 billion dollars). This was not unmanageable, particularly when it is realized that the net investment of British private capital abroad during this period amounted to approximately 3.1 billion pounds (8.7 billion dollars) and that this will yield increasing earnings in the future.†

But the pace of economic recovery in Great Britain was much less than abroad and its gold holdings by the end of 1963 amounted to only 2.5 billion dollars as compared with Germany's 3.8 billion dollars. Britain, as a key cur-

* The invisible items include such classifications as government expenditures, shipping and aviation, travel, other services such as insurance, interest, profits, dividends, and private transfers.

† British earnings from overseas investments increased from about 500 million pounds in 1952–1953 to 782 million pounds in 1963.

rency country, had the obligation under the Bretton Woods agreement to redeem upon demand, holdings of sterling by central monetary institutions of member countries of the IMF. These amounted to about 6.7 billion dollars at the end of 1963. But there was also a moral obligation to redeem private holdings of sterling if this was requested. In consequence, the gold reserves were relatively too small to support with safety the short-term deposits which had been left on loan by foreigners, both public and private, in the British banks. This placed the pound in jeopardy from the continental bankers and the currency speculators of all countries. If the latter took fright and withdrew their balances, Britain would be plunged into serious trouble. Should this carry Britain off the gold standard, the pound would then depreciate and fall below its value of approximately $2.80. As the prospect for such a development became more ominous, a selling of British securities by speculators would inevitably set in. The proceeds from this could then be rather quickly converted into claims for gold by the familiar chain of deposits in the foreign central banks and their subsequent conversion into gold. In this way, fortunate foreigners would get $2.80 for each pound rather than take the risk that sterling would depreciate further. This very fear that the pound might be devalued, of course, would whet the desire of depositors and money speculators to get their hands on gold rather than on pounds. As is always the case under a fractional reserve system, fear breeds fear, intensifies runs, and gives an opportunity for the least worthy sections of the financial world not only to save themselves but to profit at the expense of the community.

1964 was a bad financial year for Great Britain. The deficit in the balance of payments increased rapidly until it amounted to about two billion dollars at an annual rate. The volume of foreign claims against Great Britain rose while the gold reserve shrank to its lowest level since 1961.

Beneath the surface, a dangerous condition was developing. The Conservative government, already in bad odor with much of the electorate and facing an election in which the odds seemed at the time to be heavily against it, tried to cover up the real situation and took little or no corrective action prior to the October election. For had they done so, they would not only have been held responsible for Britain's predicament, but they would also have made further enemies by the remedial steps which they might have been compelled to take. It seemed to them politically wiser, therefore, to postpone any action until after the election of early October was over. Then, if they won the election, they would be safely in power for some years and could ride out any immediate storm of popular disapproval, while, if they lost, then the blame would not fall upon them but instead on their Labour successors.

The Labour Party did win the election with a wafer-thin majority of four votes, although the handful of seats won by the little Liberal Party gave them, on most issues, a slightly greater margin of safety. When out of office, the Labourites had criticized the actions of the Conservatives in giving priority to the defense of the pound at $2.80 over the need for domestic expansion. But with so narrow a majority and with the suspicion and hostility with which most of the financial and business community of the country and of Western Europe viewed them (although basically patriotic in their genuine desire to protect the prestige of their country), the Labour Cabinet decided not to devalue and instead to make the defense of the pound their primary concern. The Cabinet decided to put national interests above any ideological tenets or economic theories.

On October 26, 1964, they therefore announced an initial program which was intended to correct the big deficit in the balance of payments. The first item was an increase of fifteen percentage points in the tariffs on all imports except those on food, cigarettes and cigars, fuel, and certain other basic materials. It was estimated that this would reduce Britain's imports by about 840 million dollars a year and raise an additional 560 million dollars in taxes. This sudden increase roused a storm of criticism from Britain's fellow members in the European Free Trade Association and the increase was later reduced to ten percent. A corollary step was to grant an export bounty of one and a half percent on all exports. This was estimated to cost about 200 million dollars a year, or three-eighths of the revenues added by the original tariff increase.

The promise was also made that government expenses would be materially reduced. Although not directly stated, it was understood that the costly supersonic air transport venture was to be closed down and that military expenditures would be cut. Finally, greater mobility of labor from surplus to deficit areas was to be encouraged by means of subsidies, while the government pledged itself to work with labor, management, and capital to increase efficiency and to reduce costs per unit of output.

On the whole, it is difficult to see how the Labour Government could have been more reassuring to the financial community. But the old hostility continued beneath the surface and this was intensified two weeks later when the new budget was introduced. In accordance with the long-continued campaign pledges of the party, the central feature of their program was an increase in the very low old-age pensions and the insurance benefits for unemployment and sickness. This was to cost a total of 840 million dollars a year, of which less than a third was to be borne

by the government. Welfare grants to the destitute were
also to be increased and most charges for medicines prescribed under the National Health System were to be
abolished. The combined cost of these last two benefits
was estimated at 130 million dollars a year, or a total increase of just short of a billion dollars a year.

But this was to be more than recouped by an increase
of just under seven percent in the basic income tax, which
was to net an additional 342 million dollars,* and by an
increase in the gasoline tax, which was to raise another
260 million dollars.

These proposals certainly could not have been attacked
as fiscally irresponsible since they were designed to raise
revenues by more than the amount of the proposed increase in benefits. But they offended the well-to-do because they proposed to help the poor at their expense. The
financial groups were also offended by a proposal to impose
a tax on their capital gains which had hitherto completely
escaped from taxation.

Many of the monied groups, both in and out of Britain,
therefore began to convert their claims on sterling into
foreign exchange. This movement snowballed as the belief
spread that Britain would soon be compelled to depreciate
the pound. The currency speculators therefore began to
move in for the kill. The rush for the exits gathered speed
as men sought to get $2.80 for the pound before it fell
still lower.

To check this drain, the Bank of England, which is under
government ownership and control, announced on Mon-
day, November 23, 1964, that it would raise its interest
rate from five to seven percent. This was precisely what

---

* This was an increase from seven shillings nine pence in the pound to
eight shillings three pence, or from ninety-three to ninety-nine pence and
from 38.7 to 41.3 percent.

the Labour Party had previously criticized the Conservatives for doing. But, instead of treating this as clear proof that Prime Minister Wilson and his Cabinet were determined to defend the parity of the pound at $2.80 and, in doing so, to sacrifice their hopes of stimulating industry and employment by lower interest rates, the financial world treated it as a panic reaction and the runs from private and not official sources continued at an extremely high rate for the next day and a half. The total gold reserve had fallen in a few weeks from two and a half to one and a half billions of dollars. This was regarded as almost the absolute minimum to which the reserve could be allowed to fall. To make matters worse, even a large part of this reserve was pledged to repay previous foreign borrowings. At the rate at which the withdrawals were being made, the pound could not have been defended for more than a few days.

In the meantime, however, a rescue operation had been mounted by the monetary authorities of the West, led by the United States, and when the details were announced early in the afternoon of Wednesday, November 25, the panic ceased and, within the hour, the run on sterling had stopped and the immediate danger was over.

What had happened was that the British had drawn one billion dollars of credit from the IMF from a line of credit which had previously been authorized, while, in addition, the remaining members of the Group of Ten, plus Austria, Switzerland, and the Bank of International Settlements, had granted Great Britain an additional three billion dollars in credits which were to be good for from three to six months. The group made it clear that these credits were "to back up Britain's determination to defend the pound sterling."

The United States contributed one-third of this rescue

fund, or one billion dollars. Three-quarters of this, in turn, or 750 million dollars, was in the form of a swap of currencies while the remaining 250 million dollars was a loan from the Export-Import Bank. The French are believed to have made a rather generous contribution and at this stage were fully co-operative.

In January of 1965, General de Gaulle announced his intention to call for the redemption in gold of approximately 300 million dollars of foreign exchange to be apparently evenly divided between the dollar and the pound. These claims were carried out in the next few months.

In order to lessen the strain on the pound, the government reduced expenditures for housing and defense, postponed some capital improvements, and dampened down overseas investment. On the other hand, the Bank of England reduced its interest rate from seven to six percent, or one percent above what it had been prior to the sterling crisis of the previous November. So far as the foreign trade in physical commodities was concerned, Britain had cut the deficit during the first half of 1965 by nearly one-fifth in comparison with the previous year and did still better in the month of July.

But the First National City Bank of New York estimated that, while the deficit in the balance of payments for 1965 would be reduced to only about one billion dollars, or slightly less than half that for 1964, a balance could not be reached before the end of 1966. Moreover, the gold drain in late 1964 and early 1965 (which some believed had been as high as three billion dollars) had only been met by large borrowings from the International Monetary Fund and from the United States, amounting in all to over three billion dollars. An overhanging problem was how these debts were to be met when they came due in a little over three years.

A table published in the fall by the *London Economist* showed losses of about 750 million dollars of gold during the six months from the last week of February to the 20th of August, 1965.*

In the spring and early summer of 1965, another run on the pound seemed imminent. The forward quotations on the pound sterling fell and with the heavy seasonal imports of food and raw materials coming up in the late summer and fall, there was grave danger that Britain would be unable to meet the claims upon it and, hence, would finally be forced to devalue the pound. To avert this, a second rescue party was organized which pledged an additional sum, believed to have been well over another billion dollars, to back up the pound. Our contribution was approximately one-third of this, but this time France ostentatiously held aloof and refused to make any contribution whatsoever. It is known that the British guaranteed the lenders against any losses which might result from a subsequent depreciation of the pound itself. Backed up by the reassurance given by the pledges of its allies, the pound again rallied and the immediate danger subsided.

Nevertheless, the question remains as to whether the British gold reserves are in fact adequate in relation to the demands which can be made upon them. The basic facts can be simply stated. In March of 1965, the British gold reserve amounted to 754 million pounds, or 2.1 billion dollars. It had supplementary resources of 200 million dollars in American dollars. Against this there were total short-time foreign claims, both public and private, of no less

* *The Economist*, October 16, 1965, pp. 295–297.

than 5.2 billion pounds, or approximately 14.5 billion dollars. The gold reserve was therefore only a little over fourteen percent, or one-seventh, of the potential claims which could have been made upon it. This of course was far too small for comfort.

But in reality the situation was not as dangerous as it appeared. For Great Britain had offsetting short-time claims against foreign countries of one and one-sixth billion pounds, thus reducing its net liabilities to four billion pounds, or 11.2 billion dollars. On this basis, the ratio of gold to net liabilities was nineteen percent.

Furthermore, no less than five billion dollars of the short-term indebtedness was held by the Central Banks of the sterling area countries. These institutions would be unlikely to pull down upon themselves the pillars of Britain's financial house. Approximately four billion dollars of these obligations were held by the loyal Commonwealths of Australia and New Zealand * which, though using their reserves to expand internally, can probably be depended upon to stand by Great Britain.

The real danger to the pound, therefore, came—in ascending order of urgency—from: first, the Central Banks of countries outside the sterling area which held just short of two billion dollars of claims, of which only 300 million dollars was in the hands of the Bank of France, and an equal sum in the combined holdings of Belgium and Holland; second, the approximately seven billion dollars held by private individuals, banks, and corporations in foreign countries; and, third, the raids which could be engineered by currency speculators who could sell British securities, transfer the proceeds to foreign banks, and then put pressure on British reserves.

* In recent months the economic and financial position of New Zealand has deteriorated.

But one should note the hidden resources of Great Britain. The government, for example, retained at the beginning of 1965 one and a quarter billion dollars' worth of the American industrial securities which it had obtained from its own nationals during World War II. It is believed that some of these were quietly sold during the year to meet certain outstanding debts and claims. During 1965 British exports increased more rapidly than her imports so that her trade balance improved. She also paid off most of her American debt.

British private investors and companies also own a large stock of long-term foreign assets. The First National City Bank of New York estimates these to be worth some twenty-five billion dollars. In a great emergency, these could also be drawn upon as a last line of defense for sterling.

While the true facts about the foreign exchange crisis were well concealed at the time, it is now apparent that Great Britain narrowly escaped devaluation in 1964 and again in 1965. During 1964 and the first nine months of 1965, there was an unfavorable balance of trade which, with capital investments overseas, amounted to about 550 million pounds, or 1.54 billion dollars. This put pressure on British reserves. Then, in addition, the sterling countries, because of deficits at home and fears of devaluation in Britain, drew down their balances by about another 260 million pounds, or 720 million dollars. Finally, private depositors and currency speculators withdrew 429 million pounds up to September, 1965, or 1.2 billion dollars.

The sum of all these claims amounted to no less than 3.5 billion dollars. Britain's gold reserves were not large enough to cover these and previously acquired liabilities so that, had it not been for the large loans by the IMF, the Federal Reserve and other international institutions, Britain would have been stripped of all of her gold and forced off the formal gold exchange standard. The resulting devaluation would have been severe and an international panic might well have spread over the Western World. But the loans of about 3.5 billion dollars saved her and then 482 million pounds or 1.35 billion dollars of the speculators' money came back and about 112 million pounds was redeposited from the sterling area, making a total of just under 1.7 billion dollars.

While Britain, at the end of March, 1965, had total reserves of 2.3 billion dollars, she owed the Monetary Fund and others more than 3.5 billion dollars.

Two comments on this tangled history are appropriate: First, Britain was primarily saved directly and indirectly by the United States. The United States provided the main leadership in organizing support for the pound, and the direct American aid of a billion dollars was essential. Our behavior was in sharp contrast to that of France, which in 1965 refused to help Britain and was, in addition, busily trying to weaken us by withdrawing as much gold as she could conveniently get her hands on. We have never flaunted our rescue operation and we should not do so. But it was certainly unbecoming for Edward Heath, the leader of the Conservative Party, to stir up anti-Americanism in the March, 1966, elections by his complaints that we were seeking to make Britain dependent on us. We, of course, want no such thing and we would be happy if we did not have the extra strain created by the British difficulties.

The second warning from the British experience is that it will be difficult for the pound to survive another crisis such as that of 1964–1965. Britain now owes to the Fund and central banks more than three billion dollars, or an amount exceeding her entire reserves. Her deficit from trade and investments overseas in 1964 amounted to about

2.2 billion dollars. Chancellor Callaghan in his policy speech of March 1, 1966, stated that in 1965 this deficit had at least been cut in half, to not more than 1.1 billion dollars, and later official statements have lowered this figure still further. The deficit in commodities alone had been reduced to half by the tariff duties of first fifteen, and then ten percent on imports. The rate of increase in imports decreased from fourteen percent in 1964 to a rise of only one percent in 1965. Exports, on the other hand, aided by the export bonus, increased by 7 percent. Capital investments abroad were also greatly reduced largely because of restrictions imposed by the government.*

The Labour government is expecting during 1966 to close the gap completely on the balance of payments and, if not then, to do so in 1967. Whether it can accomplish this is problematical since, in order to make further export gains, it would have to energize management and also reduce wage and salary costs per unit of output. These have been weaknesses in British industry for over a half century but, while some progress has been made, it has been minor compared with the need. Unless Great Britain can put her industrial house in order in terms of costs and selling prices, she will either be compelled to ask for a further credit transfusion or accept a further devaluation of the pound sterling. It is not certain that the United States and the IMF can continue for many more years to bear a continuing burden of Britain's heavy exchange deficits. If the deficits continue and if Britain receives little or no help from the creation of an international currency, then the currency speculators, unless checked, can be expected to resume their built-in wrecking practices. And

* The speech by Chancellor of the Exchequer Callaghan in the House of Commons on March 1, 1966, gives some of these details which are supplemented by comments in the *Economist* for the following week together with the *Quarterly Bulletins* of the Bank of England for December 1965 and March 1966.

then the Western nations will have to decide whether they will once more come to the relief of Great Britain.

For, while the temporary difficulties of the pound can and should be shored up by massive foreign assistance, this is no permanent answer to Britain's industrial and monetary problems. The brutal truth is that England's industrial equipment is partially obsolete, its business methods and management commonly inefficient, and its trade unions wedded to maintaining a widespread network of restrictive rules and practices. During the twentieth century, Britain, as a whole, has tended to rely in the economic field upon its past glories and entrenched position and, except in a few lines, failed to keep pace with modern developments. It has been weighted down, moreover, by a class structure which emphasizes family connections and school and university affiliations rather than competitive efficiency. The self-protective customs of landed feudalism have penetrated deeply into the worlds of industry, finance, and trade, and it is small wonder that the world of labor has tended to follow the practices of the society in which it lives. Each group is anxious to reform the habits of the others, but zealously defends its own practices. Only if there is a general transformation can this immensely talented people with its long and inspiring history and with its magnificent contributions to the civilization of the world, but deprived of the most essential raw materials, hold its own in the international market for goods and services. The Labour Government is urging such a transformation on Great Britain, but it remains to be seen how the various groups will respond to the call for a "new deal." The burden may well be so heavy that Great Britain cannot carry the added weight of being one of the two key currency countries.

19

America's Balance of Payments

In the days of the mercantilists, international trade took the form of only material goods. If the commodities exported by Country "A" exceeded in value those which it imported, then "A" had a "favorable" balance of trade and, consequently, of payments. Were we to judge by only this standard, the United States would be in a very strong position indeed. For, in 1964, we exported 25.3 billion dollars' worth of goods * and imported only 18.6 billion. Our favorable "balance of trade," therefore, amounted to 6.7 billion. Even deducting the 2.5 billion dollars' worth of goods (mostly food) financed by our government, the surplus was still over four billion dollars. In 1965, our exports of goods amounted to approximately 25½ billion dollars as compared with corresponding imports of 20.9 billion dollars or a somewhat smaller surplus of 4½ billion dollars.†

We have had such a surplus of exports over imports ever since World War II and during that time we have exported over nearly 90 billion dollars more of material goods than we have imported.

It is worthwhile to examine this trade in commodities more minutely and to see what kinds of goods we ex-

* This excludes approximately 800 million dollars' worth of goods transferred under military grants.

† *Economic Indicators,* January, 1966, p. 24.

port and import and in what amounts as well as to see the relative importance of our trade with the main areas of the world.

Let us begin with a summary table which shows the main categories of our exports and imports and then proceed to a more detailed analysis. Due to difficulties in classification, the statistics do not precisely balance, but the general picture which they give is approximately accurate.

Value of Our Exports and Imports—1964
(In millions of dollars)

Category	Exports	Imports
A. Agricultural	6.3	4.1
A(1) Crude agricultural products, i.e., fibres, etc.	2.0	
A(2) Crude foods	2.5	
A(3) Manufactured foods	1.7	
B. Other crude materials, i.e., wood, ore, coal, etc.	0.8	2.6
C. Semi-manufactures	4.1	4.0*
D. Finished manufactures	14.1	7.3
E. Other commodities		.6
Total	25.3	18.6

* These statistics are based on those presented in *U.S. Foreign Trade 1957–1964*, prepared by the U.S. Department of Commerce, August 1965. The figures include about two billion dollars' worth of our exports (mostly food), which were government financed by other agencies than the Export-Import Bank.

It will be seen that nearly sixty percent of our exports consisted of manufactured goods while agricultural products formed only a quarter of the total, with semi-processed goods the remainder. This is a far cry from the nineteenth century when we chiefly exported wheat, cotton, and tobacco and imported manufactured goods in return.

Now our chief exports are such capital goods as machinery, both electrical and non-electrical, including trucks, automobiles and auto parts, aircraft, agricultural and earth-moving machinery, and metal products and the like. The next most important group among our exports are chemical goods including medicine and drug products, plastics, manufactured fertilizers, together with soaps and oils. The final main group of manufactured goods is a miscellaneous group of primarily consumer products such as paper, rubber, textiles, clothing, scientific and photographic equipment, films, printed matter, etc. In the main, it is the mass production goods in which we excel both in the field of capital and consumer products.

On the other hand, we still continue to export large quantities of farm products, notably 850 million bushels of wheat worth 1.5 billion dollars, 5.2 million bales of cotton worth 700 million dollars, 12.6 billion pounds of soybeans valued at nearly 600 million dollars, 480 million bushels of corn at 650 million dollars, 100 million bushels of grain sorgham, 1.9 million tons of oil cake and other animal food worth 200 million dollars, and 2.9 billion pounds of rice at 200 million dollars. Here again it is the farm commodities produced with modern machinery for both planting and harvesting, together with an intensive use of commercial fertilizer in which we excel.

Balancing this are our imports, now consisting primarily of raw materials and semi-manufactured goods but falling short in the aggregate during 1965 by over four billion dollars to pay for our exports.

First are the tropical products of sugar, tea, coffee, cocoa, and fruits amounting in 1964 to nearly two billion dollars. Then beef and fish coming to another 800 million dollars. Then amongst the raw materials 1.6 billion dollars' worth of wood and wood pulp and newsprint primarily from Canada, together with an equal amount of metallic ores, iron, manganese, and bauxite, 200 million dollars' worth of wool, mainly from Australia, two billion dollars' worth of petroleum from Venezuela and the Persian Gulf, 200 million dollars' worth of natural rubber from Malaysia and Indonesia, copper from Chile and tin from Bolivia and Malaysia. The prediction made twenty years ago by the Paley committee that we would become increasingly dependent on foreign supplies for our raw materials has been largely confirmed by the development of events.

But Europe is still strong in the production of capital goods requiring precision, such as small automobiles, luxury products such as Scotch whisky and French wines, the finer textiles, glass, and pottery, cameras, optical and photographic goods, clocks, and watches, and autoworks. In recent years, moreover, Europe has more than quadrupled its sales to us of iron and steel products due largely to its adoption of the oxygen process and of continuous casting. And in 1965 it markedly increased its sales of steel to us.

It may also be well to show the relative volume of our trade with the different geographic areas of the world.

Canada is the country with whom we have the greatest volume of trade since, in 1964, we exported 5.5 billion dollars' worth of goods and imported 4.8 billion dollars, mostly in the form of wood, wood pulp, newsprint, iron ore, lead and zinc. We exported 4.2 billion dollars' worth of goods to the nineteen American Republics. In turn, we imported 4.1 billion dollars' worth of goods from all of these countries, mostly in the form of sugar, coffee, and petroleum, the latter primarily from Venezuela together with copper from Chile and tin from Bolivia.

We sold 9.1 billion dollars' worth of goods to Western Europe primarily in the form of manufactured goods, such as trucks, earth moving machinery, electrical equipment and agricultural machinery and specific types of other machines. But we also exported to this area large quantities of cotton, wheat, tobacco, corn, soybeans, and oilcake. In return, we imported 5.2 billion dollars of goods in the form of small autos, non-electrical and electrical machinery, whisky, glass, pottery, manufactured textiles, etc.

To the Near East and Asia we exported no less than 5.5 billion dollars of goods of which 900 million dollars went to the Near East, 1.9 billion to Japan, nearly a billion dollars' worth to India, and 360 million to the Philippines. From all these countries we imported 3.6 billion dollars of which 1.8 billion came from Japan, 400 million from the Philippines, 300 million from India, and 250 million from the manufacturers of Hong Kong. From Malaysia we imported rubber and tin, and from Ceylon, tea.

We sold about three-quarters of a billion dollars of goods to Australia and New Zealand and imported 440 million dollars' worth mostly in the form of wool and meat. Finally, we sold slightly less than a billion dollars to the African countries (excluding Egypt) of which 400 million dollars went to South Africa. Reciprocally, we imported an almost equal sum.

It is worthwhile remembering that enormous as these sums are, they form only a small fraction of our total gross national product—namely, four percent in the case of exports and three percent in the case of imports. In comparison with our internal production, these proportions seem relatively insignificant, but many of the exports, such as wheat, cotton, corn, agricultural machinery, and so forth, are of crucial importance as are many of the imports, such as oil, copper, wood products, and iron ore.

But material commodities are now only a part of the financial dealings between nations. Intangible services, such as travel, shipping, and insurance create increasing claims by nations against each other. Furthermore, during the postwar period, we have exported large quantities of liquid capital which, when spent abroad, have created money claims against us. In addition, during these same years the United States, in order to deter aggression, has stationed and equipped large military forces in Europe and Asia which, in Korea and Vietnam, have actually come into armed conflict with our opponents. Our purchases abroad to provision and equip these troops and their expenditures and those of their families have in turn become money claims which these countries have acquired against us. We have also carried through an extensive and costly system of foreign economic aid and a major share of these expenditures for the primary benefit of others have also been transformed into foreign claims against the dollar as has a large share of our military aid. To an examination of these other elements in the balance of payments, we turn now.

The following balance sheet of payments for services as distinct from commodities for the ten years from 1954 to 1963, inclusive, and for 1964, itself, seems to be substantially accurate. The payments for foreign travel for 1964 were estimated by the Bernstein Committee to come to over two billion dollars. About half the travel expenditures were for overseas travel and the remaining half was about equally divided between Canada and Mexico. The receipts from travel by foreigners in the United States in the same year came to a little over one billion dollars. It was estimated that forty percent of this was from Canadians, twenty-five percent from Mexicans, and the remaining thirty-five percent from overseas visitors. The travel items in 1964, therefore, showed a deficit according to the Bernstein Committee of about a billion dollars. The Department of Commerce estimated that the total deficit amounted in that year to 1.6 billion on travel and transportation. In 1965, this was increased by 200 million dollars.

The "miscellaneous service" item includes a wide variety of payments such as those for cables, radio and telephone service, insurance premiums, motion picture rentals, patent and copyright royalties, and so forth. On the whole, these yield a comfortable balance.

The remittance and pension item includes gifts from American citizens to foreign residents as well as pensions to Americans residing outside the country.

The estimates of expenditures for all forms of transportation are much less accurate but the Bernstein Committee seems to fix our receipts from abroad in 1964 at 2.3 billion dollars and our expenditures at 2.6 billion dollars, leaving a deficit of 300 million dollars.

The Balance Sheet of Services 1954—1964

| | 1954–1963 | | | 1964 | | |
| Type of Service | Re-ceipts | Expend-itures | Bal-ance | Re-ceipts | Expend-itures | Bal-ance |
	(In billions of dollars)			(In billions of dollars)		
Transport and Travel	24.4	−32.3	− 8.9	3.3	−4.6	−1.3
Miscellaneous Services	9.7	−6.7	+ 3.0	1.3	− .9	+ .4
Remittances and Pensions (Net)			− 7.0			− .8
Total			−12.9			−1.7

Source: Report of Review Committee for Balance of Payments Statistics, pp. 35–46.

It will thus be seen that there has been a net outflow in payments for the service items of over 15 billion dollars in twelve years (including 1965) and that this has been due to the payments for remittances and pensions and to foreign travel by Americans. The enjoyment from and the broadening experiences of foreign travel are, of course, intangible gains which cannot be measured by the coarse

thumb and finger of financial statistics. But it is apparent
that, to the people who spent the money for these purposes, they are worth what they cost, for they come to
increasing sums with almost every year. And no one would
wish to stamp out from the world the family affection and
filial obligations which lie behind the remittances.

Capital is now international and is invested in large
quantities in other countries. From 1946 through 1963, our
private investors sent abroad no less than 37 billion dollars
of capital, while our government loaned another 28 billion
dollars, making a total of 65 billion dollars. In the process
of investing this capital, dollars were sold abroad to obtain the needed foreign currencies and these dollars, when
acquired by foreigners, constituted claims upon us. In the
future, as interest is paid on these loans and the principal
itself is repaid, we will acquire, in turn, claims against
these other countries. In other words, the investment of
capital initially contributes to an unfavorable balance of
payments, but, if the investments are fortunate, then, ultimately, the accumulation of interest and profits, if transferred back to this country, will help to offset any fresh
investments. When an ultimate equality between these
two tendencies is reached, the capital sector of the international accounts is in balance. When the annual payment
of interest and profits from abroad exceeds the fresh investments abroad, the capital exporting country will have
a net volume of claims upon other nations which it can
then use for a variety of purposes, such as financing an
excess of imports over exported goods, providing for
added services such as travel abroad, and for other purposes.

When the earnings on invested capital are, however,
not repatriated to the United States but are instead re-

invested abroad, they do not immediately enter into the stream of international payments and, hence, are neutral in any effect upon the balance of payments.

There are many ways by which Americans have made these investments in foreign countries. The first and simplest is when American investors buy the stocks and bonds of foreign companies which these companies then spend or invest abroad. These then become claims against the American dollar. The same result occurs when deposits in American banks are transferred to similar institutions abroad. A second way in which American capital moves abroad is when American corporations use dollars earned or acquired in the United States to expand their investments in other countries whether these be in their own companies or subsidiaries or whether these be used for the acquisition of new companies and plants or the expansion of existing facilities.

Finally, there is still a third major source of capital transfers, namely, loans by American banks made either to foreign banks or corporations abroad. These may, of course, be for short periods of a year or less, or for longer terms. Since the short time loans are commonly renewed upon their coming due, the difference between the two types of loans is much less in practice than it is commonly represented. Reciprocal investments by foreigners in American enterprises, together with the payment of interest and dividends on foreign holdings by Americans, create counteracting forces to the total investment abroad of America. So, of course, does the repayment of principal and the repatriation of capital.

It should also be realized that some of the direct investments by Americans in foreign subsidiaries and enterprises stimulate the export of American goods, especially in the form of modern machinery and equipment.

In discussing these matters, it is important to distinguish between the comparative investment position at a given time and changes in these totals from year to year. It is the latter or annual increments which constitute the respective current claims on the balance of payments.

First, let us give a summary of the comparative total investments by Americans abroad and by foreigners here. Excluding for the moment investments in international monetary institutions such as the IMF and our gold holdings, the total of our private investments and claims at the end of 1963 amounted to 66 billion dollars. This was nearly three times the 1953 figure of 23 billion dollars. No less than 40 billion of the 1963 total was in the form of direct investments by American corporations in foreign branches and affiliates, or twice what it had been ten years earlier. About equal amounts of approximately 14 billion dollars each was invested in petroleum and in manufacturing with about equal sums of 3⅓ billion dollars each in mining and in trade, with another 5 billion dollars in miscellaneous lines.

Other American private investments abroad consisted in 1963 of about 7.5 billion of foreign bonds, 6 billion of other long-term securities, slightly over 4 billion dollars in long-term bank loans and claims, and 8 billion in short-term loans and claims. Then, in addition to the 66 billion dollars of private investments and claims, our government had slightly over 21 billion of foreign assets excluding our gold holdings of 15.6 billion (at the end of 1965, 13.9 billion dollars) and gold drawing rights of one billion on the IMF.* The combined total was 87 billion dollars and, if

---

* These consisted of 17.4 billion dollars of long-term credits and claims and of 6.8 billion of loans for foreign assistance programs, 3.6 billion for Export-Import Bank loans, 5.3 billion for the British loan and other post-war credits and foreign country balances and short-term claims of 3.4

we were to include our gold holdings, approximately 103 billion. By the end of 1965, the combined total of our private and public investments came to slightly over 100 billion and with gold holdings and rights to 115 billion.

As an offset to this, private foreign interests had in 1963 32.5 billion dollars of investments and claims upon the United States. This was only half of our private investments abroad. Moreover, only eight billion dollars of this was in the form of direct investments or but one-fifth of the corresponding direct investments by Americans. In addition, there were holdings of one billion in federal, state, municipal and corporate bonds, another 1.7 billion in long term claims and, according to the Bernstein Committee, 9.4 billion dollars in short-time investments and claims held by private banks and individuals. This was probably an understatement. Finally, foreign central banks and the IMF in 1963 had total short-term credits of 15.3 billion of which at least 12 billion dollars constituted official claims against the dollar while governments had investments and claims of 1.6 billion dollars. Taken altogether, the foreign claims against the United States, both private and official, amounted by the end of 1963 to 51.5 billion or only one-half of the corresponding total claims by the United States against foreigners. But whereas we held only eight billion dollars of private and 3.4 billion of governmental short-time claims, or only twelve percent of our total, the rest of the world held at least 25 billion in our short-term obligations or a full half of their total American assets. We are, therefore, much more vulnerable to the sudden calling of loans than are the foreign nations. Furthermore, our obligation under the IMF to redeem

billion, plus 1.2 billion of subscription to international monetary institutions.

such demands in gold or convertible currencies create an added burden and danger.

In 1963, the private long-term investments which we currently made abroad exceeded the corresponding foreign investments here by 3.3 billion while short-term loans showed an excess of 300 million dollars. There was a similar net increase of 400 million in the claims of foreign commercial banks making a net current capital outflow of four billion dollars. Our income from past investments abroad amounted, however, to 3.8 billion.

In 1964, our investments abroad rose markedly. Long-term investments increased to a net of 4.1 billion dollars and short-term loans to no less than 1.7 billion. This tremendous jump was caused, it is understood, by bank loans to Japan and Canada. The reported short-time claims of foreign commercial banks increased by 1.4 billion dollars, making a total current deficit of 7.2 billion. It was this outflow that caused Congress to pass the Interest Equalization Act of 1964 and which induced the Administration to seek the voluntary co-operation of business in early 1965. But, against this, there should be considered the fact that the net income from past investments abroad amounted to 4.5 billion dollars.

Our governmental aid abroad is of two kinds, namely, military and economic, and each of these can in turn be subdivided into loans and grants. Our military expenditures abroad during the five years from 1960 to 1964, inclusive, averaged approximately three billion dollars a year,* including an estimated 800 million dollars spent abroad by military personnel. In addition, foreign economic aid amounts to extremely large sums. The 17 billion

---

* This does not include expenditures at home for the troops and installations abroad.

dollars we advanced to Western Europe from 1948 to 1953 was in the form of outright gifts and we have followed this up with large gifts and loans to the undeveloped and less developed nations of the Near East, Asia, Africa, and South America. In all, since the war we have given over 41 billion dollars in foreign economic aid and loaned over 28 billion. This is a combined total of approximately 70 billion dollars. Our total expenditures since the war for foreign aid, both military and economic, has amounted to the enormous total of over 113 billion dollars,* making our total military aid well over 40 billion dollars. Never in the history of the world has there been anything remotely comparable to our generosity as well as to our enlightened self-interest. But this has also been the major cause of our adverse balance of payments. To the degree that we have placed ourselves in economic jeopardy, it has been from a desire to help the less fortunate and to provide greater military security both for ourselves and for the world. This may be hard for foreign eyes to read or foreign ears to hear but it is the sober and unvarnished truth.

Our adverse balance of payments did not really emerge until 1958. During the four years from 1946 through 1949, we had an actual surplus which in all totaled seven billion dollars. This was because we were supplying Europe with large quantities of food, materials, and equipment with which to repair the damage which that continent had suffered from the war. In order to finance these purchases, Western Europe sent us much of their gold reserves and foreign exchange. With the establishment of the Marshall Plan, the Communist invasion of South Korea, and the formation of NATO as a defensive alliance against Communist aggression, our aid to Europe and ultimately to

* Approximately 10 billion of this has been repaid.

other continents increased.* As a result, the balance of payments turned against us from 1950 to 1957, amounting in all to ten billion. The British devaluation of the pound also decreased our exports and increased our imports. But taking the twelve years from 1946 on, the combined deficit came to only three billion dollars and was most certainly of manageable proportion.

The real trouble began in 1958 when the surplus of our exports over imports fell off markedly and our military expenditures abroad rose. As a result, the total deficit for that year came to 3.5 billion dollars. These deficits have continued in varying amounts since that day as indicated in the following table based on the conventional or "liquidity" method of computation. These total:

Year	Deficit in Balance of Payments (In billions of dollars) (liquidity basis)	Year	Deficit in Balance of Payments (In billions of dollars) (liquidity basis)
1958 *	$3.5	1962	$2.2
1959	3.7	1963	2.7
1960	3.9	1964	2.8
1961	2.4	1965	1.3

TOTAL 1958–1965 = $22.5 billion
Average deficit: 1958–1960 = $3.7 billion
1961–1965 = $2.3 billion

* Since 1958, the accounts include certain classified transactions.

In recent years, the theoretical basis for the conventional or liquidity computations has been challenged by several experts, most notably by E.M. Bernstein. An official committee which he headed recommended that short-term private claims on the United States should not be included because first, there was no obligation to redeem

* While economic aid to Europe was virtually stopped by 1954, it was extended elsewhere and military aid was expanded.

them in gold—this being restricted to official holdings by governments and government institutions, and second, short-term claims by American private interests against foreign interests are now excluded. Since there is unequal treatment as between these two sets of claims, the committee agreed that the only symmetrical solution was to exclude such short-term private foreign claims against us just as we exclude ours against them. The Bernstein formula would give us the following deficits which, it will be noted, were appreciably smaller than those obtained by the conventional method.

Deficit as Shown by Bernstein Method (See Report of Review Committee on Balance of Payments Statistics) 1965, p. 4

Year	Bernstein Formula (in billions of dollars)	Difference Between Conventional and Bernstein Formula
1954–1957	1.3	1.8
1958	3.0	0.5
1959	2.5	1.2
1960	3.5	0.4
1961	2.0	0.4
1962	3.3	1.1
1963	2.3	0.4
1964	1.5	1.3
Total 1958–1964	19.4	7.1

The use of the Bernstein formula, therefore, reduces the computed deficit by 7.1 billion dollars from 1954 to 1964 by eliminating the short-term private holdings from the foreign account.* Since these are not legally liable for redemption in gold, some of the hysteria created during these last years by the use of the conventional deficit

* It is understood that there is little difference between the two methods so far as 1965 is concerned. The reduction for the years 1958–64 amounted to 5.3 billions.

should be reduced by this other formula which has now been approved for alternative use by the Department of Commerce.

But while the excluded short-term private foreign claims are not binding obligations for redemption in gold, they can become so by the private holders depositing them in the governmental state banks where they would then become, if demanded, official claims upon gold. They are, therefore, contingent though not immediate liabilities. The conventional method of computing the balance therefore should not be discarded, although in the interests of symmetry our smaller short-term claims against foreign countries might perhaps be included. For a time, it is well, as the government has decided, to utilize the two formulas in double harness.

The claims against the United States which are left on deposit with the private banks of New York and London by private parties of foreign countries are different in function as well as in legal rights from those deposited by central banks and governments of those countries. As we have seen, these private deposits cannot be converted into gold upon demand whereas the official deposits, under the United States policy, are a claim against our gold.

The official deposits are moreover a "reserve currency" which can be used by the depositing country to multiply its own internal creation of monetary purchasing power. For these purposes the pound sterling and the dollar are treated as being "as good as gold."

The deposits made in the United States and Great Britain by the foreign private banks, corporations, and individuals are of a somewhat different nature. Since they have no legal claim to be redeemed in gold, they cannot be counted as "reserves" in their home country. But they do instead serve as "vehicle," or, in Robert Roosa's phrase, "transaction money." They not only arise out of commercial and financial transactions, but they can be shifted about and transferred to settle surpluses and deficits in transactions between individuals and corporations. In actual practice, these private deposits lubricate international trade much more directly than the official deposits of the central banks.

The sharpness of the distinction between "reserve" and "transaction" or "vehicle" money is, however, blurred by the fact of their also being interchangeable. Thus, "transaction money" can be transformed into "reserve" money by a foreign private bank transferring its claim upon the reserve currency to its own central bank and receiving in return drawing rights upon that bank. This in fact is precisely how most central banks have acquired these reserve assets. Conversely, the central bank may sell its claim upon the reserve currency to a private bank. A second relationship is that, since such an acquisition by a central bank swells its reserve and makes possible a general expansion of credit and monetary purchasing power, this will of course serve to help finance foreign as well as domestic trade.

But, despite these interconnections, the main distinctions between these two supplementary forms of international money are still valid. It is ironical that the extremely important element of "transaction" or "vehicle" money should have been so ignored in both the statistical and the theoretical treatment of international trade and the balance of payments.

The first way in which we have met these accumulated claims against us has been by the time-honored method of shipping gold abroad. In 1953, we held 22.1 billion dollars of gold in our reserves. This was sixty-five percent of the total monetary gold reserves of the world. This total has since declined in the following fashion:

End of Year	U.S. Gold Holdings (in billions of dollars)
1958	$20.6
1959	19.5
1960	17.8
1961	16.9
1962	16.1
1963	15.6
1964	15.5
July, 1965	14.2
March, 1966	13.7

There was thus a loss of over eight billion dollars in our gold holdings over the period of thirteen years,* and of nearly seven billion since 1958. Since the total gold reserves of the world have risen to a little over 41 billion, this meant that the proportion which our gold reserves form of the world's total has declined from sixty-five to thirty-three percent, or from roughly two-thirds to one-third. Relatively speaking therefore they had fallen in half.

As I have pointed out, the remainder which we owe to other countries has been invested by them in short-time U.S. Government bonds and notes and by interest bearing deposits in American commercial banks. This brought the total of the short-time liabilities of the United States to foreigners in November 1964 to 24 billion and a year later to approximately 27 billion dollars. About 13 billion of this was in the form of official claims redeemable in gold and another 14 billion in private short-time deposits.

* The gold to which other countries have taken title has not in the main physically moved overseas. It is stored far underground in special vaults of the New York Federal Reserve Bank and held to their account.

Our private gold reserves are therefore approximately equal to the official demands which can be made upon them and are about half the total of short-time official and private claims. This would seem to be an adequate margin although, of course, we could not in practice permit ourselves to be completely stripped of our gold reserve. There is an indeterminate minimum below which we could not and will not allow our gold supply to fall. The gold drain cannot therefore be allowed to go on indefinitely and a solution must be found within the next few years although the improvement in 1965 was marked.

Formerly, as we have pointed out, we were greatly restricted by anachronistic and archaic legal requirements and shibboleths governing this gold reserve.

The basic law which established the Federal Reserve system provided that gold reserves of twenty-five percent must normally be maintained against both the total amount of Federal Reserve notes which were in circulation and the total deposits of member banks in the Federal Reserve system. By the end of 1964, the total deposits came to 19 billion dollars and the notes in circulation to 35 billion. The combined total of 54 billion dollars, therefore, called for a gold reserve of 13.5 billion. This left at the time, therefore, only about 1.5 billion dollars of free gold as a reserve against the official and unofficial foreign claims. Since the total required reserves tended to increase at the rate of approximately 750 million a year because of the normal rise in business activity and bank credit as well as of Federal Reserve notes, this meant that the margin of free gold would have virtually disappeared sometime in 1966.

A further complicating element was introduced by President de Gaulle and the French government during the latter part of 1964 and the early months of 1965. De

Gaulle became obviously anxious to reduce the economic power of Great Britain and the United States. As we have seen, France held official claims of 1.5 billion dollars against the dollar and pound sterling and large additional private sums.

In the fall of 1964, the French announced that they would ask for gold on about 300 million dollars of their claims and intimated that this was only the beginning. It is believed that they withdrew approximately 150 million in gold from us towards the end of that year. During the opening quarter of 1965, they converted no less than 540 million dollars of their claims into gold. They were followed by other countries, such as Spain, Holland, and Belgium, so that, in all, approximately 1.1 billion dollars was withdrawn within a few months. This largely accounts for the fall in our gold reserves in 1965 which was shown above. President Johnson, therefore, properly asked that the requirement for a twenty-five percent gold reserve on the deposits of member banks in the Federal Reserve system be eliminated. Since the member banks could not have converted their deposits into gold, even if they had wanted to do so, the requirement was completely obsolete. It served no good purpose and actually locked up nearly five billion dollars of gold from being used for the one remaining monetary function of gold, namely, to help ensure the international convertibility of the dollar.

If I may inject a personal reference, I tried to get Congress and the President to go even further and to eliminate the twenty-five-percent gold reserve required for the 35 billion dollars of Federal Reserve notes and thus free nearly another nine billion dollars in gold. Since gold could not be obtained for these notes, it was even more foolish to divert gold from the field of international convertibility into the fiction of a nonexistent domestic convertibility which had, in fact, disappeared over thirty years before. This gold reserve was indeed like the smile of the Cheshire Cat in Alice in Wonderland which lingered on long after the Cheshire Cat itself had disappeared from sight.

But this proposal was thought to be too strong medicine for the public to take. The mystique of gold is such that many otherwise sensible people feel safer if the gold underground at Fort Knox is somehow theoretically ear-marked for them even though they know they will never be able to get their hands on it. There is indeed a striking similarity between all this and the mythology of the Wag-nerian operas, *Das Rheingold* and *Siegfried,* where the gold was also represented as having gone underground.

So a compromise was reached that only the reserve on member bank deposits in the Federal Reserve was to be eliminated by Congress. This did free nearly five billion dollars in gold and removed the immediate danger of our being carried off the gold standard.*

Once having acted in this fashion, there is little doubt that Congress would act similarly in the case of the reserve for the Federal Reserve Notes should such a need arise in the future. The whole gold reserve can therefore be used to maintain the international convertibility of the dollar into gold. Gold will then in law as in fact be reserved for its role as an international currency.

Barring a concerted and malevolent attack by a wide spectrum of foreign governments, private bankers and currency speculators, the American dollar seems at pres-

---

* The Federal Reserve Board was undoubtedly ready to suspend the reserve requirements by a series of temporary rulings. This would have soon involved the imposition of penalties and it was much better for Con-gress to deal directly with the matter. This it did in a very courageous manner.

ent to be secure. Into what currency indeed could these various groups take safer refuge if they sought safety from the dollar? But we probably could not withstand another decade similar to the last for that would draw down our gold reserve to such a very small total as probably to cause us ultimately to go off gold and to devalue the dollar. Our very strength, generosity, and assumption of world responsibility would have been our monetary undoing.

It is important therefore that we either stop the flow or help devise and put into operation an international monetary system which will be more satisfactory than our present international gold exchange system keyed as that is to the dollar and the pound. We shall turn to these subjects in the following chapters.

20

Structural Methods Proposed and Used to Correct Our Balance of Payments

Under the former gold standard, as we have repeatedly stressed, deficits in the balance of payments tended in the long run to be automatically corrected. For the export of gold abroad tended to raise prices there and to lower them here. This encouraged our exports and diminished the volume of imports and of foreign travel by increasing their costs. This process was presumed to go on until a balance was reached or until some new alteration in the equilibrium occurred.

But modern societies do not operate under the automatic movements of the gold standard. We have not only adopted the gold exchange standard for international purposes, which in itself slows down price adjustments, but nearly all countries have, in addition, "managed" or "partially managed" currencies. Under these currencies some central control is exercised by governments and by central banks of the amount of monetary purchasing power which is issued and hence a large degree of control can be exercised over the internal price level. As a result of the experience of the two world wars and of the years which followed, the major governments are now very much afraid of inflation. As a consequence, countries with enduring surpluses in their balance of payments commonly try to prevent these surpluses from increasing the price level and instead try for stable prices.

In a similar fashion, countries with continued deficits in their balance of payments do not want to let an outflow of monetary purchasing power depress their internal prices since this would tend to increase unemployment and shrink profit margins. In other words, both sets of countries by seeking an internal stability in prices, and trying to avoid both increases and decreases, interfere with the self-regulating mechanism of international prices which was formerly relied upon to produce ultimate equilibrium in the balance of payments.

Thus, the countries of Western Europe which in recent years have enjoyed a surplus which has taken the form of added gold and foreign exchange and which in turn has sent up their bank reserves have tried to prevent this from greatly increasing the volume of their created demand deposits. This has had the effect of dampening down the price increases which would otherwise have happened.* While the central bankers in the deficit countries may desire deflation in order to make the price mechanism work, they are restrained in the democracies by the force of public opinion and, in most cases, are willing to settle for comparative stability in prices and the avoidance of inflation. The preceding paragraphs may have given a somewhat

---

* It is ironical that the conservative bankers of the Continent who constantly denounce the United States for not redressing our balance of payments should, by their refusal to allow their own prices to rise freely, be themselves largely responsible for the deficit of which they complain. They seem to be ignorant of or oblivious to the obligations which surplus countries should observe if the monetary "rules of the game" are to be followed.

exaggerated view of the obstacles to international price adjustments. Despite all the barriers imposed by the gold exchange standard and partially managed internal currencies, some forces making for at least partial adjustments are still at work below the surface. When a "surplus" nation, such as Germany, France, or the smaller countries of Western Europe, acquires a large amount of gold or foreign exchange, this may not lead to an immediate or proportionate increase in the volume of bank loans and bank credit. But it will ultimately tend to create some expansion in credit and in prices. In other words, the potential credit will sooner or later be put to work in at least a partial degree. Similarly, the export of gold from countries with an adverse balance of payments will tend to have an ultimate restraining influence on the amount of credit and consequently upon the price level.

Even with partially managed currencies, therefore, price levels will not be completely impervious to gold transfers. Thus, since 1957–1959, wholesale prices in Germany have risen by eight percent, in Britain by twelve percent, in the Scandinavian countries by between ten and thirteen percent, and in France by no less than thirty-two percent, while in the United States they had increased by only three and a half percent up until the summer of 1965. These price movements were beginning to tilt the balance of trade in our favor, although recently our price levels have been rising more rapidly.

Moreover, the export of our capital abroad lowers the margin of profitability there and, consequently, reduces the rate of return on private investment. This diminishes the incentive to invest further amounts abroad and reduces the annual increment of new capital which will be sent there. At the same time, the increase in the total investments abroad will result in an increased total of interest and profits received. This will in part be transferred back to the United States and, hence, will operate as an added force to redress the balance of payments.

From a combination of all these factors, the authors of a Brookings Institution study predicted in 1963 that not only would the balance of payments improve but that it would come into balance in five years or by around 1968.* But this prediction could be vitiated, as the authors realized, if the military and international situation requires us to spend more money abroad than was then contemplated. The military situation in Vietnam and Southeast Asia does not encourage optimistic hopes. Indeed our adverse balance of payments may increase and France, through its control of the Bank of Indochina, may come into increasing possession of our foreign exchange and hence of our gold.

With the former price mechanisms greatly impeded, we have been forced to adopt structural methods for reducing our adverse balance. Other nations with a deficit in payments have felt compelled to use similar methods. Indeed, surplus countries desiring to increase their payment surpluses still further and hence to increase their stock of gold and foreign exchange, have themselves used artificial means to improve their exchange position still further.

We have not adopted the once common device of increasing tariffs and paying bounties on exports. It is to our credit that we have instead sought to increase international trade, confident that on the whole our competitive efficiency would permit us to compete satisfactorily in a free market. To be sure, there have been minor departures from this general policy. Such have been the restrictions upon the importation of carpets and glass from Holland and Belgium, of cheap beef from Australia, oil from Vene-

* Salant, Walter S., Despres, Emil, and others. *The United States Balance of Payments in 1968,* The Brookings Institution, 1963.

zuela,* and textiles from Japan and Hong Kong where wages are extremely low. But these barriers have been relatively slight in comparison with the export bounties and covert forms of discrimination practiced by many other nations.

Perhaps the most important development has been in the field of labor costs. During the years from 1957 to 1959, labor costs per unit of output apparently did increase and, to this degree, were an impediment to a further expansion of exports. Since European labor on the other hand had held back during the preceding decade from obtaining appreciable wage increases, although output per man hour was rising steadily, this gave Western Europe a further advantage over us.

From 1960 on, however, wage increases for production workers in American manufacturing did not exceed the increase in hourly output and, as a consequence, labor costs per unit of output did not rise and may indeed have fallen slightly.† In the countries of Western Europe, on the other hand, money wages, so long repressed, turned sharply upwards and rose by more than the increase in output.** The increase in unit labor costs in West Germany was between twenty and thirty percent; in France for all employees by over twenty percent; in Italy nearly thirty

* The quota on residual fuels has, however, recently been cancelled.

† Mark, Jerome, and Kahn, Elizabeth, "Recent Unit Cost Trends in U.S. Manufacturing," *Monthly Labor Review*, September 1965, pp. 1956–1960. This index shows a decrease from 1959 to 1964 of one percent in unit labor costs for production workers as a whole. The total earnings of the nonproduction workers, however, went up slightly more rapidly than output. There is, therefore, some question as to whether the managerial decisions increasing the numbers and pay of the clerical, technical and submanagerial staff has been justified from the standpoint of immediate productivity.

** Chandler, John H., and Jackson, Patrick C., "Cost Trends in Nine Industrial Nations," *Monthly Labor Review*, Op. cit., pp. 1064–1066.

percent for production workers; in Sweden by eight percent and in the United Kingdom by six percent. The Netherlands had an increase of twenty-nine percent and Japan of approximately eleven percent. Canada was the only foreign country to show a decrease in unit labor costs, amounting to nine percent for production workers. *

This comparative stability of American labor costs in the face of European increases naturally improved our trading position, and this showed up with especial force from 1963 on, when the surplus in trade increased from 4.4 billion dollars in 1962 to 6.7 billion in 1964. There was, however, a slight decrease in 1965.

Precisely what share of the credit for this development should be ascribed to labor, employers, the general public and government is, of course, impossible to estimate. But it is probable that the guide lines suggested by the government, namely, that as a general rule increases in hourly rates and earnings should not exceed the corresponding increase in productivity played at least an appreciable part in the final result.

Without diminishing the number or combat effectiveness of our forces overseas, and indeed while actually increasing both, we succeeded in reducing the expenditures abroad for each unit of men and equipment. There are fewer dependents assigned overseas now than in 1957. Moreover, a still larger proportion of the supplies for our troops are being purchased and shipped from the United States rather than being bought abroad. This has increased the total costs but has saved several hundred million dollars a year in foreign exchange.

* In all foreign countries, as in the United States, the relative increase in money payments to the nonproduction staff exceeded that for the production workers, and the increase in their costs per unit of output was greater than for the manual workers.

We have also greatly reduced the very generous amounts of duty-free purchases which we had formerly permitted returning tourists to bring in. While foreign countries had imposed either rigorous limits or had permitted none at all, we had allowed no less than 500 dollars a person. In 1961, this was reduced to 100 dollars. This saved about 100 million dollars a year in foreign exchange. Finally, in 1965, this was still further reduced over the protests of the tourist industry by computing prices in retail rather than wholesale terms. It is expected that this will save an additional 50 to 100 million dollars in foreign exchange.

Our government has also tried to stimulate foreign tourists to travel in the United States and to do so has set up promotion and service bureaus both abroad and at home. This has increased the receipts from foreign travelers, but not as rapidly as expenditures by American travelers abroad. The exchange loss on travel rose in 1965 by 200 million dollars from 1.6 to 1.8 billions of dollars. About all that can be said is that the deficit in payments would have been greater without these efforts.

These measures began to produce an effect in 1961 when the deficit in "liquidity" terms fell from 3.9 to 2.4 billion dollars. In 1962, it fell slightly to 2.2 billions rising however to 2.7 billions in 1963. This was largely caused by increased investments abroad of all the varieties previously described. The differential in the open market between the yields on long-term investments abroad and at home was approximately one percent. To eliminate this differential in the summer of 1963, the administration asked for an interest equalization tax of one percent on the yield of foreign securities bought in the United States. The Canadians who had previously protested at the way the inflow of American capital was

Americanizing their country, now protested even more loudly that this would reduce their growth rate and decrease their Gross National Product. Out of consideration for them, Canada was then, by administrative discretion, exempted from the application of the act as were the undeveloped countries. But, despite the protests of Japan, this privilege was not granted to her nor was it to the countries of Europe.

While the law was not passed until the late summer of 1964, it was made retroactive to July 1 of the previous year. In the meantime, it had exercised a restraining effect on the types of transactions covered. But there were other sources of leakage and the total effect was to increase the total deficit slightly in 1963 and 1964. While the bill was being considered by the Senate Finance Committee in 1964, the alert eye of Senator Albert Gore caught the omission of short-time bank loans from the terms of the act. Pointing out these very loans had been and were being made in large quantities to Japanese and Canadian banks and were then used by them to finance domestic expansion on much longer terms of credit, Senator Gore and I argued for their inclusion in the act. The Treasury at first opposed this proposal but opinion inside the Finance Committee and the Senate itself finally forced the Treasury to agree to a compromise. Under this, the President was given discretionary powers to impose such a tax on bank loans should he deem it desirable. Senator Gore's fears proved to be well founded. There was a big increase in these loans in the closing months of 1964 and the opening weeks of 1965. The President, therefore, took advantage of his discretionary powers and imposed such a tax.

But, as we have seen, the main source of foreign investments were the direct capital outlays by American corporations in their foreign branches, subsidiaries, and affiliates. These investments had not been touched by the tax differential law and actually rose from 1.9 billion dollars in 1963 to 2.3 billion in 1964. They continued to be exceedingly high in the opening weeks of 1965. All forms of investments abroad increased by over two billion dollars in 1964 over 1963. When President Johnson applied the Gore Amendment to short-term bank loans, he made a simultaneous appeal to the heads of several hundred American corporations to dampen down their future investments abroad. He declared that he sought the voluntary co-operation of American business in obtaining this objective and neither wished nor intended any mandatory government action. The immediate response of the business leaders was very favorable and promises of co-operation were freely and fully made.

It is probably still too early to determine what the long-term results will be of these developments in the field of foreign investment. Short-term bank loans were decreased in 1965, but while direct investments by American corporations decreased in the second quarter below the high level of the first quarter, they were still planned by business at a very high level for 1965 as a whole. There was a natural desire on the part of large American concerns to get inside the tariff walls of the countries in the Common Market and in EFTA. Indeed, the experts of the Department of Commerce reported in the fall of 1965 "the total capital outflow to foreign branches and subsidiaries during the first half of the year thus exceeded two billion dollars, not much less than the 2.4 billion-dollar outflow for all of 1964." * Although Secretary Connor in middle November

---

* Lederer, Walther, and Parrish, Evelyn M., "The Balance of Payments, Second Quarter of 1965." *Survey of Current Business*, September 1965, p. 21.

reaffirmed this statement, he also declared again that he had full faith in the program of voluntary co-operation and that the administration had no intention of abandoning it. He did say, however, that it was planned to make the guide lines for 1966 more definite and to try to work them out for individual corporations as well as for groups. Taking 1965 as a whole direct investment increased by nearly a billion dollars or from 2.4 to over 3 billion dollars. This could not be said to be a srtiking success.

There is no doubt that a reduction in the rate of current investment abroad would have an immediate beneficial effect on the current balance of payments even though its ultimate effect would be to diminish the reverse flow of income from earnings, interest and dividends. When these considerations are joined to the fact that such artificial restrictions mean a smaller return to American investors, banks and corporations, we are probably safe in predicting rising opposition on the part of large sections of the business and financial community to a long-time continuance of the use of voluntary restraints and a still deeper opposition to the imposition of mandatory controls. How this conflict of purposes and interests will turn out, no man can tell.

The Treasury has also developed several ingenious methods for reducing the outward flow of capital. One device has been to encourage the development of more adequate capital markets abroad. Continental Europe and Latin America have lagged behind the United States and Great Britain in developing these financial centers where savings and investment can be brought together. As these markets have begun to take more definite form, American companies with foreign branches and subsidiaries have been encouraged to raise a larger proportion of their needed overseas capital from the countries in which they have been doing business in order to reduce our own export of capital. This has coincided with the rising nationalistic tendencies which have wanted to have a larger share in the ownership and direction of these enterprises. The nationals in these countries prefer to have these investments made in the form of stock purchases, which have voting and directive powers, while the companies themselves do not want to have this carried so far as to threaten their control and prefer to have the domestic investment contain as large a mixture as possible of nonvoting bonds, which will also be safer because of their prior claim on earnings.

Another ingenious device developed by Undersecretary Roosa were the so-called "swap" arangements in which we and certain European countries simultaneously purchased each other's currencies. By the end of 1963, we had thus obtained approximately two billion dollars of foreign currency including 500 million dollars from the Bank of England. Then when claims against the dollar were made by nationals of a given country, they would be paid off in their own currencies. This postponed the shipment of gold and hence avoided immediate trouble although, ultimately, the debts would still have to be paid.

There has also been an effort to induce European investors to put their money into long-term instead of short-term American obligations. For this would decrease our vulnerability to sudden withdrawals of foreign loans and the consequent demands for their immediate conversion into gold. By the end of 1963, approximately 300 million dollars of medium-term government bonds were sold abroad which were non-marketable for from fifteen to twenty-four months.

Finally, there has been the much disputed question of whether American interest rates should be raised to induce American investors, especially those who tend to put their capital in short-time investments, to invest at home rather than abroad. There is no doubt that European interest rates are higher than ours, although the difference is less than sometimes appears on the surface. Part of the excess is in many cases compensation for extra risk. Differences in the rediscount rates which are sometimes used as a basis for comparison are highly unreliable. Thus when the Federal Reserve rediscount rate was four percent and the British six percent, the real difference was much less since our rate was below the rate charged the so-called prime borrowers while the British rate was above. There are, moreover, arbitrage charges on the shifting from one currency into another and there is always the impalpable but real factor of risk and possible currency devaluations. It is probable that real interest rates are on an approximate equality as between the United States and Canada but that there is a differential as between ourselves and Western Europe.

The bankers and financial interests would like to eliminate this differential by raising our rates to an equality with those of Europe and to effect this through Federal Reserve policy in restricting the growth of the money supply. I personally believe that this is also the desire of Chairman Martin of the Federal Reserve Board and his followers. This is also the remedy which the European bankers and the "gnomes of Zurich" would like to have us utilize. While there is a great deal of obvious self-interest in this position, the arguments in its favor deserve to be stated and considered.

First, it is argued that the continuing tendency of modern capitalism is towards ever more perfect markets within which there is an equality of price and that this should be as true of the money as of the commodity markets. It is moreover pointed out that there will be a gain in utility as measured in money terms by transferring capital from areas where, because of its lower price, it apparently meets less pressing needs than where its rates of return are higher. This is really more of an argument for the free flow of capital between countries than for artificially raising American interest rates by governmental policy. For, on this basis, such an increase could only be justified on the basis that it would choke off investments of low utility in this country and accumulate a stock of savings which would have no place to go unless the foreign countries, by special concessions, took them in.

The second argument is keyed directly to the balance of payments. It is contended that the raising of our interest rates would reduce the flow of our investments abroad whether these were short-term or long-term and start a reverse flow of capital back to the United States. Thus, Chairman Martin, in justifying the increase in the rediscount rate from four to four and a half percent which he put through in early December, 1965, by a four to three vote of the Governors of the Reserve Board, stated that one of the reasons for his action was to improve the balance of payments position of the United States.

Such views, however, disregard the essential fact that money and bank credit is not like other commodities and cannot properly be treated as identical with them. For it is the medium of exchange and the instrument through which the general system of prices, costs, and rates of return is measured and, to some degree, influenced. A rise in our interest rates would make business more costly and hence would tend to dampen down the demand for short- and long-term loans and, consequently, of the amount demanded of raw materials and of semi-finished and finished goods. This would create unemployment and result

in reduced incomes for those formerly employed. They
would be compelled to buy less and this would bring into
play the familiar cumulative forces of economic breakdown involving the ever-widening destruction of monetary
purchasing power, the decrease in demand and the increase in unemployment.

Is not all this more important, it is argued, than merely
inducing some liquid capital to be shifted here from
abroad? Our economy is now approaching an annual rate
of production of over 700 billion dollars, while the
volume of mobile money which moves back and forth
across national boundaries at the behest of the currency
speculators is estimated at no more than two billion dollars and may indeed be less. Thus, a five percent reduction
in our Gross National Product would mean a loss of
35 billion dollars of goods and services which would far
outweigh any bad effects upon the balance of payments
from a speculative shifting of deposits. As a matter of fact,
these might well be frightened away from us by a recession.
It is indeed curious how many money managers are blind
to these comparative effects which would also affect them
and seem instead to be chiefly interested in the activities
of some of the least estimable of men, namely, the speculators in money and foreign exchange. Perhaps, like so
many others, they may have fallen prey to the shibboleths
which underlie all activities and which frequently prevent
men from obtaining a balanced view of realities.

The advocates of such a policy of raising interest rates
by governmental action tend, moreover, to ignore the
possibility that the banking officials of other countries will
be moved by the same motives as ours and will also try to
attract back to their nations the mobile capital which has
left them for us and to do so by raising their interest rates.
There is, in fact, good ground to suspect that one reason

why European bankers are so insistent that we raise our interest rates is that they know that this would give them a good excuse for raising theirs. In the last two years, as the Federal Reserve has successively raised its rediscount rate from three to four and half percent, a close study of European rates does not however indicate any close or immediate response from Europe although there may well be a delayed reaction. If such a competitive increase in interest rates occurred, it would of course leave us in no better position in terms of foreign exchange and could lead to a world-wide contraction of demand, production, and employment.

The dispute between these theories is still raging in this country and no one can predict how it will turn out. Perhaps there would be some advance in public discussion and wise eventual action if each side would consider more carefully the arguments of the other. This would at once reduce the heat of the discussion and add to its light.*

The deficits in our balance of payments have also exercised a restraining influence upon both our economic and

---

* Of course, the conflict over increases in the interest rates does not hinge solely on their effect on the balance of payments. The question of inflation as compared with a possible recession is also involved. Mr. Martin believed that our economy was approximately at full employment and maximum utilization of the factors of production and that an appreciable expansion of credit would inflate prices and pave the way for a speculative fever which would lead to an ultimate depression. Those who take an opposite point of view say that with nearly four percent unemployment and with nine percent of fixed capital idle, there is still an unutilized surplus of idle labor that can be put to work with idle capital turning out goods that otherwise would not be produced. The growing efficiency of government financed training methods and the possibility of a greater use of second shifts would seem to make possible a moderate further expansion without an appreciable increase in prices. There was some merit in the statement of J. L. Robertson, a dissenting director of the Federal Reserve, that Chairman Martin and his followers were "afraid of prosperity."

military aid to other countries. The first defensive measure which we took was to substitute to an increasing degree loans for grants. While initially the low interest rates of one-quarter of one percent made the difference between the two much less than it seemed on the surface, this was later raised to two and a half percent after ten years. But the requirement for ultimate repayment as well as the interest rate not only made for greater self respect among the recipient countries, but also somewhat dampened down the volume of applications.

The State Department has, however, refused to terminate or appreciably reduce aid to Egypt, India, and Pakistan despite their hostile words and acts. This is more than justified to the degree that such aid is necessary to save millions of people from starvation, although it is proper to require in return steps to help these countries raise more food through the production of more chemical fertilizer, and so on. But it is humanly hard to continue to give such help under the continuous revilement which is heaped upon us as when Mr. Krishna Menon denounced our gifts of food, which is saving millions of his fellow countrymen from starvation, as arrogant, "immoral" and unjustified. Some improvement in the Indian attitude has been evident lately as the magnitude of their impending famine has dawned upon them. Certainly we should and will give of our surplus to prevent wide-spread starvation. The recent military revolt against the Indonesian Communists moreover gives us some hope for a change in policy by that country.

As we have indicated, the degree to which we can reduce our military expenditures and aid abroad hinges on the future of our relationships with the Communist world. At the moment, the outlook is unfavorable. The war in Vietnam and the troubled situation in Southeast Asia will almost certainly require the annual expenditure of additional billions of dollars. About 12 billion dollars a year is now being budgeted for this purpose. A considerable fraction of this will inevitably result in eventual claims on the dollar. The deficit in our balance of payments, therefore, threatens both to increase and to continue for a long period to come. While this is far less to be feared by free people than an increase in Communist domination over the world, it is still something to be reduced wherever possible.

While our gold reserves are sufficiently strong to meet ordinary demands for a considerable time to come, they might be put in real jeopardy should some powerful country in the Free World stage a determined effort to strip us of our free gold and if it were successful in getting private investors and other countries to join them. At present, such a danger can only come from France which has already shown signs of adopting such a policy, under the guise of returning to the pure gold standard.

Up to now we have followed the policy of disregarding the possibility of such demands being caused by hostile motives. We have met the French demands for gold without protest or reproach. For under the gold exchange standard, creditor countries are legally entitled to ask for gold in return for their short-term claims on dollar exchange. So were the holders of bank notes and currency in the days when the dollar was internally convertible into gold. But those who in periods of stress took full advantage of their legal rights, put the public safety in danger. And so it may be that certain nations will imperil world stability. Perhaps a full answer to these hazards must wait upon the development of an adequate international monetary system. But there are defensive steps which we can

take, in the meantime, under existing rules of the game
to protect ourselves from any monetary raids by De Gaulle
and the Bank of France. Thus I urged in early 1965 that
we could reduce our dollar expenditures for the support of
troops stationed in France to help protect that country.
In 1964, we spent 231 million dollars in this fashion and
this claim could be reduced by moving many of our command and military installations either to West Germany
or to Holland and Belgium. The French attitude towards
NATO will indeed force us to do precisely this. As we
withdraw, however, we should ask for adequate compensation for American owned housing and military installations left behind. Similarly, we can cut down on or even
eliminate our aid to former French possessions in Africa
which still have their finances handled in Paris. In 1964,
we spent nearly 200 million dollars on these territories,
but there would seem to be no good reason why we should
assume so much responsibility for these countries for
which, with one or two exceptions, it would only be proper
for France itself to bear the financial liability.*

We now spend approximately 50 million dollars a year
for transportation on French vessels and airlines. We can
reluctantly but quietly shift our government transportation of persons and things either to our own ships and
airlines or to those of more friendly and co-operative
countries. Without initiating any public boycott, American tourist agencies can be quietly encouraged to book
their clients on other lines. American tourists, who spent
approximately 120 million dollars in 1963 in France itself,
can also be encouraged either to travel at home or to
substitute the Caribbean, Italy, and Greece. All of these

* The State Department refuses to consider such a step and have
turned down the suggestions which I have made in this direction. It is
still obviously hoping for a change of heart by France.

items total together approximately 600 million dollars a year. In addition, we should eliminate the drain resulting from the activities of the French Bank of Indochina in Southeast Asia. If we can cut all these to the bone, we can eliminate our unfavorable balance of payments with France and possibly even turn it into a net favorable balance. If the latter, it would only be proper if we in turn then ask France to make her payment in gold.

It is greatly to be hoped that these possibilities may impress President de Gaulle and cause him to be less disruptive in his financial tactics. We should welcome any change in the basic trade and financial policies of France whether under President de Gaulle himself or a more international-minded successor. But we cannot wait much longer. And President de Gaulle's re-election in December of 1965, even with a greatly reduced majority, diminishes our hopes for such a happy result. Only a change of policy by that strange and self-assured man can avert a further break-up in the Free World. But this is scarcely to be hoped in view of his withdrawal from NATO and his demand that our protective forces leave French soil.

As Chairman of the Joint Economic Committee, I discovered in 1963 that the ocean shipping rates were much higher on our exports than on our imports even on the same goods on the same ships plying between the same ports. This was true on virtually every basis of comparison for both Atlantic and Pacific shipping. It was also true on goods shipped to third countries such as those of Latin America. For in these cases the shipping rates were much lower per ton mile on goods coming from foreign ports than from ours.

All this naturally tended to restrict our exports and increase our imports. Perhaps the basic reason for this discrimination is the fact that most shipping rates are fixed by international shipping conferences in which the American lines are in a small minority and yet are bound by the decisions of the cartels. For a long time, in fact until the investigations of the Joint Economic Committee, the Maritime Administration actually served as an indirect enforcing agency for these decisions by its policy of withholding subsidies from American lines that declined to adhere to conference regulations and rates.

It has been very difficult to break up these discrimination practices since the shipping lines are at once powerful and cohesive. Moreover, Great Britain and other foreign governments have refused to authorize inspection by the Federal Maritime Commission (the U.S. regulatory authority) of records and documents relating to rates on American commerce carried from foreign ports. This is exactly the type of supervision required by Congress of shipping conferences as a condition for their immunity from domestic antitrust laws. Until recently, the Maritime Commission did not even try to exercise such supervision. In the last two years, under prodding from the Joint Economic Committee and under fresh and able leadership, it has pushed in this direction even though denied the right of inspection. The British-based conferences have partially co-operated by furnishing summaries which, in the main, bear out our contentions. But it is still uncertain whether in practice remedial action can be obtained and the rates on American exports reduced. This would certainly be one step in reducing our unfavorable balance of payments. But the European nations seem determined to maintain these discriminations in order to improve their balance of payments and under the protective covering of national sovereignty may be able to perpetuate them.

The capacity of the conferences to discriminate against

American exports is also increased by certain pooling arrangements providing for a sharing of profits. Where such arrangements exist, and they are apparently quite general, competitive forces, already greatly reduced by conference price practices, are altogether eliminated. Before the investigations of the Joint Economic Committee, pooling agreements were approved as a routine matter whenever the participating lines requested it. I take satisfaction in having helped to bring about a reversal of this policy, along with new administrators in the Department of Commerce and new leadership in the Maritime Commission and in the military shipping authority. Today pools are not permitted unless the participating lines can establish that their proposed arrangement is in the public interest. This imposes a heavy yet proper burden of proof on the lines which none as yet have been able to meet. Moreover, most of the pools previously approved are being re-examined to determine whether they are in fact in the public interest.

If we are able to eliminate the deficit in our balance of payments or even keep it down to not far from a billion dollars a year, we will probably be able to keep our exchange problems within manageable limits. If we become deeply involved in a world struggle with Chinese or Russian communism, then such issues will be very minor in comparison with the ultimate safety of this nation and the preservation of freedom in the world.

But, if peace, however uneasy, were to continue and the deficit were once again, despite all our efforts, to mount to between two and three billions of dollars yearly, then we and the Western World would be forced to make some hard decisions.

There is undoubtedly waste in both our foreign aid and our overseas military establishments. If detected, this could be eliminated without any loss of efficiency. But some waste seems inevitable in every large undertaking, whether it be public or private, and it is doubtful whether the unfavorable balance could be reduced in this way by more than a few hundred million dollars. The hard choice of whether we should effect a severe cut would still remain.

I do not rule out the possibility that this may become necessary. But it would have such grave international consequences that it should not be decided upon either lightly or prematurely. It might mean in many sections of the world, notably, Asia, Africa, and Latin America, that communism would take over, either by outright military conquest or through a collapse of the present government. This would probably mean an increasing alliance between the Eastern European or Chinese Communists and the peoples with darker skins which would marshal over two billion people against those of North America and Western Europe. The future of the world under these conditions and tensions would be an unhappy one.

It would, therefore, seem both wise and prudent to use every effort to prevent this from happening. But this is not a responsibility for the United States alone but for Western Europe, as well.

If Europe, for example, would permit us to furnish them with more farm products, such as wheat, meat and soybeans, and so forth, with which we could pay for more of our military expenses abroad, that would help. But, at present, there is little evidence that this will be done. On the contrary, the tendencies are all in the opposite direction.

The situation would also be eased if France and Germany would permit their price levels to rise more rapidly. For this would promote a further increase in our exports and a decrease in our imports. This would happen under the old gold standard. If this standard is partially replaced by a system of managed currencies, then to make the new system work, the monetary authorities of the various countries must carry out certain implicit rules of the game. As we have repeatedly insisted, the countries with surpluses in their payment accounts must be prepared sooner or later to allow their price levels to rise, while countries with deficits must prevent general price increases, so that the deficit countries may be brought into balance by an increase in their exports and a slowing down of their imports. But the European nations, having twice experienced the terrors of inflation and being anxious to build up big reserves of gold and foreign exchange, are very reluctant to permit even a modest adjustment of international prices. When their prices do rise, they tend to speak of it as "imported inflation" and imply that we are ultimately responsible.

There are at least three other ways in which the European nations could co-operate in what, after all, should be a common responsibility. That would be to assume a greater financial share in the defense of the Free World in order to take some of the burden of foreign aid from our shoulders, and, second, to add at least the French franc and the German mark to the dollar and pound as the key currencies with which gold can be supplemented as an international medium of exchange. Or in the third place, they could depend more on fiscal policy by raising taxes and less on monetary policy by raising interest rates. This would tend to lower the interest rates in Europe relative to those in the United States thus contributing to a reduction in the movement of capital from the United States to Europe.

That we are bearing an undue share of the defense burden of the Free World is evidenced by the following statistics on the comparative number of men under arms and the proportion which our military expenditures form of the Gross National Product and of the total national governmental budget. Even after making allowances for our higher level of material prosperity and for the fact that European budgets furnish a larger proportion of the cost of local government than ours, the disparity is striking. I believe our friends in Australia and New Zealand should consider whether they should not bear a larger share in the war in Vietnam than the few troops they are contributing. And should Great Britain and France allow their traders to provision and supply the North Vietnamese? These are questions to which the consciences of these nations should respond.

The record is somewhat similar in the field of foreign aid. Great Britain and France confine their aid almost entirely to their former colonies which they wish to keep affiliated with them in a common monetary and economic system. Germany provides its aid in the form of loans at high interest rates netting them an average of more than four percent. We, on the other hand, are still making at least forty-five percent of our foreign aid in the form of outright grants to countries which are not our possessions and which we do not intend to acquire, while most of the so-called loans are at extremely low interest rates for long periods of time. Thus, for several years our loans were only at three-fourths of one percent a year for forty years. Recently, at the instance of Congress, they have been raised to one percent for the first ten years, and then to two and one-half percent for the next thirty years. This is in sharp contrast with German and French practice.

As long as Great Britain is undergoing her present difficulties, it would seem improper to ask her to step up her overseas obligations, although it is to be hoped that she will not curtail them. But, if France and Germany could

Comparative Share of Military Expenditures Since 1964

Country	Calendar 1964 Number of Men in Service Per 1,000 of Population	Calendar 1964 Per 1,000 Males 15-49 Years	Calendar 1964 As Percentage of Gross National Product (GNP)	Calendar or Fiscal Year 1964 or 1965. As Percentage of Total. Central Government Expenditures	
United States	13.9	62.5	8.3	52.3	FY '65
Great Britain	8.3	36.0	6.2	22.8	FY '65
France	12.0	53.7	5.5	24.7	Cal. '64
West Germany	7.2	32.4	5.0	35.6	Cal. '64
Italy	7.5	29.9	3.6	18.4	FY '64
Belgium	11.2	49.7	3.2	14.6	Cal. '64
Holland	10.0	40.8	4.5	16.9	Cal. '64
Sweden	9.2	38.1	4.7	18.1	FY '65
Norway	9.2	39.0	3.6	16.8	Cal. '64
Denmark	9.6	42.1	2.8	12.9	FY '65
Canada	6.1	26.3	3.9	24.3	FY '65
Australia	4.8	19.8	3.0	11.8	FY '64

Source: Department of Defense and A.I.D.

be induced to recognize a greater degree of economic responsibility for the backward countries which were not formerly affiliated with them, the situation would be greatly eased.

Furthermore, if the smaller countries among the democracies would also take on some of the burdens of foreign and military assistance instead of enjoying a comparatively free ride at the expense of the stronger powers, and notably of ourselves, it would be a real contribution to international good will and stability.

It is one thing to hope and to ask for such international co-operation, but it is far more difficult to obtain it. Thus far, despite our quietly polite pleas for a greater assumption of the burden by our allies, their response has been largely negative.

Should this attitude continue, we in the United States will be faced with a grave decision as to whether we can continue to bear so large a share of the world's burdens. Our own security and that of the Free World, joined with the ethical duty which the fortunate and prosperous owe to the poor and deprived, may come into conflict with the rigors of international finance. Since monetary and financial systems should be the servants and not the masters of nations, it is appropriate to inquire whether improvements cannot be made in the system of international payments which will permit both us and other nations a broader range of choice.

The tenets and spirit of mercantilism are still so strong in the modern world that governments, for reasons of prestige and internal politics, inevitably seek to obtain a surplus in their balance of payments. They also desire to accumulate as much of the international currency as possible as a reserve against possible contingencies and, like the medieval monarchs, as an aid in time of war. But it is clearly impossible for all countries to have such a surplus, since for every sale there must be a purchase and for every claim an obligation. It is no more possible for every nation to show such a surplus than it is for every college football team to win all its games. Just as every victory carries with it another's defeat, so does the surplus of one nation require that others must show deficits.*

This proved to be a hard lesson for nations to learn as they emerged from medievalism. It seems to be almost as hard for them to learn it today. For nations are still primarily self-centered and feel that they are living in the midst of a world of competing rivals which seek not only absolute but comparative power and prestige. While, ultimately, each will benefit as all go forward, it is still true that, as in private life, one country can gain a differential advantage over others. And it is indeed all too easy for a nation to adopt such a policy instead of trying to work out a rational solution which will permit the fundamental advantages of the international division of labor to operate.

Thus, when a nation pays an export bonus to stimulate sales abroad, it not only makes a present to its foreign purchasers, but it also reduces the reserves of the importing countries. And when it raises the tariffs on imported goods, it not only increases the cost of living to its own citizens and reduces its own ultimate ability to export, but it also improves its own immediate position so far as its reserves

---

* It is almost equally impossible for every nation to effect a precise balance at all times. There are bound to be temporary surpluses and deficits if for no other reason than capital exports and return payments of interest, et cetera.

are concerned. In so doing, it obtains an immediate financial advantage over other countries even though it weakens the absolute and comparative prosperity of its citizens.

Faced with such practices, it is hard for other countries which do not resort to these methods not to follow suit. Just as unilateral disarmament in the face of a determined and relatively implacable foe is an unwise and impossible policy for a nation to follow, so quietude in the face of trade discriminations and refusals to co-operate is impracticable for any protracted period.

Ultimately, virtually every nation will be forced to retaliate in kind. There are just not enough saints to enable a nation to follow for a long time the other course of returning good for evil. And, in so doing, the policy of seeking security by "beggaring one's neighbor" will be universalized to the ultimate detriment of all. This is why proposals, such as the mutual reduction of tariffs, as evidenced in our negotiations within GATT as well as those with the Common Market, are efforts in practical and constructive statesmanship as are efforts to obtain guarded and properly inspected mutual disarmament. The chances for success within the Free World on trade and international finances have indeed a much greater chance of success than those with the Communist world because there is a common basic interest instead of the basic hostility to the Free World to which China and Russia seem to be pledged.

Thus far, with certain exceptions such as the imposition of import quotas on oil, lead, zinc and textiles, we have in the main followed the path of seeking international co-operation. Should our efforts in these lines fail and our reserves be drawn down excessively low, we may be forced by circumstances to adopt in reprisal similar methods of self-defense. There is, therefore, not much time for the Free World to lose in developing more effective methods of co-operation in the fields of both trade and an international currency.

Sometimes critics also charge that the efforts of various nations to promote tourism in their countries and to sell more of their products abroad are mutually cancelling on the ground that one nation gains, another loses. But this would only be true if the total quantity of goods to be produced and demanded was of a fixed quantity and an equal quality. To this degree and to this degree only do such promotional efforts cancel out and, even then, one nation could not safely forego them.

But such efforts can stimulate worthwhile new wants and hence increase the psychic income of a people. It can and commonly does also put pressure upon rival producers to improve quality and reduce costs. Thus, the desire to attract tourists has had some effect in improving the quality of British cooking and the amiability of French innkeepers and their entourage. To the degree that this is so, it has not only given more pleasure to the tourists, but has increased the amenities for the British and French themselves. Similarly, our attempt to draw foreign tourists has forced us to develop less expensive and more considerate accommodations.

There has been a similar pressure to cut costs and improve quality in the fields of both capital and consumer goods. The reduction in costs is ultimately reflected in a decrease in price and consequently an increase in the amounts demanded and produced. That this force spreads has been evidenced by the way that the virginal developments in Austria of the basic oxygen process and continuous casting in steel production have been adopted on most of the Continent and are forcing similar improvements here. The constructive elements in the promotion of exports and of tourism and in the competitive system can therefore be made to outweigh any mutually cancelling effects. In any event, any nation in the modern world cannot properly forego them. On the whole, the decrease in the deficit in our balance of payments to 1.3 billion dollars in 1965, shows that these structural measures have effected a temporary improvement. Whether they can be relied upon permanently is uncertain. If military expenditures abroad rise sharply it will be difficult to keep our deficit down and an added burden will be imposed upon us. One wishes that other countries would assume more of the burden of defending and aiding the world. But it is much easier for them to save their money and energies by not acting and then to enjoy the pleasure of criticizing us for being so active.

21

Two Rejected Proposals—
Devaluation and
Floating Exchange Rates

We have not discussed thus far two proposed changes in the international monetary system; namely, a return to the pure gold standard and the adoption of freely fluctuating instead of stable exchange rates. Neither of these proposals finds much favor in either the financial or banking worlds and neither will probably be put into effect in either the immediate or intermediate future. Because of their intrinsic importance, however, they deserve to be considered and weighed by the general public.

One of the few advocates of returning to the former international gold standard is the able French economist, Jacques Rueff,* whose theories seemed at one time to have the support of President de Gaulle and may still.

Dr. Rueff has been attacking the gold exchange standard for over thirty years and has centered his criticism upon the charge that it has a built-in bias towards inflation. He points out that the credits, which countries with surpluses in their payments have on deposit with the "key currency" countries with a deficit, are counted as part of their

---

* See his collection of essays, *The Age of Inflation*, Regnery, 1964.

legal reserves and, hence, enable them to expand their own circulating medium by creating further bank deposits. But these very credits in the key currency countries are also invested in government or private indebtedness. Credit is thus built upon credit in both the surplus and deficit countries with the inevitable result, according to Rueff, that severe inflation results during the period when the foreign exchange holdings are increasing. But when the financial resources are overextended, as in 1929, the nations then try to exchange their holdings of key currencies for gold, and deflation not only sets in but is accentuated by the shrinkage in reserves. Thus, Rueff blames the gold exchange standard for the Great Depression of the 1930's and predicts that we will experience a similar catastrophe in the relatively near future unless we eliminate this surplus element of foreign exchange in the international monetary system and return to the old gold standard for international transactions.

Rueff has been an intimate financial adviser to President de Gaulle and, in January, 1965, the latter announced his support of the Rueff policy. To help carry out such a program, France almost immediately converted 150 million of its dollar holdings into gold and followed this up with additional conversions of 332 million dollars in March. The stated program was to convert into gold all additional dollars which came into French hands, which was estimated at around 500 million dollars a year, but also gradually to reduce the some billion dollars of U.S. foreign exchange held by the French government and the Bank of France. Eventually, Rueff apparently hopes that the some 25 billion dollars of claims on the dollar and pound would be paid off in gold until the international currency would again consist entirely of gold—at present valued at 41 billion dollars.

Such a shrinkage of approximately thirty-five percent in the total volume of international currency would almost inevitably create a sharp fall in prices and probably a world depression. This would be still further intensified if the advocates of a further return to the internal gold bullion standard were to have their way. For this would mean making all the internal currency and checkbook money ultimately convertible into gold. The 40 billion dollars of monetary gold in the world would not be sufficient to support the heavy superstructure of three hundred billion dollars of bank credit and paper currency. It would seem inevitable that prices in this situation would fall further and that the consequent depression would be still further intensified.

To all this, the advocates of the gold standard make two replies. The first is that the reduction in the key currency element in the world's monetary stock could be carried through gradually. The fall in prices would, therefore, not be sharp but, instead, graduated. But even this would have a depressive influence on production and employment. Depressions tend to be longer and periods of prosperity shorter when there is a long continued decline in the price level. The experience of the period after the Napoleonic Wars and from 1871 to 1896 seems to bear this out.

The second proposal is to increase the money equivalent of the gold stock by raising its price per ounce to compensate for the decrease in the quantity of the claims on the "key currencies." The present world monetary reserves of gold consist of approximately 1,140 billion ounces of gold at 35 dollars an ounce. By raising the price to 60 dollars per ounce, the same reserve would have a monetary value of 68.5 billion dollars. This would be a slight increase over the present combined total of 65 billion dollars for gold and official foreign-exchange holdings of key currencies, i.e., reserve monies.

But this seemingly plausible suggestion opens up a further Pandora's box of difficulties. Should this compensatory action of increasing the price of gold to offset the shrinkage in the holdings of key currencies be continuous or all at once? If the former, then frequent alterations would have to be made in the price of gold. This would lead to speculative withholdings of mined gold from the monetary stock because of expected increases in its price. Since we not only buy, but also sell gold at 35 dollars an ounce, there would also be speculative purchases of our gold which would then be hoarded in expectation of a further rise in its price. There would not, therefore, be a fully compensatory action. If the price increases occurred only rarely but then in much larger amounts, this speculative danger would become even greater.

The advocates of the return to gold will urge in reply that the higher price of gold will cause a much greater stock of gold to be mined since it will open up many mines which are now unprofitable and will cause a more intensified utilization of existing mines.

The two countries which would be most benefitted from an increase in the price of gold would be South Africa and Soviet Russia, since they produce most of the world's supply. These are the last two nations whom we should seek to reward, for South Africa is the most blatantly racist country in the Western World, while Russia is a determined foe of Western democracy. The fact that our own existing stock of gold would have a higher dollar value should not blind us as to who would benefit from a higher price being set on the current output. Those countries would be Russia and South Africa. Is there any good reason why they should be rewarded?

If the full increase in the price of gold and the elimination of the reserve currencies were put into effect all at once, this would require an increase of approximately sixty percent in the price of gold or a rise from 35 dollars to approximately 57 dollars an ounce. This would raise the value of our existing stock of gold from 14 to approximately 22.5 billion dollars. If this were simultaneously accompanied by the cancellation of an equal amount of foreign exchange claims held against us, it would be a great boon to the United States. For we would thus eliminate claims drawing hundreds of millions of dollars in annual interest. But, if the world were to return to a pure international gold standard, there is little prospect that the other nations would agree to this technique. What they would want to do instead, would be to first present their foreign exchange claims against us and, after having them redeemed in gold, then have the world go back to a gold standard. They would then have our 14 billion dollars in gold and we would be more or less stripped bare. Great Britain would go through a similar experience. The major portion of the gold supply of the world would then be in the hands of what are now the nonreserve countries, primarily those of Continental Europe which would make a huge profit from the transaction. While these countries do not at present hold a large proportion of official reserves in the form of foreign exchange, they have, as we have constantly pointed out, large quantities of such private deposits which can quickly be converted into official claims.

The advocates of the return to gold will, however, object that this takes much too pessimistic a view of the character of the foreign nations and that, in practice, they would not carry out such a program, particularly under the eyes of the world. But, even if such public disapproval were to develop, it would have little more ability to with-

stand the temptation to make twenty-five billion dollars of
profit than unorganized public opinion has to stop determined aggression by one or more countries or to halt the
arms race. Moreover, most of the non Anglo-Saxon world
would also profit from such prior withdrawals and later increases in the price of gold. With profits widely distributed,
disapproval would be muted and good reasons could
always be found to justify bad actions.

Furthermore, since any such action in a world community of over a hundred nations could not be put into effect
immediately upon its being proposed, and since a protracted period of discussion would necessarily be required,
there would be ample time within which to carry out such
withdrawals by degrees. A permanent embitterment between the New World and the Old World would result.

The hoarders and gold speculators who have been withholding gold from its monetary uses would of course reap
a huge and unearned windfall. Nor are they the type of
persons who should be singled out for such large and
unique benefits. A return to the pure international gold
standard would, therefore, seem to be a mistake from both
a national and world point of view.

It is sometimes proposed, however, that either Great
Britain or the United States should unilaterally devalue
its currency. It is urged that, if we were to devalue our
currency so that each ounce of gold would represent 50
dollars instead of 35 dollars as now, we would make a
profit of forty-two percent on each of the 400 million
ounces of gold which we hold, or a total gain of six billion
dollars. It is also argued that we would attract further
gold from hoardings and that we would obtain an export
advantage because American goods selling abroad for
1,000 units of a foreign currency would then net us more
dollars than before. This would follow because each unit

of foreign currency would then be worth more dollars than before.

Countries being drained of their gold either because of a long-continued deficit in their payments or by inspired speculative runs may be forced to go off gold and, in doing so, to devalue. But while this policy may be justified in special circumstances, it should, in general, be vigorously avoided.

In the first place, the potential increase in the circulating medium in the devaluating country would inevitably cause an internal price increase which would be heightened by the added uncertainty which such a step would necessarily create. All this would reduce the initial export advantage which devaluation would bring.

Second, any competitive advantage which one nation might hope for would be speedily swept away and possibly reversed by defensive devaluations which would inevitably be carried out by other nations. Other countries would not sit passively by and watch their foreign trade being hampered by such action on the part of any other strong country. Moreover, devaluation by one country would cause the currency speculators to call for gold from other countries in anticipation that they would later be forced to devalue, just as in the old days the failure of a few banks caused disastrous runs on others. So, if one major country goes off gold and devalues its currency, a crisis of confidence would be engendered which might break down the financial structure of the world.

Finally, our export trade does not need any such artificial stimulus. We already have a surplus of nearly five billion dollars a year in our trade in commodities. Our prices are more stable than those of Europe as are our labor costs per unit of output. The costs of raw material of power and fuel are also lower.

Luckily, there is little chance that we would voluntarily accept any such program, although, if Britain were forced to devalue and if our payment deficits were to continue to be very large, we might be forced to follow suit.

It is better therefore for the nations to go forward together than to be fragmented again into separate entities, each seeking in a frightened and hostile fashion to protect and aggrandize itself at the expense of others.

As we have repeatedly pointed out, the International Monetary Fund has been built and operated upon the basic principle that, except under the gravest emergencies, exchange rates should be constant and stable. The Fund may give temporary help to a nation but, ultimately, the responsibility is thrust upon each country to prevent appreciable inflation and fundamental disequilibrium. When aid is given, it is generally made conditional, at least in the case of a nation making drawings beyond its gold reserve, that it prevent further inflation and bring its international accounts on the road to balance.

But the founders of the IMF at Bretton Woods did not foresee the difficulties which would be created for the two key currency countries, the United States and Great Britain, nor how the system would only be able to function if they ran large deficits in their balance of payments. Nor did they fully envisage how these countries would feel impelled to keep up their interest rates in order to prevent a run on their gold reserves with a consequent dampening effect on production and employment. Moreover, the IMF faced the difficulty that it was very hard to maintain constant exchange rates when differences in price levels developed between countries and were maintained for long periods of time. The natural corrective for this was a movement of exports and imports which would redress the balance so that countries which had enjoyed a surplus in their balance of payments would later experience a countervailing deficit. But countries which have once strengthened their position by a trade surplus are, as we have said, reluctant to replace this by a deficit. The founders of the IMF did not fully realize that the central banks would seek to dampen down and delay the increase in prices which they expected to follow from increases in the amounts of gold and foreign exchange which a country acquired because of surpluses in its balance of payments.

Finally, the founders of the IMF did not foresee that their wartime eastern ally, Russia, would take an aggressive course against the West and compel the United States to spend huge sums overseas to help provide a shield of freedom both for Europe and for the emerging nations of the world. For this, as we have seen, is one of the major reasons for the deficit in our balance of payments.

As a result, attention should be given to a proposal, long advocated by such competent economists as J.E. Meade and Milton Friedman, that exchange rates should not be fixed but instead be permitted to fluctuate according to market pressures of supply and demand. Under such a plan, the gold exchange standard would be abandoned as an international monetary system. The various national currencies would be no more redeemable in gold externally than they now are internally. Gold would then be used only in the arts or as a reserve against catastrophe. Its presence in the vaults of government and of central banks might help to quiet the latent fears of mankind just as the gold under Fort Knox is presumed to do. But neither the holders of internal currency nor foreign creditors could ask that their claims be paid from this reserve.

The rates at which the various national currencies would exchange for each other would then be determined in the free market according to the relative demand for and the supply of the various currencies. These forces would be strongly influenced by the relative present and anticipated purchasing power of the various currencies. Countries whose price levels were higher for goods internationally traded would have lower exchange rates and those with lower prices would have higher exchange rates. A country like our own with a large and hitherto persistent deficit in its balance of payments would have a smaller volume of claims upon foreigners than the volume of claims against it by foreigners. Hence, for example, we would bid up the price of foreign currencies in relation to our own. The dollar would, therefore, depreciate and the mark and the franc would appreciate. If our price levels rose, this would cause a still further fall in the international value of our currency. Fluctuations in the exchange rates would therefore according to Meade and Friedman produce a more or less automatic balancing of international payments and would replace the present method of transferring the ownership of gold and foreign exchange.

The advocates of floating exchange rates believe that the results obtained in free, competitive markets are far superior to the collective decisions of men and that they will reflect more accurately actual economic values. They will, moreover, be flexible and can shift as situations change.

Another advantage claimed for flexible exchange rates is that they would enable each nation to adopt those price and employment policies which seemed most advantageous to them and would not sacrifice domestic needs to an implicit international veto. If, for example, we wished to follow an expansionary credit and production policy, then we could do so even if it meant an increase in our price level. All that would happen would be a decrease in the exchange value of the dollar. Then we could decide which policy we wished to follow—whether it should be domestic expansion up to the point of comparatively full employment, or price and exchange stabilization at a lower level of employment.

Similarly, we would not be compelled to alter wise international policies because of exchange difficulties. If it seemed wise to continue to station a million troops overseas or even increase that number and to continue a plentiful stream of foreign aid in order to maintain the cohesion of the democratic alliance, we could do so even if it created an initial "unfavorable" balance of payments. For this deficit would be removed by the decrease in the international value of the dollar. Because of this, it would, however, require more dollars to buy the same amount of supplies and equipment abroad.

It would also permit our capital to flow abroad freely in response to interest rate differentials or greater profit opportunities in other countries than at home, although fluctuating exchange rates would also tend to increase the risk of loss and thus reduce capital outflows.

It is obvious that such a program has strong persuasive powers. It would permit the marketplace of finance to adjust the differences in international prices without the national and international controls which the gold exchange standard necessarily forces upon nations. On the surface, it would solve the problem of the balance of payments. It appeals at once to advocates of full employment, to nationalists resentful of foreign or international intervention, as well as to believers in the ultimate wisdom of decisions made by and in the free market.

But there are very powerful objections which need to be considered before floating exchange rates are adopted either as an international or national policy. In the first place, they would introduce a large element of uncertainty into transactions across national lines; namely, the fear that, before a transaction could be completed and paid for, the comparative exchange rates would alter and that one of the parties would consequently lose. It was indeed the disruptive experience with floating exchange rates after World War I with the accompanying inflation and the drastic currency conditions of the 1930's, which furnished the driving force for the Bretton Woods agreement and the creation of the IMF.

Part of the uncertainties created by flexible rates could be removed by the practice of trading in the forward exchanges. By this method, those with claims against a foreign currency which would come due in ninety days, six months, or a year could protect themselves against any future depreciation in that currency by selling an equal amount of the currency in the present and thus offsetting any possible future loss. This process of "hedging" against possible depreciation in exchange rates would, however, involve a net cost to the traders in order to compensate for the insurance gained—and this is a cost which, at present, is minimized by the system of relatively fixed exchange rates supported by the IMF. Moreover, forward trading or hedging is primarily applicable to transactions of short run or intermediate duration. It is of very limited use in connection with long-term investments in fixed capital. For, in these cases, it is almost impossible to predict what the comparative exchange rates will be in ten, twenty, or thirty years. Hence, it would undoubtedly restrict such long-term investments which are greatly needed by the less developed nations.

The basic opposition to flexible exchange rates, however, probably arises from the fear that they would remove a further safeguard against inflation. One such deterrent has already been removed by making domestic currencies inconvertible into gold. But the basic requirement of international convertibility is still a restraining force. Opponents of flexible exchanges are afraid that, if this were eliminated, those who favor seriously unbalanced budgets and unlimited domestic credit expansion would get the upper hand. The results, they believe, would be that prices would rise rapidly and exchange rates would fall.

While the decline in exchange rates would be a deterrent to inflation, it is feared that this would not be adequate since it would affect only a comparatively small fraction of the population. Believers in a completely managed currency will reply that the domestic hardships caused by inflation will still be an adequate restraining force against appreciable inflation and that national pride will seek to prevent any great depreciation in the foreign exchanges.

This question may become more and more of a practical issue in the years which lie ahead. If it were to be adopted, it would obviously be better for it to be put into effect internationally than by separate national action. But it will, of course, be extremely difficult to obtain any such agreement since it would be in direct opposition to the cardinal principle upon which the Monetary Fund was founded and which guides its operations. If the experiment is to be tried, therefore, it will probably have to be by an individual nation * and preferably by one which can lead from financial strength rather than be forced into it by already existing inflation and exchange weakness. The risks of such experimentation will be great.

* Canada experimented for a decade (1950–1961) with fluctuating exchange rates but returned to the fixed parity system. It found that the variable exchange rates did not insulate it from the economic fluctuations of the United States and that the importance of monetary policy was intensified. See Robert A. Mundell, *Problems of Monetary and Exchange Rate Management in Canada*, Brookings Institution, pp. 77–86.

The possibilities of domestic gain by lessening the present credit restrictions upon production and employment are real but conjectural. It is not likely that any nation will make the venture from the sheer desire to experiment. If tried out, therefore, it is likely to be only after a financial emergency has developed and, hence, at the most unfavorable of times and in the most unpromising of circumstances.

While freely fluctuating exchange rates seem too dangerous to adopt, it is probable that the present zone, within which exchange rates are permitted by the IMF to fluctuate, could be safely and profitably widened. At present, the basic limit is one percent on either side of parity, but narrowed by general practice to about three-quarters of this. There would seem to be no good reason why this zone of tolerance could not be extended to three, four, or even five percent. Minor and correcting fluctuations in the exchange rates could therefore occur without imposing on the country in question either the penalties of a loss in exports or expulsion from the honor roll of "stable" countries. But the rigid believers in exchange stabilization, or economic total abstainers, will object that, like moderate drinking, this will tend to create an unappeasable appetite for more. It should, in my judgment, be adopted by the Monetary Fund in the near future in order to loosen the tight financial corset in which various countries, notably Great Britain, have been placed.

22
Towards an International Currency

The idea of an international currency other than gold has been advanced by numerous writers, notably by the English publicist, H.G. Wells. It was urged in 1944 by J.M. Keynes at Bretton Woods * and more recently it has been given prominence by Robert Triffin, E.M. Bernstein, Reginald Maudlin, Dr. Zolotas, and many others. While these plans have differed in details, virtually all have had the common feature that an international financial institution, whether the International Monetary Fund or another, should have the function of creating an additional amount of monetary purchasing power to lubricate trade.

These proposals were at first looked upon coldly by our Treasury Department, which believed that a reduction in our payments deficit together with the ingenious devices of Undersecretary Roosa and a further strengthening of the reserves of the IMF by conventional means would be sufficient to meet our own difficulties. But the British crisis of 1964, the insistence of the Labour government that greater international liquidity was needed, and the slow but determined pressure of the Congressional Joint Economic Committee have gradually led the Treasury to

---

* Keynes apparently favored the creation of these "bancor" notes as an indirect means of using the gold in American hands to finance the purchase of food, raw materials, and machinery by England.

adopt a more constructive attitude towards such proposals. The Continental bankers were also induced to look more favorably on the idea of greater liquidity by the imminent possibility that the United States would eliminate or greatly reduce its payments deficit and that a substitute or supplement for the dollar exchange should be created if international trade and finance was to flourish.

The ten countries in the General Agreement to Borrow created, in the summer of 1964, a study group to explore the need and possibilities for the creation of added reserve assets.* This report was issued in August of the following year. Without taking a stand on the issues involved, this report outlined the main problems which it believed were involved and the arguments for and against each. These issues have emerged from the background into the foreground as representatives of the major industrial countries have been meeting to exchange views on the creation and functioning of a new system of international currency. At the meeting in February, 1965, a more detailed discussion took place in which Frederick Deming, the American Undersecretary of the Treasury, presented a concise statement of a tentative proposal. While the text of the Deming proposal has not been made public, it is believed to have

* See Ministerial Statement of the Group of Ten and Annex Prepared by Deputies, August 1965, p. 23.

Report of the Study on the Creation of Reserve Assets, Rome, August 1965, p. 113, also reprinted in "Balance of Payments—1965, Part 2." Hearings before a Subcommittee of the Senate Banking & Currency Committee, 1965, pp. 1104–1204.

For a further comprehensive examination of the issues involved from an American viewpoint, see *Guidelines for International Monetary Reform,* Hearings before the Subcommittee on International Exchange and Payments of the Joint Economic Committee, 1965, 2 Vols., p. 601. See also the excellent report of the subcommittee on this subject which was largely the work of Congressmen Reuss and Ellsworth and the able staff expert Dr. Gerald Pollack.

suggested a dual program for granting additional rights to draw for all members of the IMF, together with the creation of a new reserve unit based upon a composite pool of currencies or gold contributed by a group of advanced countries. We may not be too far from some such a development although French opposition will probably continue and it is therefore important that the many complex and interdependent issues which are involved should not only be analyzed, but that certain tentative decisions be taken in respect to them. It is recognized that many of these issues are interdependent and many extremely complex. But it is hoped that the discussion which follows will advance consideration and lead to wiser ultimate decisions.

Perhaps the central question which developed was whether the institution to create more of the international currency was to be the International Monetary Fund, itself, or a body dominated by the major industrial powers, such as the forty-year-old Bank for International Settlements (BIS) which is at present purely a Western European organization but which could be enlarged to include other industrial nations.

In the beginning, the continental countries largely favored the latter alternative. For they would exert much greater control over such a body than if their strength were reduced by their lower voting quotas in the IMF and by the corresponding greater voting rights of the less developed countries. In the IMF, moreover, they feared that commercial banking would be called upon to finance long-term capital investments in the less developed countries.

The United States, on the other hand, came to favor the IMF because it would give the less developed countries a voice in the conduct of world finance and would prevent them from feeling excluded and alienated from the international credit-creating process. It would also avoid the disadvantages of having two international bodies deal with substantially the same set of issues. The Treasury would have been less than human if it had not also realized that American and British strength was likely to be greater in the IMF than in a new institution where voting rights might be apportioned on the basis of either the combined holdings of gold and foreign exchange or even on gold holdings alone, and that our strength would also be much greater than in a revised BIS.

This issue is likely to be a central point of difficulty and, if it can be resolved, the other problems will more or less automatically tend to fall into place.

Another fundamental issue which is frequently ignored by writers upon the subject is whether the new arrangements will be confined to the creation of additional monetary reserves for the various nations or whether they will foster the conduct of international trade by the rediscounting of approved commercial paper arising out of such transactions. The chief advocate of the latter alternative is Eliot Janeway. This was the original purpose of the Federal Reserve System as developed by Paul Warburg. In later years, this purpose has fallen into disuse and has been replaced by open market purchases of government securities. Through the process by which these added reserves are credited to the account of the private banks, they are then enabled to expand their own loans in the form of created deposits by from six to seven times the amount of their added reserves. Mr. Janeway believes that the new functions should provide for the creation of new currency units which would probably be credited to the central banks which had originally presented the paper and which, in turn, would, in all probability, have already rediscounted the original loan made by a private bank within the member country. The IMF would thus be a secondary bank of rediscount which could protect itself by its claims against the appropriate central banks and could also protect itself against further depreciation in the foreign exchange of the given country by providing that the loan was to be repaid in currency of an equal exchange ratio.

Opposed to this, some authorities question whether such an international agency should involve itself in specific transactions between exporting and importing countries. They argue that it should instead confine itself to providing, under proper safeguards, additional international reserves to lubricate the general processes of trade and then allow specific credits to be handled solely by private banks within the various nations or by international loan agencies, such as the World Bank, the International Development Association and various regional banks. The added international reserves would then be used to help finance trade and transactions in general without direct reference to specific transactions.

Whatever the merits of the Janeway proposal, it has found little favor with the money managers of Europe or the United States. The Europeans want to confine any new purchasing power to the creation of new national reserves within the international monetary system in order to strengthen countries against temporary deficits in their balances of payments. They would build upon the present system, and the maintenance of exchange stability would thus continue to be the primary purpose of the IMF, with its indirect reassurance to private traders and bankers, rather than the direct aid to specific groups and transactions which would be provided by the Janeway plan. The new official reserves would therefore be added to the existing reserves of gold, plus the official foreign claims upon the dollar and claims on sterling.

The points in dispute naturally relate to which nations will be credited with this additional purchasing power and on what basis. There is no doubt as to what the European gold bloc would prefer. They would like to have the new reserve units (which can be called CRU's for "composite reserve unit" or "collective reserve units") issued solely on the basis of the gold reserves of the various nations. This would, of course, give them the major share of the new purchasing power and would largely confine the benefits of the new currency to two groups. First, would be the countries of Western Europe, notably France, West Germany, Italy, Belgium, the Netherlands, or, in short, the Common Market with its combined gold reserves of 15 billion dollars, or thirty-five percent of the official gold reserves of the world. If Switzerland were to join the IMF, this would add a further 2.7 billion dollars to the official gold reserves and thus increase their claims upon the new reserve units to approximately forty-one percent. The second beneficiary would be the two reserve currency countries, namely, the United States and Great Britain which, between them, hold approximately 16 billion dollars of gold, or approximately thirty-seven percent of the world's official monetary supply, though still somewhat less than the continental gold bloc.

While such an arrangement would in the short-run be favorable to these groups, it would leave out in the cold those countries whose reserves are primarily in the form of foreign exchange claims upon the dollar and pound sterling and those countries whose total reserves are low in comparison with their foreign trade or their need for added trade and investment. The nations which would suffer from such an arrangement would not only be the undeveloped and less developed countries of the world, but those loyal members of the sterling bloc such as Australia and New Zealand, and the Latin American countries which belong to the dollar bloc.

It is to the credit of the United States that both the Treasury and the Joint Economic Committee have rejected the thesis of the gold rich countries and have insisted thus far that the creation of the new reserve units should be based on some other basis than that of gold. We have thus become the champions of the undeveloped and less developed nations of the world as well as of those countries which are in the dollar and sterling blocs.

An alternative proposal which is widely favored is that the apportioning of the new reserve units should be relative to their assigned quotas in the IMF. This would reduce the shares of France and West Germany which, at their own demands, were not increased in proportion to the growth in their own gross national product or to the even greater growth in their international gold reserves. I do not see how our French friends, for example, can legitimately ask to be accorded two contradictory favors: to keep their contributions to the reserves of the IMF much lower than their own financial and economic position in relation to other countries would justify; and, at the same time, to be rewarded for their raiding of the international monetary system by receiving a disproportionately large share of the newly created international reserves.

Apportioning the new reserve units in proportion to the gold holdings of the various countries would, moreover, directly reward those nations with a favorable balance of payments, which need the new reserves least, and minimize the assistance to deficit countries which need added reserves the most. For, as has been already shown, the transfer between nations of the gold stocks of the world since 1958 has been largely caused by deficits in the American balance of payments and to some degree in those of Britain. The reverse side of the coin has been the simultaneous favorable balance of payments enjoyed by France, West Germany, Spain, Portugal, etc. This favorable balance has been due largely to American military and foreign aid and to our direct military expenditures abroad to defend the Free World from Communist aggression. Here again, the proposal to apportion the reserve units according to the possession of gold would not only reward those who need them least instead of those who need them most, but would also reward those who have been making lesser international sacrifices in preference to those who have been making greater.

The alternatives to apportionment on the basis of gold are to use the relative *quotas* in the IMF or to apportion the total official reserves of the various nations as credited in the IMF consisting not merely of the 42 billion dollars of gold, but also of the 23 billion dollars of official holdings of reserve currencies, nearly all in the form of dollar and sterling exchange, plus possibly the 5.6 billion dollars of reserve positions in the IMF. The use of this latter basis would be especially beneficial to the undeveloped and less developed countries and to the loyal members of the dollar and sterling blocs.

Finally, selective increases could be made to especially hard-pressed countries which, while trying to maintain an ultimate balance of payments, nevertheless find themselves in temporary difficulties. This would be especially helpful to the less developed countries which need added reserves. It also would be of great assistance to Britain should that nation once again find herself confronted with a run on the pound resulting either from a continuing unfavorable balance of payments or from speculative attacks on sterling. In a sense, these selective purchases would be closely equivalent to the open market purchases of goverment securities by the Federal Reserve System. In my judgment, however, they should not be used additionally as internal reserves upon which further bank credit could be expanded within the nations in question. That could produce a dangerous inflation.

It follows from all this that the new currency (CRU's) should not be convertible into gold on demand, since this would permit the gold-rich and gold-hungry nations to denude the deficit countries of their reserves, just as France and other nations have been decreasing American gold reserves by presenting their dollar claims for conversion into gold. The international monetary system might therefore find itself greatly weakened. On the whole, therefore, it would be better if the new currency were either inconvertible and hence a completely independent form of an international currency; or, if convertible, only into units of national currencies. In the latter case, then, the given national currency should carry with it full protection against any depreciation in the national exchange rates.

Obviously, the interest of all the industrial and trading nations of the world is in assuring an orderly expansion of international reserves in line with the needs of an expanding world economy. But if the new arrangement itself encourages or permits sudden and large-scale conversions into gold of existing reserve assets, we can hardly achieve the needed expansion. Much of the increase in the new reserve assets would be offset by the disappearance of the old, and, further, such conversions would seem inevitably to intensify the pressures that already exist on the United States and Great Britain. The result might well be an actual diminution of international liquidity rather than an increase.

Central to the negotiation, therefore, must be arrangements to encourage central banks to hold foreign exchange as well as gold and the new international reserve unit in their reserves. We should not encourage countries to abandon their present voluntary holding of the dollar nor of the pound as a form of reserve. Such action would completely negate the purpose of the negotiations. At the same time, it is difficult to see either the dollar or the pound bearing as heavy a burden in furnishing international liquidity in the future as they have in the past. However, if we are relieved of carrying the entire burden of creating reserves, it will make it easier for us to eliminate our balance of payments deficits and to sustain the strength of the dollar. After all, the objective of international monetary reform is emphatically not to find a device for enabling the United States or Great Britain to finance balance of payments deficits painlessly and endlessly. Furthermore, as the new international reserve unit expands in volume with trade and commerce of the world, the proportion of dollars and gold in international reserves will inevitably decline, thus taking care of the present fears of some concerning the composition of the outstanding balances in their reserves.

The new currency, moreover, should originally be confined to the settlement of foreign trade and exchange balances and insulated from internal use. As I have said, it should not be counted as reserves for internal monetary systems since this would make for added internal inflation. If the world progresses to a greater degree of cultural, economic, and political unity, then perhaps such a true world currency may develop. For the predictable future, however, it is desirable to confine the new currency to settling payment balances between nations. Consequently, the new composite reserve units will consist of credit balances in the IMF and, upon occasion, in the central banks of the member nations rather than in the ultimate reality of gold which is buried sight unseen in deep vaults in the earth. The new Composite Reserve Units (CRU's) need not indeed take the physical form of printed bank notes but consist instead of credit balances on the books of the appropriate financial institutions, comparable to the deposits created by commercial banks when they extend credit.

Whatever may be the method of apportioning the amount of the reserve units which will be created, and I favor as a compromise using initially the IMF quotas rather than the relative reserves, the next question is, inevitably, how much should be created and whether the initial and subsequent decisions should follow a more or less automatic formula or whether they should be selective and, if so, what standards should be followed.

First, it would seem desirable that the new reserves created under a revised International Monetary Fund be distributed to all members of the Fund under criteria established and applied equally and universally, so that all those meeting certain minimum standards of international financial conduct would receive the immediate benefit of the new reserves. Such standards might include the convertibility of the currency of the country concerned and the absence of indebtedness to the Fund above some level related to the country's quota in the Fund. Distribution in the first instance would, of course, be proportionate to each country's Fund quota. To make this system work equitably, however, it will be necessary to revise the present system of quotas.

As the Subcommittee on International Exchange and Payments of the Joint Economic Committee has pointed out, the present structure of the quotas is unsatisfactory.

The quotas of most of the Group of Ten are in the range of 78 to 96 percent of the statistical calculations used for each country during the original Fund negotiations, while the average quota for members of the Fund not in the Group of Ten is about 132 percent of the comparable statistical calculations. Quotas of certain leading countries, such as France and Germany, have lagged far behind improvements in their relative economic positions in the world. It should be an objective of United States policy therefore to achieve a better sharing of international financial burdens and responsibilities. In the process, the Western European countries would receive, as a by-product, greater voting rights within the IMF and a larger share of the new created reserves.

It would also seem wiser to make the initial amounts of additional reserve units generally follow a given formula and for this formula to be the principle guide for later increases. However, some selective increases to specific countries to help deal with emergencies or permanent disadvantages would have to be permitted. A safe general rule is that the total supply of international reserves should not increase at a more rapid rate than the growth in world trade.

In other words, if the physical volume of world trade increases by 3 percent a year, then the increase in (a) the countries official holdings of gold, plus (b) dollar and sterling exchange or any other reserve currency which may be added, plus (c) the reserve positions in the IMF, plus (d) the new collective reserve units (CRU's) should not exceed 3 percent annually. The increase in the CRU's would, therefore, not exceed the amounts by which monetary gold plus official reserves fell below the rate of increase in foreign trade.

If it should develop that international reserves need not

increase as rapidly as world trade because the various national balances were being brought more closely into equilibrium and international settlements formed a diminishing percentage of the volume of international trade, then the overall rate of increase could be taken as a fraction of the rate of rise in international trade. Then the increase in CRU's under the formula would be determined only by the amount by which monetary gold and other official reserves failed to equal this fraction. In other words, the volume of world trade would only be taken as a rough and preliminary measure of the need for international reserves.

However, there also should be room for selective increases. While each nation must ultimately stand or fall on its own feet, and while additional reserve units should not be created to protect fundamentally unsound economies, two sets of exceptions can properly be made. The first is in the case of a country like Great Britain whose financial solidity is essential to the world's financial system and whose monetary collapse would imperil not only her own currency but also the currencies and exchange rates of a wide range of other countries. In other words, since Britain is an integral and important part of the world's monetary system, in order to protect that international system, it is necessary to protect Britain. Such aid can come more effectively from an international institution like the IMF than from the voluntary and more or less disconnected efforts of a series of national sovereign states.

Of course, even here there is a limit. The new reserve units should not be created to shore up an economy which is continuously out of balance with the rest of the world. The aid can be prolonged since it will be protected by the collective reserves of the IMF and secured by pledges or transfers of the national currency guaranteed against any depreciation in exchange rates. But such reserve units should not be used to underwrite or pay for keeping the balance of international payments in perpetual deficit.

If France and other nations were to be successful in bringing the dollar under such serious attack as to make its devaluation imminent, then similar aid to us would not be improper.

The second group of possible exceptions are the developing countries. These nations need large amounts of capital in the form of machinery, transportation facilities and the like, and they are not able to get private capital to make the necessary investments. The IMF would be exposed to excessive pressure if it were to grant such credits directly to specific nations. But it would seem wise to create a given amount of the new CRU's which would then be credited to the World Bank, which makes the "hard" loans, or, in especially important and pressing cases, to the International Development Association which makes much "softer" loans. These institutions could then apportion these sums to specific countries according to judged need. This would at once reduce the political pressures upon the IMF and engage the efforts of the World Bank and the International Development Association which are experienced in administering such aid. In this way, both greater security and greater collective responsibility would be obtained.

The more the new reserve units can be created and apportioned by some mathematical formula, the more the system will be made self-operating and the less important decision making will become. But some important decisions will still have to be made. The reserve mechanism cannot be fully automated. It is important, therefore, to consider the mechanism by which these fundamental decisions are to be made. Since these will either be by the body of delegates to the IMF themselves, or by committees chosen by them, the whole question of control largely hinges on the method of voting and of decision making in the legislative body. The French naturally will favor the principle of unanimity which would give to any one nation the right of veto. This is bad enough within the Common Market with its six members. It would be utterly impossible within the IMF with its 103 members. The smaller states would undoubtedly like to have votes on the same basis as that in the Assembly of the United Nations—each nation to be given one and only one vote. But this would give control to the small Asian, African, and South American countries which contribute relatively little to the funds of the IMF, but which would wish to be liberally financed.

The best method would be to adopt the present voting system weighted according to the relative national quotas. This would, in itself, give some protection to the less developed countries whose quotas tend to exceed their relative national resources.

A further protection to minorities could be given by providing that a two-thirds weighted vote would be required for the more fundamental decisions, such as the adoption of a formula for expansion and the selective granting of added reserves.

It is highly probable that President de Gaulle and France will refuse to enter such an international arrangement in which France would not have veto power but would have instead a relatively minor voice and in which the new reserve units would not be tied to gold. France's probable attitude should not prevent us or the rest of the world from undertaking the venture. While the presence of France is highly desirable, it is not indispensable. The door should indeed be left open for France to change its mind and to be admitted later in a full and honored status. Perhaps some such experience may be necessary to develop a more co-operative attitude on the part of President de Gaulle and his associates.

Bretton Woods was not the last word. The Free World needs to push on. The historical evolution of currency and credit as well as the present condition of international balances calls for the creation of an institution similar to that which I have outlined. It is possible that some essential features of a new international monetary arrangement have been omitted, and it is possible that some of the specific suggestions which I have made may have to be modified. But fears of complexity should not be allowed to frustrate the will to build. If we can send instruments and even men to the moon, is it beyond our power to create a better international currency?

23
Summary and Conclusions

It is time to draw from this rather lengthy discussion some recommendations for public policy.

It is most certainly clear that there are great economic advantages in the broadest possible trade between ever wider geographical areas. The wider the market, the more minute the specialization and the greater the productivity. Each area can, moreover, concentrate on those products for which by reasons of climate, geography, and history it is best adapted. Moreover, the competition between areas lessens the power of local monopolies and promotes competition. Competition, in turn, is a stimulus to invention and innovation and leads to the development of new processes to reduce costs. This leads to lower prices and, hence, to a broadened consumption and to a higher standard of living.

There are also spiritual advantages to such broader trade. While competition has its shady features, if it is held to straightforward standards of quality, frank and aboveboard declarations of terms and decent conditions of labor, it can promote healthy and constructive rivalry between sellers and producers in improving their respective products. This can build character as much as can athletic, artistic, or scientific rivalry. Broader trade, freely conducted, brings buyer and seller more closely together and makes them better acquainted with and more sympathetic toward the needs and problems of others. By making people more interdependent, it makes them broader and deeper in their interests. It helps to lessen parochialism and indeed the cruder forms of nationalism.

Men have come to see this so far as trade within a nation is concerned. They partially see it so far as trade between nations is involved. Every year the volume of world trade increases until it is now over three times as great as it was seventeen years ago.

Trade creates the necessity for money as a medium of exchange, a standard of value and a standard for deferral payments. This need takes more and more insubstantial forms moving from metals to paper currency to bank credits to balances of debits and claims. The process is complicated enough within a country. It is far more complicated as it grows out of trade between countries. For each country has its own units of currency and its own financial institutions and operates within an institutional framework prescribed by the sovereign state. But there is no international unit of currency as such, and no sovereign world government. As a substitute, there are a series of incomplete institutions of a decentralized character where the emphasis is upon obtaining the voluntary agreement and co-operation of the many.

All this takes place within a world torn by two sets of cleavages. The first is ideological; between those who believe in a relatively free and diverse society and those who strive for a dictated monolithic state. The second cleavage is geographical; between those who generally live in the tropical zone and are not industrialized and those who dwell in the temperate zone and who are industrialized and much more prosperous.

Nor is this all. The dominant industrialized nations

within the group of free societies are only partially united in aim and conduct. Nationalism is still strong among them and, being deeply rooted in human emotion, will remain so. Many nations still seek to advance by taking advantage of their neighbors rather than by promoting mutual prosperity. What would be bad manners and unethical for a man in his private dealings becomes, all too often, an accepted standard of conduct when he becomes a statesman. Nor can those who desire a more harmonious world neglect the interests of their country or ignore the times in which they live. We live in a real and not an ideal world and we must deal with human beings and institutions as they are and not as we would like to have them.

As we strive therefore for greater world prosperity and for a smoother world financial system, we cannot and should not neglect the interests of our own nation. If we are repeatedly rebuffed after continuing efforts to induce one or more other countries to co-operate in a program of mutual betterment, it would be unseemly and ineffective for us to persist. It would then be better to proceed without the dissenter and to try without rancor to build as wide an area of co-operation as we can. Sometimes, also, a touch of reprisal brings nonco-operators to a more healthy sense of reality.

I would suggest, therefore, that on the trade front we proceed simultaneously in two allied steps: First, we should seek to get the Common Market to admit, either freely or with greatly reduced tariff barriers, such farm products as wheat, corn, soybeans, meat, and such industrial products as coal. To obtain these concessions, we should offer still further reductions on industrial products. Second, we should adopt what has become known as the Douglas-Reuss amendment, under which we would be willing to remove all tariffs on commodities, if other countries did likewise, where eighty percent of world trade is carried out by the United States, the European Common Market, and EFTA.* It was a great tragedy that this amendment was defeated but it may not be too late to revive it. Had this been done, we could have had a free trading bloc on most of the important products of the temperate zone which would cover nearly 500 million people and which would form an economic community for the major portion of the Free World.

We should then seek to widen this community by taking in as soon as possible the peripheral European countries; the Near Eastern countries of Greece, Israel, and Turkey; Canada and Mexico, the Central and South American countries; and Japan, Australia, and New Zealand. This would make the economic alliance nearly complete.

If France refuses to allow our farm products and coal to be admitted to the Common Market or is able to impose higher tariffs than those presently in force, we could then offer the same terms to the other members of the Common Market individually and to EFTA. If they chose to come with us, we would still have an area of over 400 million people and, in all probability, France would then reconsider and enter.

If the other five members of the Common Market chose to stay with France rather than come with us, we should then seek a trade alliance with Great Britain and the other EFTA nations, together with Canada, Australia, New Zealand and, in a qualified fashion, Japan. This would create a trading area of over 400 million people

___

* It will be remembered that, in addition to Great Britain, EFTA includes Denmark, Norway, Sweden, Portugal, Austria, Switzerland, and Finland.

which would be stronger than the Common Market. We would hope that these steps would also lead us to broaden these agreements as rapidly as possible to include all of Latin America and the other British Commonwealths, and ultimately to seek reconciliation with the Common Market, itself. All this might involve a modification of our "most favored nation" clause, since reductions in tariffs should not be immediately extended to nonco-operating countries but confined to those within the new alliance. This would increase the incentive for nations to join.

If the Common Market seeks to go further in antagonism and imposes added punitive tariffs on our products, as it did with frozen chickens, it should be warned that, in self-defense, we might be forced to apply reprisals. If the Common Market should persist, then we might markedly increase the tariff on automobiles, which is their most vulnerable export to us. Reprisals are, however, dangerous and should be used only as a last resort. We should seek to have any such reprisals approved by GATT. We should not be supine if excluded from Europe.

So far as China and Cuba are concerned, they are showing by word and deed their determined and uncompromising hostility to the United States and, indeed, to world peace. I submit that it would be foolish to strengthen them through trade even though our traders and producers might gain temporary profits. In this connection, the Hong Kong trade should be closely examined to see if vital goods are slipping from and to China through the embargo.

The evidence is still overwhelming that Russia's ultimate intentions are much the same as those of China and Cuba. Therefore, unless and until there is clear, and convincing proof of a change in intentions, it would also be a mistake to widen to any appreciable degree the areas of trade with the Soviet Union and its hard-core satellites. There may be some peripheral Communist countries which actually want peace with the West and desire added trade with the outside world in order to make themselves more independent of Russia. Yugoslavia may have become such a country. Rumania may want to become one. In these circumstances, a greater degree of trade may well be desirable, but caution should be used lest the products sent to such a Communist country be secretly and quietly transferred to and sucked up by Russia itself. We naturally hope that there may be some fundamental change in policy by the Communist countries and we should try to encourage this if it can be done without appreciable danger to our own security.

So far as the less developed countries are concerned, we should seek to add to their social overhead capital by low-interest development loans from governments and international institutions and use such loans also to a limited degree and at higher rates if the nation in question seeks to develop its manufacturing and to utilize its resources. We should try to get private capital to make larger investments in the industries within the less developed nations and, for a time at least, should not repeal the fourteen-percent tax cut on investments south of the border in the Western Hemisphere. Outright grants for education will ultimately be very productive if they are accompanied by a local willingness to spend.

We should furthermore encourage the importations of more tropical products, such as fruit, nuts, sugar, coffee, tea, and cocoa. Most of these products, although not all, are now duty free. They should be kept so and others added to the list as rapidly as possible. There is no over-riding reason why we should not take advantage of the lower production costs in the tropics of these products.

While it would probably be politically inexpedient for us to withdraw from the coffee pool or entirely abandon the sugar quota system, we should be very careful about entering a cocoa cartel which might greatly boost the price of chocolate. In the case of sugar, it would be well if we set aside the quotas now assigned to territories outside the Western Hemisphere and merge them into purchases on the free market, with the offsetting taxes equal to the difference between the free market price and the American price. These offset duties would go into the public treasury. Since the added purchases would also raise the free market price, this would bring double relief to Eastern Hemisphere countries outside the present favored circle.

In short, I would advise extreme caution about entering into further world cartels on tropical products. Regional customs unions within the tropics, like that of Central America, can be encouraged as a means of developing manufacturing and a more broadly based social and economic structure. But it would be foolish for these new nations to raise their external tariffs and to deprive their people of the chance to buy much cheaper manufactured goods from the more advanced countries. The benefits of world trade are many-sided and are good for the tropics as well as the temperate zone. The proposal that the North should admit tropical products free of charge but that the tropics should levy heavy tariffs against the products of the North is completely lacking in reciprocity and cannot be expected to be explicitly adopted by the Northern nations. It is however being put into effect for those countries, like Mexico, which refuse to join GATT but to whom we nevertheless give most favored nation treatment. These obtain tariff favors from us for which they make no explicit return. We suffer this from a desire to help them.

Similarly, the contention that the industrialized nations should pay an indemnity to the nations producing raw materials for the recent fall in their prices gives every evidence of having been advanced primarily for bargaining purposes.

So much for a suggested policy on tariffs and trade. What, then, about the balance of payments?

First, there is no other immediate way than to reduce and, if possible, eliminate the deficit in our international payments. The major sources of this deficit, foreign aid—economic and military—and capital investments, have helped to provide political and economic stability and progress. They have also provided the monetary lubricants for a greatly expanded world trade. But we cannot be asked to bear interminably all, or even the major burdens of the world. While sacrifices will have to be made and disputes will arise as to the proper mixture of economic, cultural, and political retrenchments which should be made, self-defense requires us to shorten our sails.

Assuming that France continues on its present international course, one of the first prunings could be in our direct and indirect aid to French Africa. This would save 200 million dollars a year and would compel France to face more fully the need for more generous treatment of her African associates. Military aid to Latin America, India and Pakistan could also be pared. I have not seen any evidence that our economic aid to Egypt has made Nasser more friendly. We may now be reconsidering aid to Indonesia. If and when there is a change in the internal power structure of these countries and a greater willingness to co-operate internationally, as has apparently occurred in Indonesia, such cuts might be restored. But, for the time being, some retrenchment would seem to be in order.

Similarly, while there are undoubted cultural advantages to travel, some abridgment may be temporarily necessary. It would be highly desirable if this were voluntarily curtailed and if a further shift from the Riviera to the Caribbean were carried out. If the situation still remains serious, the possibility of an exit fee should be at least considered. This, however, would weigh most heavily upon lower income travelers who, in many cases, are the most appreciative. It should not be applied unless proportionate sacrifices are asked of those with larger incomes.

In the field of trade, the greatest stimulant would be the removal of the present discriminatory ocean freight rates which charge American exports more than our imports on identical products on identical ships between the same ports. An equalization of these rates by lowering the charges on what we ship out, and raising or equalizing import charges would add several hundred million dollars to our balance of trade. But, to effect this, our government will really have to get tough with the powerful international shipping cartels, protected as these are by the various European governments.

Finally, so far as investments abroad are concerned, I see no reason why the interest equalization tax should be abandoned on foreign loans and investments in securities. The problem of restricting expansion by American companies in their branches and subsidiaries abroad is more difficult. We are seeking to obtain this through the voluntary co-operation of American business and we have every hope that this will be successful. If it is not, then few, even in business, can doubt our need to explore other more formal methods.

The whole problem of military and economic aid would be greatly simplified and reduced if other nations would contribute a larger share. We are bearing much the heaviest burden, namely, about nine percent of our Gross National Product, and, unless there is a satisfactory peace in Vietnam, this bids fair to increase rather than to diminish. In contrast, the payments by England come to only about 7 percent, France 6½ percent, Germany 6 percent, and Italy 4 percent, while the smaller countries of Europe, such as Belgium, the Netherlands, Denmark, Norway, Sweden, and Switzerland are paying much less, generally from three to five percent.* The burdens of Canada, Australia and New Zealand are also relatively light. While such other factors as relative isolation, lack of direct international involvement and income per capita rather than total Gross National Product should be taken into account, it is apparent that the other countries, and particularly the smaller ones, have allowed too heavy a share of the burden of defending the world to rest on the shoulders of Uncle Sam.

We have tried through diplomatic channels to call these facts to the attention of our associates. The responses have been meager. Fuller publicity of these basic facts is needed so that the general public in other countries may come to feel a greater degree of responsibility.

If a permanent international police force could be created, it could greatly simplify operations and reduce ultimate costs. Such a force could operate as in the Suez crisis, the Congo, and Cyprus. It could act as a fire department to put out the brush-fire wars which commonly help to start the big conflicts. It conceivably could help to keep the peace in Southeast Asia. The small countries should be willing to make a special contribution to such a force to compensate for their own small contributions to national arms and economic aid.

If Russia and France were to continue to veto the development of such a force under the direct control of the United Nations, is it beyond the realm of possibility for us

* These include economic and military aid.

to propose a league within the UN to which nations could voluntarily belong and through which they could make their contributions to such an international force? This could give greater and more palatable international security at less cost to us than the present practice. A pooled police force is safer and more economical than a series of private armies. This was a lesson slowly learned in the Renaissance cities. It is even more true today. Such an international police force possibly could not be used effectively to stop major conflicts, but it could be of great use in many areas of the world. It could help to stop small wars which have a way of growing into great ones.

The recommendations in international finance would seem to be fairly clear.* We should push for a new international arrangement within the International Monetary Fund, with the power to create monetary purchasing power which would then be made available to assist in settling international balances. In such an institution, the developing countries should have adequate representation but not control. They should take part in the preliminary conferences of organization. Once established, neither the unanimity rule nor a simple majority rule should prevail, but a weighted voting requirement for fundamental decisions might be substituted.

The new international reserve unit should be initially created in a proportion to be agreed upon by negotiation related to the economic strengths and liquidity needs of various countries. Units should be distributed in proportion to revised quotas in the Fund. Annual increases should be provided, part of which would be automatic and part of which would be determined by the usual voting processes within the IMF. The initial amount of

* For somewhat similar recommendations, see the Report of Subcommittee on International Exchange and Payments of the Joint Economic Committee, 1965.

the new medium created and the additions in subsequent years should be directly related to the needs of the world for liquidity in connection with settling international balances created by expanding world trade and finance among the member countries.

The new institution would deal directly only with national central banks and not with private individuals or corporations. Its credit and currency would be transferable from one central bank to another.

In the case of the developing countries, credits should not be issued for long-term capital loans.

The holding of the national currencies by the IMF and other central banks should be guaranteed in units of stable exchange value as a protection against devaluation. National sovereignties in all internal matters would be unimpaired. Gold would still be a form of reserve, and the dollar would be used in private transactions.

Some of these suggestions may be superfluous. Some may be in error. Others may be needed. But this is at least a working agenda for the immediate future. It is important that we all consider the issues involved. Inattention or neglect may be fatal.

By and large, there has been a loss during these last years in the will of nations to co-operate in the field of trade and international finance. If we are not to revert to a period of crass mercantilism, we should move forward on as wide a scale as possible. Thus far our own national record has been a good one. Despite all the frustrations and provocations, we should not be weary of well-doing. It is in the broader interests of the world to co-operate. Let us do so with those nations which show an honest will to take part in these mutual endeavors and at the same time let us be on guard against the efforts of those who would tear down the international fabric of fair trade and mutual helpfulness.

Bibliographical Note

Adam Smith's *Wealth of Nations* (Cannan edition, Book V, Chapters I-IV; Book IV, Chapters I-VII) is the classic exposition of the advantages of widened trade. Ricardo's *Principles of Political Economy,* and John Stuart Mill's *Principles* are vital on the historical development of the theory and advantages of international trade. Jacob Viner's *Studies in the Theory of International Trade* is a modern classic, and Heilprin's *The Trade of Nations* is a cogent modern exposition of the advantages of a wider market.

Heckscher's two volumes on *Mercantilism* and Furniss' *The Position of the Laborer in a System of Nationalism* are the best modern works on mercantilism. I have used both of them extensively in quoting other writers in this area.

Morley's *Life of Cobden* and Trevelyan's *Life of Bright* give the exciting details of their struggle to repeal the British Corn Laws. Ashley's *Modern Tariff History* tells the story during the 19th century. Taussig, *Tariff History of the United States* is a classic. Humphrey's *The United States and the Common Market* is a good account of developments prior to 1962.

Wilcox, *A Charter for World Trade* (1949) describes the principles of and the struggles to establish GATT and the efforts which failed to create an International Trade Organization.

Piquet, *Aid, Trade and the Tariff,* describes the detailed tariff situation which faced us in 1953.

Wendell Gordon, *International Trade* (1958) is a clear discussion of the major principles involved.

On the grievances of the undeveloped nations, see Report by Secretary-General Prebetsch of United Nations Conference on Trade and Development (1964) and the *Final Act* of that conference. Also Theobald, *Free Men and Free Markets* (1965).

For some of the problems of international payments and exchange stability during the period 1935–1950, Brown, *The International Gold Standard Re-interpreted*, 2 volumes, Gardner, *Sterling-Dollar Diplomacy* (1956), and Bell, *The Sterling Area in the Post War World* are all solid pieces of work. For problems during recent years, see Hearings Before Joint Economic Committee 1962, and 1965 on the Balance of Payments, 3 vols., and Report of Review Committee, the *Balance of Payments Statistics of the United States* (1965).

For further discussions of the world's monetary systems and proposals for improvement in the international gold exchange standard, see Triffin, *Europe and the Money Muddle* (1957), *Gold and the Dollar Crisis* (1960), and *The Evolution of the International Monetary System* (1964). Also, Harrod, *Reforming the World's Money,* Hansen, *The Dollar and the International Monetary System* (1965), Roosa, *Monetary Reform for the World Economy* (1965), also Hearings before Subcommittee of Joint Economic Committee, *Guidelines for International Monetary Reform* (1965), two volumes, and the cogent report prepared by the subcommittee. Congressman Henry S. Reuss has written a penetrating book on the various allied problems which well repays study, namely, *The Critical Decade.* The articles by Charles A. Coombs, Treasury and Federal Reserve Foreign Exchange Operations, *Monthly Review of Federal Reserve Bank of New York,* March

1965, pp. 42–50; October 1965, pp. 199–208; and March 1966, pp. 47–57, are excellent in treating the currency crisis of 1964–65. See also the budget speech of the British Chancellor of the Exchequer, James Callaghan, *Hansard,* March 1, 1966.

The Council of Ten of the General Agreement to Borrow has also prepared an excellent analysis of some of the issues involved in the creation of a supplementary international currency. The monthly, International Financial Statistics published by the International Monetary Fund is the best source on the amounts of gold and foreign exchange held as official reserves by the various countries and of changes in their composition. The monthly Federal Reserve Bulletin also has valuable national and international monetary information.

Index

Act of 1846, protective tariffs, abolished by, 77
Act of 1945, importance of, to reciprocal trade, 92
Adenauer, Chancellor
  conflict of, with France, 135, 142
  high farm prices maintained by, 110
advalorem duties, 21–22, 24, 102
Africa
  British activities in, 13, 70
  coffee production in, 186
  communism in, 316
  CRU tie-in with, 353
  emerging nations in, 104
  exports from, to U.S., 16, 42
  French in, 70, 223
  IMF effect in, 256
  living standard in, 170
  U.S. aid to, 285, 312
Africa, French, U.S. aid in, 362
Agriculture, Department of, U.S., Common Market viewed by, 145
Algeria
  French in, 13
  labor migration from, 119
Alliance for Progress, U.S. aid through, 190, 193
American Revolution, mercantilism cause of, 54
Argentina
  industrial progress in, 167
  IMF effect in, 229, 255
  U.S. imports from, 23
Asia
  British domination of, 13
  communism in, 316
  CRU tie-in with, 353
  exports of, 23, 42
  foreign intervention in, 71
  gold reserves in, 247
  IMF relations with, 256
  labor costs in, 27
  living standard in, 170
  nationalism in, 258
  silver standard in, 204
  U.S. aid in, 278, 285
  U.S. trade with, 277
  See also Southeast Asia

Atomic Energy Authority, Common Market's similarity to, 115
Australia
  British development of, 11, 70
  British pound relationship to, 221, 250, 268
  British trade relations with, 73–74
  Chinese trade with, 163
  Common Market's effect on, 117
  exports of, 42
  GATT membership of, 102
  industrial progress in, 167
  IMF membership of, 231, 255
  Janeway proposal influence on, 344–345
  Russian trade with, 157, 158, 159
  U.S. trade with, 275–276, 277, 358
  world aid contribution of, 318, 364
Austria
  economic development of, 323
  EFTA membership of, 118
  GATT relationship with, 103, 105
  Germany's relations with, 69, 72
  GNP in, 120
  IMF membership of, 265
  Russian trade with, 157

balance of payments, 30–33
  Bernstein Committee studies on, 278, 283, 286–287
  British, 213, 254, 257–272, 332, 345–346
  Brookings Institution reports on, 298
  CRU effect on, 345, 346, 365
  Department of Commerce, U.S., regulation of, 287–288, 303
  French, 242
  German, 242
  gold and, 31, 211

IMF stabilizes, 234
  United States, 239, 254, 266, 273–324, 332, 335, 345–346, 362–366
Ball, George, 125
Bank of England
  international gold standard affected by, 213, 266
  "swap" arrangements with, 305
Bank of France
  gold reserves affected by, 268
  U.S. gold reserves affected by, 312, 326
Bank of Indochina, 298, 313
Bank for International Settlements (BIS)
  CRU tie-in with, 341
  Great Britain credit from, 265
Batista, Cuban revolution led by, 164
Battle Act (of 1951), 155–156
Bavaria, 69, 142
Belgium
  British pound related to, 268
  Common Market membership of, 107, 109, 111, 186
  Congo exploitation by, 70
  GATT membership of, 102, 127
  gold reserves of, 245
  IMF related to, 254
  sterling devaluation effect on, 221
  U.S. relations with, 91, 127, 242, 292, 298, 312
  world aid contribution of, 364
Benelux
  Common Market membership of, 107, 114
  GATT membership of, 102, 103, 127
  unemployment in, 119
  U.S. tariffs effect on, 127
Benton, Thomas Hart, Western expansion stressed by, 11
Berlin Blockade, 154

371